The People Time Forgot

The People Time Forgot

by

Alice Gibbons

MOODY PRESS

CHICAGO

©1981 by
THE MOODY BIBLE INSTITUTE
OF CHICAGO

All rights reserved

ISBN: 0-8024-8692-4

Library of Congress Cataloging in Publication Data
Gibbons, Alice.
 The people time forgot.

1. Missions to Uhunduni (Indonesian people) 2. Missions to Dani
(New Guinea people) 3. Christian and Missionary Alliance—
Missions—Indonesia—Irian Jaya. 5. Gibbons, Alice. 6. Gibbons, Don.
I. Title.
BV3373.U35G52   266'.023'730951   81-9466
ISBN 0-8024-8692-4   AACR2

2 3 4 5 6 7 Printing/LC/Year 87 86 85 84 83

Printed in the United States of America

To my husband, Don,
and to my five daughters,
Kathy, Joyce, Lori, Helen, and Darlene,
who have shared a life of missionary adventure
as a family

Contents

Part 1

Part 2

Part 3

Map 1

N

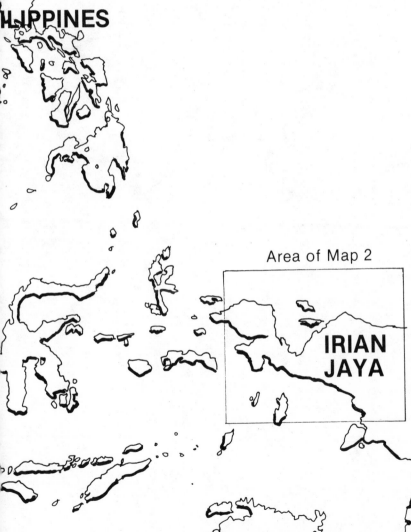

ᴴ.IPPINES

Area of Map 2

IRIAN JAYA

AUSTRALIA

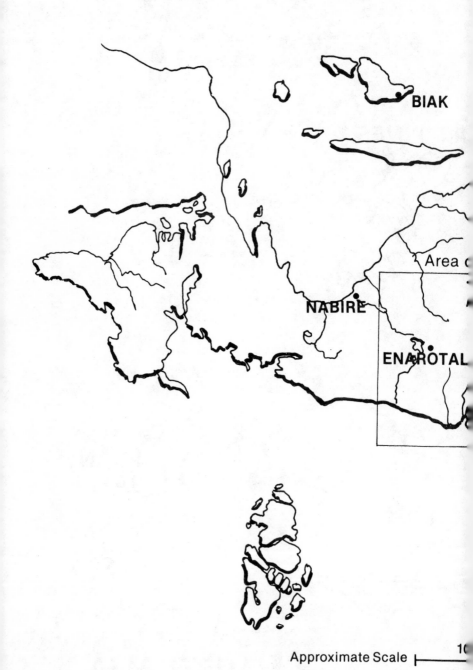

BIAK

Area o

NABIRE

ENAROTAL

Approximate Scale |———— 10

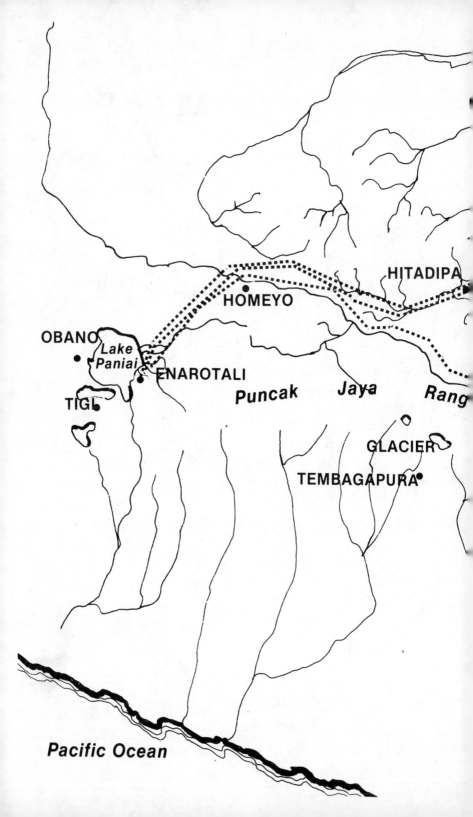

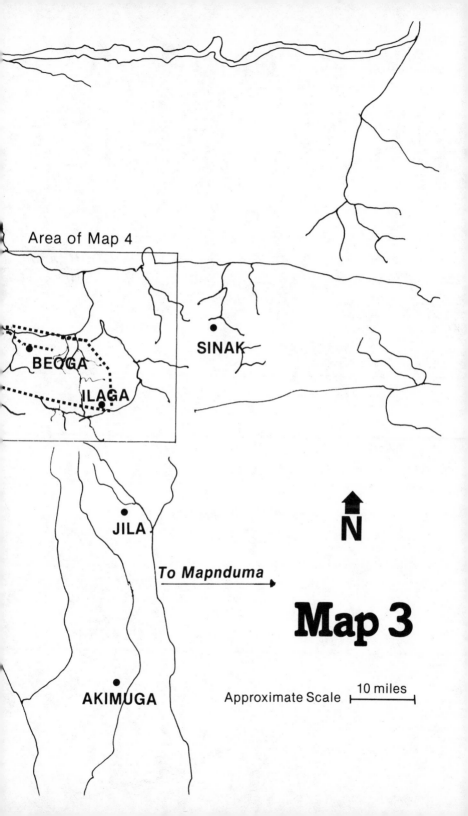

Map 4

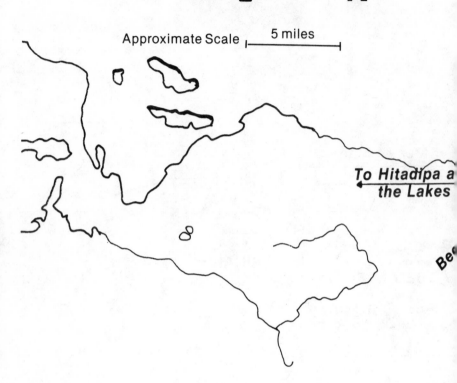

N

Approximate Scale |____| 5 miles

To Hitadipa and
the Lakes

Be

Pu

GLACIER

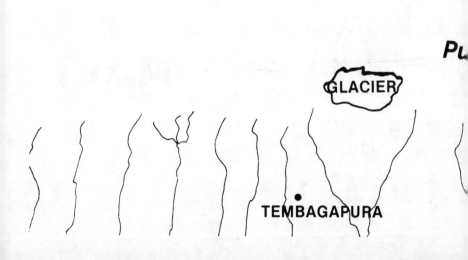

•
TEMBAGAPURA

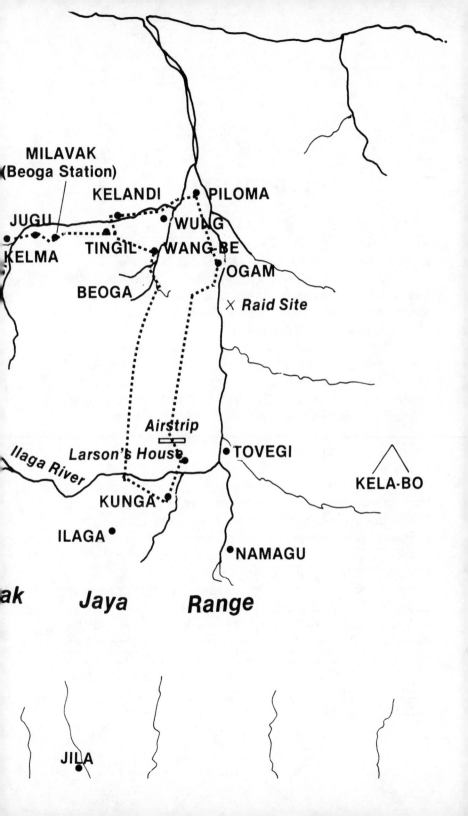

Foreword

Future historians of Christianity will remember the advance of the gospel into central Irian Jaya as one of the greatest breakthroughs in the saga of our faith.

In spite of awesome geographical barriers and the imponderability of Irian Jaya's complex languages and stone age cultures, a relative handful of missionaries have established some 1400 churches in less than twenty-five years. These thriving tribal congregations average at least 200 members each. They are pastored entirely by tribal church leaders and are already sending their own cross-cultural missionaries to other tribes. In fact, they have sent out approximately one such missionary for every eighty church members. It would not surprise me if investigation revealed that to be an all-time historical record for missionary zeal.

In addition to their numerical strength, the churches of Irian Jaya are remarkable for the quality of their indigenity. For example, even today many tribal pastors still stand before their congregations wearing only the traditional gourds. Originally all of them did. Some now wear Western clothes through their own decision to adapt to the encroaching majority of Indonesia—which by its own choice has adopted Western clothing styles.

Don and Alice Gibbons are pioneering members of that incredibly efficient and sensitive missionary task force. I am delighted that Alice has chosen to capture part of that major historical breakthrough in the following narrative. I have read her account with fascination and recommend it to all who think that the day of missionary pioneering is past.

The Damal people among whom Don and Alice and their colleagues have lived and labored are now almost entirely Christian. They received the Christian gospel with perhaps greater spontaneity than any other people in history. How had God prepared the Damals to understand the gospel? What dangers did the missionaries face? What methods did they use? And how did God bless their vision? Turn to the following pages and discover the answers for yourself.

Don Richardson
Director, Institute of Tribal Studies

Introduction

In *The People Time Forgot* Alice Gibbons has given an absorbing inside account of a missionary family's experiences in taking the gospel to an unknown tribe in the interior of Irian Jaya. The story is about the establishment of a vibrant church among a people who, until the Gibbonses arrived, had never seen a person from the outside world and had never heard the gospel.

The scope of the book and its intimacy, as well as the remarkable breadth of the reportage, give it an unusual importance for those engaged in the study of missions and cultural anthropology. Here is a wealth of factual information about a stone age people in practically every detail of life as they live it. The strange and sometimes startling account of birth, death, tribal wars, witchkilling, food preparation, nakedness, housing, marriage, divorce, polygamy, and the rites and appeasement of evil spirits are all set forth in a remarkably lucid manner. Skillfully interwoven are matters of human interest such as the family's braving incredible dangers and enduring great loneliness before they witnessed the great power and success of the gospel among the Damal tribe.

Anyone who supports overseas missions, is interested in becoming a missionary or in studying the problems, techniques, and effectiveness of missionary work, or who would enjoy a novel-like story of adventure, ought to read *The People Time Forgot*. It would be difficult to find a more informative and interesting book.

Louis L. King
President, The Christian and Missionary Alliance

Acknowledgments

To share the story of what God has done in the lives of the Damal people has been my husband's and my dream for many years. Although we have played an obvious part in this drama, another group of people has also played a very important role—the hundreds of men and women who have followed our work through our general letters, have prayed specifically for the requests, and seen God answer prayer. Many have encouraged me in this venture of writing a book, and I thank each one.

I want to thank Grace Cutts, my closest missionary neighbor, for her encouragement as well as her practical criticism and suggestions. She read the chapters as they came out of my typewriter. Since she has served with her husband in the Moni tribe for many years, she thoroughly understood the heart of my story.

Most of all I want to thank my husband for his loving encouragement. He has added much to an accurate portrayal of the Damal people. His insights are invaluable, for he loves and understands them as few foreigners ever will.

The book is written, but the story of the Damals is not ended. We will continue to serve the Damal people as long as God keeps the door open.

Prologue

The village of Tovegi at the eastern end of the Ilaga Valley in New Guinea lay shrouded in the blackness of night. It was June 28, 1954. Already the Dani and Damal tribesmen who lived there had retired to the little round huts that dotted the landscape. The warmth of the fire inside each hut felt good on their bare, black skins. No one was asleep, though, because there was too much to talk about. They were not alone in their village this night, for two *tuans* and their sixteen Ekari and Moni carriers had come to their village that afternoon.

Pitched off to the edge of the village was a two-man pup tent, and inside curled up in sleeping bags lay Gordon Larson and my husband, Don Gibbons. They too were talking about the events of the day.

"Our carriers were certainly against moving down to this lower end of the valley," Gordon said. "They'd rather go over the mountain trail into the center of the Beoga Valley—or they'd like better yet just to turn around and go home."

"They really were pushing for that," Don replied. "But I think the Danis are telling them there is danger if we go along the river trail to the Beoga just because they want to keep us here in the Ilaga and have us spend all of our axes and cowrie shells here. I feel we should follow the Ilaga River on around as it loops back into the Beoga. If we don't, we won't know who lives down there or how many Damals live in the Beoga, and that's why we came on this trip."

"I agree with you, Don. I don't think there is any real danger. One thing that made the carriers uneasy this afternoon was the crowd of people that kept pushing around us and touching everything. There must have been three or four hundred of them. I suppose they are just curious, but it's hard to tell. It would help if we could really talk to them. There was only that one Dani man who could interpret from Moni, and you wonder if he really does it carefully or adds some of his own ideas."

"Listen," Don broke in. "I thought I heard a sound outside the tent."

Don crawled out of the tent in time to see three boys running off. He turned back to inspect the carrying tins of supplies stacked beside the tent. Shining his flashlight on the supplies, he reported to Gordon. "The carrying tins are all here, but they've slit the gunnysack and taken several cans of food." Nothing could be done, so Don went back to bed.

Sometime after midnight Gordon roused Don and whispered, "I hear someone outside again."

Don jumped up and was out of the tent in a flash, determined to catch the thieves this time. He spotted a black figure running down the hill and across a sweet potato garden and bolted after him. The man jumped over the fence, so Don vaulted after him and landed squarely on top of the startled Dani. Still determined to bring about justice, Don thought he would drag the man back to the village chief. The Dani began calling out, and after several minutes of struggling in the darkness Don decided he had better turn the fellow loose before all his friends came to his rescue.

When he returned to the tent, Don found that this time the Danis had stolen an entire load of supplies packed in a carrying tin. After pausing to think, Don realized that as two missionaries alone, and fourteen hiking days from their home base without a radio or any means of communication, they had better not try to force the Danis to return anything.

The next morning the carriers were even more apprehensive about going on down the river trail, but Don and Gordon persuaded them to continue. A crowd of noisy men jostled them all the way down to the Ilaga River. They had to cross the river on a swinging vine bridge that was in poor repair. It was no easy job to get across it while carrying a thirty-five-pound pack. The Danis discovered a way they could unnerve the already frightened Moni and Ekari carriers. When a man got to the middle of the bridge they hooted loudly and threw large rocks into the river, splashing him with water.

On the far side of the river the party entered a village. The chief there advised them at that point to take a trail that led up over a 11,000-foot mountain and into the center of the Beoga Valley. He said if they continued down the river trail the party would be raided, their goods would be stolen, and they might be killed. However, several other men who claimed to be Damals reported that there were Damals living on the river trail and said they would guide the group to that village. Since the whole purpose of the trip was to survey the areas where the Damal people lived, so that a mission station could be opened among them, Don and Gordon both felt the thing to do was to continue on down the river.

The Ilaga River wound through a narrow canyon with a series of mountains rising sharply on either side, and the trail followed the river. The men walked single file over the path that had been followed by travelers before them—not a broad walkway, but rather the line of least resistance— through mud, tall grass, and brush, climbing up and down and around obstacles that blocked their advance.

There were no villages now, but still fifty armed men from the Ilaga continued to crowd in among them, chanting as they walked. The missionaries chalked up their actions to curiosity, but the Ekaris and Monis did not. Seeing that the carriers were quite fearful, Gordon asked the Danis to turn back, but obviously they had no intention of doing so. It also became evident that the men who had offered to guide them were neither Damals at all nor had they any thought of serving as guides.

One of the Danis suggested he would help an Ekari by carrying his load for him for a while. That arrangement worked well for a couple of hours until suddenly the Dani vanished and so did the carrying tin with all the salt and sugar. There was nothing to do but go on.

At noon they came to a Dani village where the people insisted they spend the night. In the morning they must backtrack a half hour to cross the river, for the main trail led down the other side of the river at that point. No one was in a mood to spend a night in a Dani village! Finding a well-used path leading out of the village they pressed on—and so did their Ilaga tormentors.

Before long the trail petered out into a garden. Obviously the main trail *was* on the other side of the river. Don spotted a tall tree on the opposite bank and decided to try to build a bridge using that tree. He put an ax head in his pocket and swam across. A Dani man on the other side helped him fell the tree, but as Don was watching the tree fall the Dani disappeared with the ax. The fallen tree proved to be too short, and Don swam back across the river minus one ax.

Retracing their steps, they came to the bridge. Again the Danis saw their chance to harass the party, and they swarmed around until it was almost impossible to cross. Regrouping on the other side, Don and Gordon decided that the fears of their carriers had been valid. These Danis were bent on getting their goods one way or another.

They closed their ranks with Gordon leading the procession and Don bringing up the rear. That kept the Ilaga men at a little distance as long as the trail led through heavy undergrowth, but soon they came to a section where they climbed over rocks along the edge of the river. A Dani man moved in and snatched the personal net bag from the neck of the Ekari carrier walking next to Don. The little bag contained a number of cowrie shells—the man's cash with which he had planned to buy a pig.

The carrier raised his bow and arrow, and immediately the cry rang out from the other carriers, "Don't shoot! Keep on going. If anyone shoots an arrow at them they'll kill us all." Although every one of the carriers had a bow and a full set of arrows and knew how to use those lethal weapons, they also sensed that, being two weeks' trek away from

23

home in enemy territory, they would have no chance of survival.

The party hurried on, but in half an hour their tormentors were back, demanding a payment of shells before they would allow the group to continue on the trail. Don and Gordon were still debating about what they should do when the Ekaris and Monis began to hand out shells and steel knives from their personal net bags. The missionaries added a few more shells as payment and urged the carriers to pick up their loads and keep going.

The Danis allowed them to go on, but they did not turn back. Their chanting increased, and when they came to an open area the excited Danis grabbed two tins from the backs of the carriers. They pulled the lids open and the contents spewed out on the ground. The Danis dove for the things, each man grabbing whatever caught his eye.

Don watched one husky man dash off with his red pullover sweater. In an instant, memories of that sweater flooded his mind. I had given it to him on his twenty-third birthday. He wore it often that fall, because it was my gift, and because he did not own another. The sweater almost became famous when the registrar at Simpson Bible Institute asked his secretary, "Who is the new student who always wears that brick red sweater?"

"Oh, that's Don Gibbons," she said, "the boyfriend of Alice Rhoads."

Now the sweater was worn and the elbows had been mended, but the cords of sentiment pulled at Don's heart as the Dani darted off with it.

"Go on with the carriers," Don yelled to Gordon. "I'll try to hold them back a little."

While the Danis gathered up the last of what they wanted, including the tins themselves, Gordon and the carriers dashed off down the narrow trail. Don let the yards widen between himself and his party. The Danis were all yelling at him because they soon understood what he was doing. Of course Don could not understand a word of their language, but before long they changed their tactics so that he could understand. An arrow flew over his head, and another one hit off to his side. It was time to catch up with the others, Don decided, and he was soon close behind them.

When they came to a wide place in the trail, they were surrounded again, and there was the twang of bow strings as the Danis let arrows fly over their heads. Suddenly an Ekari cried out in pain. "They've hit me. They've hit me in the shoulder." The arrow did not have the razor sharp point used in war, but only a three-pronged point of an arrow designed to shoot birds. It broke the skin and drew blood but did not go deep into the flesh. It had the desired effect, however—pandemonium broke loose. The carriers dropped their loads right where they were and ran for their lives. They were sure this was the end.

"Oh, Lord, You may let them take our things," Gordon prayed. "But save our lives for the sake of our families—for the sake of Peggy and our two girls—and for the gospel." And Don added, "Don't let them kill us, Lord. Don't let Alice become a widow—not now."

The Danis tore open the carrying tins, and every man grabbed for what he could get. Sleeping bags, medicine, food, papers—everything was strewn out on the ground. Gordon snatched a bundle of his language analysis papers while the Danis were taking things they wanted. In the confusion he also got hold of one sleeping bag and the tent.

Don looked for the two smaller carrying tins containing rice and the bulk of their cowrie shells and beads. He spotted them lying together a few feet ahead on the trail and the lead Ekari carrier standing nearby. "Take these tins of rice," Don shouted in Moni. "The Danis don't want our rice."

The Ekari was a mature man, and he accepted Don's challenge to defy the Danis under the guise that both tins contained rice—something that they would not want because they had no way of cooking it. He also knew that in the second small tin all the trading items were packed—the

25

very thing the raiders wanted most.

It was every man for himself as the Danis grabbed their loot and the missionaries and carriers ran for their lives. Twice more a small band of Danis overtook the fleeing men, but they got very little, and the party pressed on. When darkness fell they were free from their pursuers and in an unpopulated stretch by the river. Just when they could see to walk no more they reached a huge overhanging rock—the campsite of hundreds of native travelers before them—and stopped for the night.

Sitting around the campfire eating supper, the carriers began to take from their net bags things they had salvaged during the raid. From one bag came a cracker tin containing a dozen knives and sixty shells. Others produced cans of meat and dehydrated soup, some clothing, soap, and two flashlights. For Don the most important discovery was his second pair of hobnailed boots, for the pair on his feet was falling apart. The two smaller carrying tins had come through intact, with rice in one and cheese and dried fruit packed underneath the barter items in the other. Having the cowrie shells and beads meant they could buy food along the way both for their carriers and for themselves.

One by one the Ekaris and Monis curled up beside the fire and went to sleep. It was cold in the mountains at 6,000 feet above sea level—cold as soon as the equatorial sun disappeared. The carriers had no clothing, but this was not the first time they had slept in the open with only a fire to warm their bare skin, nor would it be the last time. They were satisfied with a sweet potato to stay their hunger and a fire to keep them warm.

Don and Gordon sat by the fire. Although they were tired, they were not ready for sleep. "You know," Don said, "in a way I almost envy them. They can be content with so little. There are so many things that we think we must have just to stay alive."

"It's true," Gordon agreed. "So many things are essential for our survival—but wasn't God good to give us enough of

26

those essentials to see us home? And yet, you still wonder why God permitted those Danis to raid us."

"I guess we can't answer that one now," Don said, "but we can really be thankful that no one was killed. Once arrows start flying, anything can happen. Two years ago those two TEAM missionaries* were killed when they were exploring up in the northwest corner of the island, and the only motive seemed to be the stealing of their goods. Tomorrow is my third wedding anniversary—I kept thinking about that today, and what it would mean for Alice if I were to be killed."

"I thought a lot about Peggy, too." Gordon said. "I'm glad they know nothing about what happened today. They'd be worried sick. We've got a lot to be thankful for. Let's pray before we turn in."

The two men prayed for their wives and children, for help to get home, and also for the Danis who had raided them. Gordon rolled up in the tent, and Don crawled into the sleeping bag. The rushing Ilaga River nearby lulled them to sleep, and the giant boulder towering overhead was "a rock in a weary land."

In years past you may have heard the Damal tribe referred to by the name of "Uhunduni," for that was the name used for them before 1962. The Ekari tribe was formerly called "Kapauku." In 1962 the western half of the island of New Guinea became a province of the Republic of Indonesia, the fifth largest nation in the world. Tribal names and the government have changed, but the people remain the same.

Many of you who will read this book have followed the work of the Christian and Missionary Alliance† in Irian Jaya through the years. You have prayed for the missionaries and supported them with your gifts. This book is a report to you. May it also be a challenge to some who are young enough to answer Christ's call to learn a foreign language and go with the gospel to those who have never heard—whether they live in a crowded city or remote jungle village. God in His sovereignty allowed my husband and me, with our five girls, to have a part in what *He* is doing among the Damals— a people whom time forgot, but God did not!

*In 1952 Edward Tritt and Walter Erikson, missionaries with The Evangelical Alliance Mission, were killed while on a trek near Manokwari.

†The Christian and Missionary Alliance, Box C, Nyack, New York 10960.

PART 1

This story begins in the year 1933 in the Beoga Valley. You may ask, How do we know an accurate date, when the Damals had no system of reckoning time? Don has a hobby of determining the age of some of his special friends by questioning them about their family history. He asks several related people questions like this: What event coincided with the birth of your first child? Are you older or younger than this neighbor of yours? How big were you when that government officer walked into the Beoga? (We know that this officer trekked into the Beoga in 1941.) Every person alive at that time knows the point in his life when this first explorer from the outside world appeared in the Beoga. By approaching a given point from several angles a fairly accurate date can be found. Thus our story begins in 1933.

1

Another Hearth

Meyong buried the sweet potatoes for the evening meal in the ashes on the hearth. Then, picking up small pieces of wood, she crisscrossed them over the ashes. Her black eyes sparkled as she blew the coals on the hearth into flames. The heat from the fire felt good, for all she wore was a short grass skirt. Meyong was a small girl for her eleven or twelve years. But what she lacked in size she made up for in spirit.

This was a quiet time of day. The *dedel* cicada had chirped their thirty-second chorus in unison. Every evening without fail, the beetles sang together just at dusk. Their song was as much a part of the peaceful descent of night as is the chime of a clock in a church tower. Meyong's older brother, her father, and her uncles had already gone into the men's hut for the night. Only Meyong, and her sister, mother, and baby brother were left in the women's hut.

Meyong's mother laid down the net bag she was weaving with her fingers and got up to close the door. "I'm cold," she said. "It is starting to rain." She took the three rough boards that served as the only door into the low hut and wedged them into place. Now that it was closed, the warmth and cheer of the fire filled the hut.

Meyong sat staring into the fire, thinking about the young man who was to be her husband. She had mixed emotions about Wolo. He was a strong young man, and that attracted her. Wolo had already grown a beard, and he was a member of the adult men's group. Meyong was flattered by the indirect attention she was receiving from him, but she was still a little girl both physically and emotionally. She was not ready for the life of a married woman.

Wolo had never actually spoken to her, but she was well aware of the bride-price payments he was making to her family. For many days now he and his brothers had put aside all thoughts of garden work and had been bargaining with her family. The two groups of men would go off into the privacy of the tall grass to talk. Sometimes their angry voices drifted back into the village yard. "That's not enough . . . I want another big pig . . . She is not deaf and dumb . . . This cowrie shell isn't good enough . . . She is worth far more."

Meyong had seen the string of at least sixty cowrie shells sewn on a belt that her mother had received. The belt had been woven, with the aid of a bone needle, of string made from bark. Many hours had been spent grinding off the top of each shell on a rock. Blackened beeswax had been carefully pressed into the center of each shell, highlighting its size and whiteness. Finally the shells had been sewn onto the belt, so they could be displayed more easily. The most valuable cowrie shells, called indo, were not sewn to the belt, but were kept separately in a cocoon case. The indo shell was larger, with more pronounced bumps on the top. It was worn white and smooth through generations of men's handling and rubbing it, trading and loving it. Four other shell belts had been given to Meyong's father, brother, and uncles, and two large pigs had been delivered to her father.

Meyong realized that in a way she was the center of attention. And yet in another way she was completely ignored. Her father, brother, and uncles were not interested in her and her happiness but only in the shells and pigs for which they so greedily bargained night and day. Which one of them would get the most beautiful indo cowrie shell? They had no interest in the little girl's wishes at all.

Meyong's thoughts were interrupted by the cries of her baby brother. Her younger sister, Nakal, had been playing with the baby, keeping him entertained. Now he cried. "Give Me-Tal to me," Meyong said. "I'll make him happy." Taking the baby she cuddled him in her arms and sang softly:

Dear little brother, I love you
Dear little Me-Tal, I love you
I'm your big sister, I love you
I'm Meyong, I love you
Don't cry, Me-Tal, I love you
Dear little brother, I love you.

Finally his whimperings could no longer be appeased, and he broke into a loud cry. "Bring the baby here to me," her mother said. Meyong carried the baby around the fire to her mother, taking care to bend her head lest she touch the hut's low framework covered with black, shiny tar from the smoke of many fires. Her mother took the baby and held him to her breast. Soon his stomach was full, and he went to sleep for the night. The two girls sat side by side watching the dancing flames of the fire. Nakal chattered about this and that, but Meyong was lost in her own thoughts.

Meyong was still a girl in appearance, but within her the bud of womanhood was forming. In time the blossom would begin to unfold. Sometimes she daydreamed about being Wolo's wife and having a baby of her own, but for now she was content to remain under the shelter of her mother's love. She had her baby brother to love and care for. The blossom and desires of womanhood had not yet burst the green leaves of youth that bound them.

Her mother broke the silence. "The sweet potatoes are cooked. Take them out of the ashes, Meyong."

Almost without thinking, Meyong picked up the wooden tongs and began to push the remaining wood and coals to the edges of the hearth. Slowly she began to poke into the ashes with her tongs. When she found a potato, she lifted it out and laid it on the clay protruding around the hearth's edge. She continued to dig out the potatoes one by one, tapping each with her hand so that the ash dust fell back into the fire. Meyong divided the potatoes into three piles and left them to cool.

Meyong's mother laid her sleeping baby on a palm leaf

mat by her side and covered him with her net bag. The potatoes were still steaming hot as the three broke them open and began to eat in silence. Meyong's mother reached behind her for the gourd of drinking water, removed the leaves that served as a stopper, and drank. Wiping off the neck of the gourd with the palm of her hand, she passed the gourd to her daughter.

Then she pushed two logs of wood into the center of the fire, added two sticks, and blew on the coals until they began to burn.

The girls spread their palm leaf mats beside the fire and lay down. They chattered about the grasshoppers they had caught and roasted that day. "I know where there are a lot of frogs," Meyong said. "I'll show you the place tomorrow, and we can catch them together."

"I can almost taste them now," Nakal said. "We'll go tomorrow."

The smoke curled up from the fire through the grass-thatched roof. The only sound was the ever present roar of the river and the soft sound of the falling rain. They slept.

The next morning Meyong was still enjoying the warmth of the fire when she heard a commotion outside. As she stepped out to see what it was all about, she saw Wolo running toward her. Instinctively she turned and ran, but he was too quick for her. Wolo grabbed her arm and shouted, "I've paid pigs and shells for you, and I'm taking you to my village. Come on with me."

Kicking and screaming, Meyong cried, "I don't want you! I don't want to marry. I want to stay with my mother."

All the men in Meyong's family were around her, shouting too. "The bride price is paid. Do you think we want to throw away all we've been paid? You have to go. We've already spent the shells and can't return them. You must go."

Meyong's mother watched her struggling daughter, and the passions of a woman rose within her. In an instant the life of all Damal women flashed before her—the life that was hers from childhood until now. What could be done?

Nothing! It was a man's world. They bought and sold their women to satisfy their greed and passion. The men stuck together, and by force they did what they pleased with their women. Meyong would settle down and bear children, and then her world would revolve around her children. That had been her mother's life, and the life of her mother before her. Nothing could change it. *Meyong will get used to her new life. After all,* she thought, shrugging her shoulders, *I have been given the shell belt, and there will be wedding pork to eat.*

Wolo picked up Meyong and tossed her over his shoulder just as he would carry a pig, as he climbed over the stile in the village fence and started toward his home. Meyong, struggling to free herself, fought and screamed, tore Wolo's head net off, and pulled his hair. She gouged at his eyes and broke the brittle gourd he wore for trousers. She tore at the shell necklace around his neck. She scratched and tried to bite him, screaming all the time. She fought like a wild pig.

Meyong's fighting only made Wolo more determined to take his bride home with him. She was his, he had paid for her, and he would have her for his wife.

With all the screaming and shouting a crowd of men and boys was soon following them. After a time Meyong was exhausted, and so was Wolo. He put her down at the top of the hill. When they started again Wolo pulled her along behind him. She still cried out in protest, but not as often now. What was the use? There were men walking in front of them and behind them. Meyong knew there was no chance to escape.

When the sun was high overhead they arrived at Wolo's village. He took her to the hut of his sister-in-law, who was there waiting to receive the new bride. She gave Meyong two cooked sweet potatoes to eat and offered her water. Meyong took the potatoes and water, but said nothing. She lay down, exhausted.

In some ways life in Wolo's village was not very different from what Meyong had always known. She ate and slept and went to the garden as she always had. She lived in her sister-in-law's hut with the other women. Wolo would not build a house for her until she had children and wanted to live alone. But Meyong longed for her own family. Much of the time her thoughts and emotions were those of a girl rather than of a woman. She missed her sister so very much. Here there was no frog hunting or roasted grasshoppers; there was no running off for an hour just to do nothing or to have intimate talks with her own sister. Meyong missed the loving care of her mother, and she missed her baby brother and the fun she had loving and playing with him. Me-Tal had been her real live doll. In this new home there were only adult women who expected her to think and act like they did. No one loved her, and she loved no one.

One afternoon her sister-in-law demanded, "Meyong, go get some water for me." When Meyong did not respond she burst out, "You lazy little girl, go get water right now!"

Meyong just sat there. She thought of running away to the river and committing suicide. Then they would all cry and mourn for her. And their pigs and shells would all be wasted. That thought did not last long, though. Meyong had too much life and fire in her to give up so easily. She did not want to die—not really. Angrily she replied, "Go get your own water. I don't have to listen to you. I'll do what I please."

In the days that followed Meyong joined the other women in their daily routine. Each morning they started up the steep mountain with their empty net bags. Keeping her balance on the steep mountainside was not difficult for Meyong. Her bare feet clung to the rough ground almost like a second pair of hands. All her life she had gone to gardens like this one, so steep that the garden might slide down the mountain at any moment.

Wolo had sharpened a potato digging stick and given it to her to carry with her to the garden every day. When it became blunt he sharpened it again for her or made her a new stick. Providing this short digging stick was one of the ways Wolo acknowledged that Meyong was *his* wife, and by keeping it in good condition he expressed his affection, making her work a bit easier.

Meyong weeded in a potato garden that was just now ready to harvest. First she dug out the weeds around a plant with her stick. Then, probing into the ground with her digging stick, she located a large potato and dug it out without disturbing the plant. With her hands she carefully pushed the soil into a mound around the plant and went on to the next potato vine. That was the first potato crop. In two more months the rest of the potatoes would be ready to dig.

When their nets were full of potatoes the women picked a net of potato leaves and spinach, which were always a part of the afternoon meal. It was time to return home. Meyong hoisted the heavy net bag of potatoes onto her back, slipping the carrying strap across her forehead. With one hand on each side of the net band to help bear the weight, she bent forward and started down the mountainside.

Just before she reached her village, she came upon three women washing their potatoes. Meyong eased her net to the ground and dumped the potatoes into a stream of water that trickled from the side of the hill. Pulling a tuft of grass to help her scrub the potatoes clean, she sat down and scrubbed them one by one. The women were all talking and laughing as they worked. No one was in a hurry to leave. Meyong looked forward to this part of her day.

When she returned to the village, Meyong prepared the afternoon meal for Wolo. While the food was steaming, Wolo came into the hut, and they talked. Affection was beginning to grow between the two of them. She was getting used to her new home.

One day when Meyong returned from the garden later than usual, the other women had already cooked the evening meal of greens. Wolo, his two brothers, and their wives were taking the greens out of the cooking pit. It was raining, and the group did not hear Meyong outside. She stood in the rain listening to their talk.

One of the women was saying, "Meyong is just a lazy little girl. She never does her share of work in the garden. Why did you ever bring a worthless child like that to our village?"

Then a brother spoke. "She's just a skinny splinter of wood. She doesn't even have any breasts. She'll never give you any sons like a mature fruit-bearing tree. I tell you, Wolo, she's just a skinny splinter of wood. Why don't you send her back to her father?"

After a silence Meyong heard Wolo's voice. "No, if I send her home I'll never get all my shells and pigs back. Besides, although an older woman might work better, I want a young innocent girl for my wife. She'll grow up someday."

Again the brother spoke. "Well, I suppose you can always take a second wife. I still say that skinny little runt will never give you any sons."

Meyong heard the slurping sound from inside the hut. They were eating. If she didn't go in now there would be no greens left for her. She took off her rain cape, crawled through the low doorway, and began to eat.

2

Wolo the Warrior

Wolo listened to the village news with interest. His cousin, Adak, had stolen another man's wife from the upriver village of Jugu. Adak and the stolen wife fled downriver to his home at Wang-Be. Rumor had it that the offended husband was gathering his relatives and clansmen to attack the downriver people. Wolo knew his clansmen would be ready if they were attacked, and he was hoping the attack would come, for it would give him his first chance to prove his bravery in war.

That night, the two men's houses at Tingil were packed with men who had heard the rumors about an impending battle. Excitement grew as the older men told stories of their adventures and bravery in past wars. One man started singing, and the rest joined in with a chant-response in rhythm. He created the song line by line as he went along. The man sitting next to him sang the harmony part to his chanted tune. While the tiny hut was filled with the repeated chant-response, the leader formed the next line of the song in his mind. The veteran warrior sang of his prowess in battle:

> I was in the forefront of the battle, but I was not afraid.
> The spear was thrown at me, but I dodged it.
> It was my arrow that felled the enemy.
> When my comrades scattered, it was I who regrouped them.

Another verse gave advice to the young men:

> When you go to the battle, be fearless.
> Never lose courage when you are attacked.
> It is up to you to kill the enemy.
> Be brave and daring in the fight.

39

Toward the middle of the night, the urge to sleep grew stronger than their desire to sing and tell stories. One by one, the men lay down and slept.

In the morning the men were aroused by the singing of the birds. Sweet potatoes were taken from net bags and put into the hot ashes to bake. Soon the women came with more hot potatoes, and everyone shared until all had had enough.

Outside, someone shouted, "The warriors are coming," and broke into a rhythmic hooting that resounded across the mountainside. Another man took up the cry, and then another, until the word of attack passed down the valley, echoing from one village to another. Men poured from the houses, grabbing their bows and arrows and spears as they came. The air was filled with their shouting.

A line of warriors streamed single file over the hill, whooping in rhythm as they ran. Their black bodies, greased with pig fat, glistened as the sun's rays struck them. Now they were silhouetted on the skyline with their spears held ready over their heads and their bows drawn for attack.

Wolo and the downriver warriors were out to meet them. Both sides broke file and scattered into the heavy brush that covered the mountainside. Soon arrows were flying in every direction. The upriver men had expected to make a surprise attack. They were not prepared for the large group that met them, and they were not accustomed to fighting in heavy brush and trees. As the sun rose higher in the sky, they gradually withdrew up the hill and down the other side.

When they reached the stream flowing down the side valley, they came to a more open field. Here they regrouped in closer formation. The opposing warriors advanced, and volleys of arrows flew back and forth. Dodging arrows, the men dashed forward, shot at the enemy, and quickly retreated.

To an onlooker it might have seemed an animated game until one of the downriver men shouted, "Tugu. I've hit the mark." He had been close enough to throw his spear, and it entered the chest of his enemy. A man named Tiop fell to the ground, dead.

Cries of anger and revenge poured from the upriver men as they saw their comrade fall. Then an even more pressing emotion filled their hearts. They wanted to give their dead brother the honor and respect of proper mourning and cremation. It was past noon, and since everyone was tired, both groups turned toward home by common consent.

The downriver warriors regrouped before they topped the crown of the hill that led into their village. The men ran over the hill in single file, just as their attackers had done that morning. Running into the village yard, they shouted, "We killed a man. We killed Tiop." They ran in a circle dance, shouting and waving their weapons, while the women and children joined them by running on the outside of the circle. This was a victory dance for them.

Upriver, the warriors returned, but there was no victory dance in their village. They had tied the body of Tiop on a pole, and two men carried it home, slung between them. The warriors came straggling home—tired, hungry, and defeated. The death wail rose from the women as the body was lifted over the pig stile and into the village yard.

Tiop's wife and two sisters came crying. They fell on the ground and began to caress the body. The wife held the still form in her arms as her body shook with sobs of hopeless sorrow. Children stood in the background, not knowing what to do. Other women gathered, and their voices joined in a high-pitched, pulsating wail.

Men began to construct a support for the body in the men's hut. They pounded stakes into the earth floor, and with rattan tying vine and boards, they made a crude reclining chair. When it was finished, they washed the corpse and carried it in, propping it up in the chair. In life, Tiop had never sat in a chair. Now, in death, his body rested in one for all to view.

Men, women, and children crowded into the hut to sit with the corpse. Tiop's wife sat next to the body, shooing away the flies with a long tuft of jungle grass. The voices of the women rose and fell in a high wail that could be heard throughout the village. His sister started to sing in a quiet voice, while others in the house took up the chanted response.

> Oh, my little brother, why have you gone away and left me desolate?
> Your death reminds me of how I used to carry you in a net bag.
> I wiped away your tears when you cried.
> Now I am crying and there is no one to comfort me.
> I remember how you hunted birds as a boy and when they were cooked, you shared them with me.
> As a young man, you wove a yellow belt for me, and I wore it proudly.
> Oh, how these memories make me weep.
> When I walk the paths where you left your footprints, I will wear the mud of mourning on my face.

When she had finished singing, everyone wept uncontrollably for some time. Then Tiop's young widow took up the refrain:

> Oh, father of my son and daughter, why have you left me?
> Who do you think will care for your widow and your orphans?
> How I will miss the little gifts you brought me so often.
> You made gardens for me, and we had plenty to eat.
> You bought pigs, and I raised them.
> Then, at the feasts, we had pork for our family, and extra to share with friends.
> Where are you now? Are you ascending the Ba river, or are you approaching the Kela mountain?
> When you arrive at the abode of my dead ancestors, tell them I am still weeping for them.
> Dear father of my children, speak to me through the voice of the juwi bird.
> Sing to me and comfort my heart.

Women plastered their faces and bodies with mud. The more miserable they made themselves, the more fully they expressed their hopeless grief. Even the children must feel the pain. In a burst of sorrow, Tiop's brother grabbed his two-year-old niece and chopped off her little finger at the second joint. She, too, must mourn.

On the third morning, the body was to be cremated. Men chopped lengths of firewood and piled them in layers, alternating the direction of each layer. When the rack was chest high, they brought Tiop's body and laid it on the pyre. More layers of wood were added to the top, and the fire was lit. The wailing of the mourners died away with the last embers of the fire.

The funeral was over, but the war had just begun. To the Damal, adultery is punishable by death to both partners involved, or war can follow if the time is ripe for fighting. The family of the wife-stealer, Adak, could have chosen to execute him and thus prevent war. Instead, they chose to defend him. They were ready to fight.

In war, the fighting continues until an equal number of men have been killed on each side. No one really wins the war; it is simply a matter of revenge—killing until both sides are satisfied. When the fighting is over, life returns to normal, with trading and travel as usual. In one war two villages may be enemies, and in the next war they may be allies. The division of sides is made according to what starts the fighting and where the family and clan ties lie.

A small group of Dani tribesmen lived in the area between the two groups who began this war. Part of those Dani people had business ties with the men upriver, and others had ties with the downriver group. Although the Danis were closely related to one another, some joined the upriver confederacy, and others joined the downriver group.

Another unwritten rule in the game of war is that the two sides must have an equal balance of power, with the same number of warriors on each side. The downriver group recruited men from the Ilaga and lowlands area, each a three-day walk from the Beoga, so to make the sides even, the upriver men added recruits from the Dugindoga Valley, a three-day walk in the opposite direction.

After the first battle, the war took on a more permanent

form. The upriver people built a high war fence around their village. The only opening was a small hole in the fence, which was securely closed at any threat of danger. The men inside the fence could shoot arrows at any approaching enemy and yet be relatively free from danger themselves.

Just a half hour's walk away, the downriver group built a war fence around one of their villages. Between the two villages lay an open flat area, which had been created by a landslide from the cliffs rising 2,000 feet above. That half-mile long landslide became the battlefield for a war that lasted nearly a year.

Before going out to the battlefield each morning, the men carefully painted their faces. Wolo carried his cosmetics in his net bag: pig grease, which he mixed with special red clay, and soot for black greasepaint. After Wolo got his friend to paint alternating colored stripes for him on his face, he carefully retied the padding and net that he wore on his head and topped it by pinning on a circle of black cassowary feathers. His outfit was complete when he stuck a bore tusk through the pierced septum of his nose. Strutting like a fighting cock, he looked fierce and felt brave.

All that paint and feathers was for the benefit of the women who often came to the battlefield to watch their men fight. They stayed back just far enough to be safe but still near enough to see what was going on. Even the women who did not see Wolo would hear about how he looked— and that was important.

An observer sitting on a hill watching might think the men looked like actors in a ballet. Their physiques were beautiful in their costumes of black skin, shiny with pig grease. The red grease paint and yellow and tan war vests added color, and the yellow plumes of the bird of paradise bobbing on their heads added motion. It all made a stunning picture as they pranced about on the battlefield.

The war vest served as a protection from an arrow hitting the heart or lungs. It would even slow down a spear thrown from a distance. Weaving a war vest from rattan vine was a craft mastered by only a few men. Tediously working with stiff rattan and a bone needle, they took several months to complete a vest. The finished product was a thick, tough covering that resembled the chain mail of the medieval knights.

Not owning a war vest, Wolo carried in his net bag a shield roughly carved from a thick piece of wood. With his net bag slung over his left shoulder, both hands were free to shoot. His strategy of defense was to guess when an arrow was coming his direction, then crouch close to the ground, turning the left side covered by his shield toward the enemy. When the volley of arrows was past, he ran toward the enemy, shooting. As the arrows were returned, again he would run, dodge, and retreat.

The shaft of the arrow was made from a reed. Some arrows had a flat, razor-sharp, bamboo tip. Others were fitted with a tip carved from wood with barbs to tear the flesh when it was pulled out. Because the arrows had no feathers on them, no one could really become an accurate marksman. The object of the offense was to keep shooting a barrage of arrows until, by chance, one found its mark.

The entire performance might seem like a game of war, but it was no game. The hearts of the players were filled with hatred and a passion for revenge. Before the war started, the men on the opposite side had been their neighbors and associates in business transactions; now they were the enemy to be killed. If they could not kill a man on the battlefield, they would settle for the killing of a woman or child of the enemy group wherever they could find one.

After several months of fighting, the score was five dead on the upriver side and twelve dead on the other side. Then one of the Dani men who had been fighting with the upriver group was shot and killed. The Danis fighting on the downriver side could not bear the thought that their close relative had been killed by their allies. They decided to change sides and fight those who had killed their cousin. The Danis said to their wives, "You go upvalley and tell our

kinsmen we are changing sides." The next day they entered
the battle as usual. In the midst of the fighting, they turned
on their allies, killing two men and seriously wounding a
third. That left the score even further from being equal.

Part of the upriver forces were camped across the main
Beoga River. The river was a torrent of white water and
rapids dividing the mountains that rose on both sides of the
valley. The only way to cross the river was by bridge. In
times of peace, there was a bridge at the foot of the
landslide, but that had been cut when war began. The only
remaining bridge was upriver, more than an hour's walk
behind the enemy lines. That gave the upriver people an
island of safety for their women and pigs.

One evening the downriver men were sitting around the
fire discussing the events of the war. "Why are the spirits not
helping us? We've been fighting bravely every day, but we
have lost fourteen men and they, only six. What more can
we do?"

After a silence, another man suggested, "If we could make
a surprise attack on the enemy on the other side of the river,
we could even the score."

"The moon is full tonight," Wolo said. "Let's build a
bridge by moonlight and attack them at daybreak." The
group agreed to try the plan.

They took their axes and rattan tying vine and headed for
the river, where they found a tall tree long enough to reach
the other side. After cutting it down, they slashed off all the
branches and tied Wolo to the smaller end. By pivoting the
larger end of the pole on a boulder at the water's edge, they
gradually swung Wolo to the other side of the river. Once on
firm ground, Wolo untied himself from the pole, lashed his
end of the pole to a tree, and the bridge was begun. The men
worked on in the moonlight until their bridge, made of
three poles tied together, was ready to use.

In the early morning light, Wolo's men stole over the ridge
toward the first village. "*Wem me motako.* Warriors are
coming!" a man called out, and the war cry rose from the

village. Wolo's band had failed to surprise the enemy.

"The spirits are not helping us. The enemy will cut our bridge. Go back!" shouted Wolo.

Turning, they fled down the hill and back to their bridge. On the other side of the river, Wolo cut the vines that held the poles in place. The current swung the bridge to the opposite side of the river. For a few moments it bobbed in the current, then the anchor vines broke and the poles disappeared in the rapids.

Frustration from their failure, hatred, and grief reached the boiling point in the hearts of the downriver men. They *would* kill in revenge. They *must* kill someone—anyone— to avenge their dead.

The next day, the men fought on the battlefield with renewed fervor and determination to kill. At the same time, a small group sneaked unnoticed behind the lines and upvalley beyond the village war fence. They found three women and a boy in a garden digging potatoes. Almost before the group had time to cry out, they had killed all four of them.

Going further upvalley, they found all the villages deserted. Perhaps, they thought, there would be a party at the salt spring two hours' hike beyond the villages. Elated by their kill, they ran on through the jungle. As they approached the hut by the salt spring, they saw smoke rising and knew some of their enemies were there. When they had almost reached the hut, one of the enemy group saw them and sounded the alarm. Five men ran for their lives, and escaped into the jungle. Two were not fast enough, and the downriver warriors filled their bodies with arrows.

Running back down the trail, the warriors jumped over the logs and boulders as if they were not there at all. They were the victors! Six were dead! That made the score twelve to fourteen—almost even. Elated over their day of great victory, they decided it was time to stop fighting. This they could elect to do, because the larger number of dead was on their side. As they ran back through the villages, they shouted, "The fighting is over. We killed six people. The war is finished." When the upriver people heard the announcement, they accepted the decision. They, too, were tired of the months of fighting.

The fighting was ended. No more warriors would go to battle on the landslide. Twenty-six people were dead. Adak, who had stolen another man's wife, was now free to live with the woman as his second wife. Men would again trade shells with their former enemies and buy wives from their families. The fighting had stopped, but the heartache that the war would cause to all the people of the Beoga Valley had only begun.

3

The Skinny Splinter
Bears A Son

At last Wolo had his fill of fighting, and now he was going home to his wife. After the war had begun, he had taken Meyong to a village five hours' walk from the battlefield, for he did not want to take any chances of her being shot.

Wung village was built on the top of a mountain. Two thousand feet below, the Wang-Be River joined the Beoga River. Much of the mountain was covered with rocks and cliffs, with trees and bushes holding fast to the shallow soil. Clinging to the mountain near the top were terraced gardens that were always in danger of sliding off into the rivers below. Wolo's destination was six little round huts perched almost at the top.

Wolo gave no thought to the mountain grandeur that surrounded him. Other villages were also built on the steep mountainsides, with roaring streams not too far away. Damals and their neighboring tribes were earth's only real people, and this was the setting in which they lived. There was nothing special about any of the beauty that surrounded them, for that was life.

Wolo was conscious of his aching knee joints as he went down one mountain, only to climb up the next, feeling his leg muscles cramp. Catching a glimpse of the village, he thought of Meyong, who would be there waiting for him. She *had* matured into a young woman, and now she was going to have a baby—his baby!

When birth pains began for Meyong, she did not need anyone to explain what was happening to her. Like every other Damal child, she had never been sent away from watching anything that caught her curiosity, and that included observing every woman of the village as she had given birth to a baby.

Late that night, the old lady who was sitting with Meyong said to her, "The baby will soon be born. It is time to go outside."

Fortunately, the rain had stopped, and there was a soft light from the moon behind the clouds. The two women walked a short distance from the house into the tall grass. The older woman took Meyong's rain cape, sewn from stiff palm leaves, and spread it on the ground. "Squat on the mat," she said.

The cold night wind blew across the mountaintop, and Meyong shivered. "Why are Damal babies born outside?" she asked. "Dani women have their babies in the house by the fire."

"That's the way we Damals do it. Our babies are always born outside. Our mothers did it this way, and this is the way we must do it."

Another birth pang clutched her, and she cried out in pain. Then, it was past and forgotten. Meyong squatted silently, thinking of the baby that was to be born—her baby. She wanted this baby more than anything else in life. She would cuddle, nurse, and love it. No one else could feed this baby. It would depend on her—be her very own.

Soon the baby was born, and the old woman picked it up, wrapped it in banana leaves, and it began to cry. "It's a boy," the old woman told her. Meyong was glad.

As they waited for the placenta to be delivered, a light rain began to fall, and the wind seemed even colder. The baby cried a little as the older woman cuddled it in her arms. The cord was still attached to the baby according to Damal custom. Meyong remained squatting until the placenta had been discharged. Then the woman picked up a rock from the ground, and with a sawing motion cut the cord. "Now you can go to the house," said the old woman, and they returned to the warmth of the fire.

In the first light of morning, Wolo came to see his baby son. He was proud to have a son, but he did not tell Meyong that. Instead, he said, "Because I do not have any *mo* root in my garden, I bought some from my neighbor. I'm going to dig it now. As soon as I get it cooked, I'll bring it back for you to eat." (*Mo*, a starchy tuber, is called "taro" in English. Hawaiians make poi from the same root.)

Wolo was following the custom of his fathers. *Mo* is a specialty food, planted and cared for by only the men. When a man's wife gives birth to a baby, he cooks and serves her *mo* for a week. Wolo did not know it, but *mo* is an excellent food for a mother who is nursing a baby, for it contains calcium.

Meyong did not name her baby until he began to smile. She, like all Damal mothers, feared he would die; and if he died without a name, it would be easier to part with him.

When the time came to name her baby, Meyong remembered again the cutting words of her in-laws. "She is only a skinny splinter of wood and will never bear a son," they had said. In irony she named her baby *Kok-Me*, which means "leader of the splinters." Every time her son was called by name, her in-laws would be reminded that she, that skinny little girl, *had* borne a son.

When Kok-Me had grown to be a little boy, there was an unusual season of dry weather in his village. One day his parents had gone off to the garden, and his old grandfather was asleep in the hut. Kok-Me could find nothing to do that interested him, so he picked up some dry reeds to make a torch—it would be fun to make a fire. Taking the reeds into the house, he lit his torch with the coals on the hearth. Outside again, he was busy for some time lighting patches of grass and watching the fire burn. When the grass was all burned, he decided to light the grass on the roof of the house, to see if it would burn.

Kok-Me had no trouble reaching the roof with his torch.

Immediately the grass thatching caught fire. The grandfather was awakened by the sharp crackle of the fire, and ran outside. He tried to beat out the flames with his arms, but his efforts were in vain. The flames shot up higher and higher, and soon the whole house was burning. A mother pig had sense enough to run from the house, but her newborn piglets were burned alive. Everything else in the house was lost: a block of salt, some nets, and a stone knife.

When Wolo and Meyong saw the flames leaping from their house, they ran up the trail to the village, but it was too late to put out the fire. They were furious when they learned that Kok-Me had set the house on fire, and each of them gave him a severe beating.

The grandfathers arms were badly burned. He ran to the stream and held his arms in the cold water, trying to relieve the pain. Later, Meyong plastered her father's arms with mud to keep the flies out of the oozing sores. Wolo was totally embarrassed about what his son had done to cause his father-in-law's burns. "Kok-Me has no mind at all," he ranted. "He's senseless. How could he do such a thing?" Then Wolo caught one of his small pigs, butchered it, and presented its heart as a peace offering to the old man. In doing so, Wolo was also remembering that he still owed more bride price, and he did not want to deal with an angry father-in-law.

A favorite pastime of Kok-Me and his friends was to build dams on one of the small streams near their village. The boys collected pieces of wood and rocks and cemented them together with mud. When the water collected, one of the boys loosened a rock at the base of the dam, and the rocks and water went roaring down the hill. At the same time, the boys broke into a shout, "Ak ak ak," imitating sounds their fathers made when they had witnessed an exciting or dangerous event, like felling a tree or seeing a house catch fire. The boys thought it was great sport to be doing something dangerous, and the shouting to announce their feat was half the fun.

Another day, the boys got their bows and arrows and went hunting for lizards. They found their catch on the rocks, enjoying the warmth of the midday sun. The lizards were not very large, but they were a moving target, which made shooting them fun. Kok-Me enjoyed running and shouting and the freedom to do whatever he pleased.

Those little lizards are one of the few living creatures not edible to a Damal boy who is starved for meat, but the lizard eggs are a delicacy. One of the boys discovered a nest of lizard eggs under a rock and partly covered with sand. He broke one of the tiny eggs to see if the lizards had started to form. Finding they were freshly laid, he put the other fifteen eggs in his net bag to take home and bake in the ashes before eating them. This was a real prize!

Kok-Me's friend shot a larger lizard, which differed from the variety of little lizards that were everywhere. He called out, "Kok-Me, come see what I shot." Kok-Me came to admire his friend's prey. "Aren't you going to take it home and eat it?"

"No! Not me. I touched it, and it feels all scaly like a snake. You can have it."

"I'm not afraid to eat it," Kok-Me bragged. "It will taste good after I cook it." And he popped it into his net bag.

When Kok-Me was a little older, his father announced, "Now that you have learned to shoot lizards, you are old enough to hunt birds. I've made you this bigger bow. Go and get me some reeds, and you can help me make some arrows for shooting birds."

Kok-Me came back with a handful of reeds. Sitting in the men's house, Wolo took a reed and moved it back and forth across the open flame on the hearth. He needed just enough fire to heat the reed without burning it. Then he sighted down the shaft, bent the reed and sighted again, until it was straight. Some of the reeds broke as he bent them, and others shattered in the heat of the fire. But finally he was satisfied with the arrows he had prepared. "Now we're ready to put the tips on the arrows," he told his son.

Taking some pieces of hardwood from his net bag, and using a piece of jagged rock for a knife, Wolo sharpened the splinters of wood to a fine point. Then he hollowed out the end of a reed and poked three splinters of wood into the opening. He pushed some fiber between the splinters to spread the points and carefully wrapped the outside with a strip of rattan vine. Kok-Me watched the whole process with keen interest, for this set of arrows was to be all his own.

Kok-Me spent many happy hours hunting. He and his friends often went up to the edge of the jungle looking for birds in the tall trees. True, birds were hard to find, but when they shot one, the boys were elated. The bird was taken home, roasted on a stick, and devoured with relish.

During his growing years, Kok-Me's body craved protein; he never got enough from his basic diet of sweet potatoes. He was quick to eat anything that offered him a bit of meat, and that included several varieties of rats. Wolo taught his son to trap these little creatures, which lived in the fields around his home.

The trap was made from a green stick that was bent to act as a spring. Other sticks poked into the ground, and string made from rattan vine completed the trap. Kok-Me learned that rodents often travel along the base of a fence or near a banana tree. Working near a fence, he took a raw potato, chewed it up a bit, spit it out, and scattered it around on the ground. Then he put another piece of raw potato in the trap as bait, just behind the noose. The rodent would come along, discover the bits of potato on the ground, and then go after the bait in the trap. The rat's movement in eating the potato triggered the trap, and it was caught in the noose.

Kok-Me set a number of traps in the afternoon. The next morning when he found that he had caught two rats, he hurried home to cook them. Holding the rats with wooden tongs, he singed off the hair in the fire. Then he wrapped them in banana leaves and buried them in the ashes to bake.

While they were cooking, Wolo came into the hut and learned that his son had caught two rats. "Did you clean out the intestines before you cooked them?" he asked.

"No," was the reply. "I was in a hurry to eat them, so I just singed off the hair and put them in the ashes to bake."

"You lazy boy! You must always slit the rat open and take out the intestines before you cook it." He paused, and then continued. "And never eat them alone. Always share your food with others. If you don't, the spirits will make you die."

"Oh, I'll share them. I always share my food."

Wolo nodded and went outside.

Although the war in which Wolo had fought had been over for ten years, he was still deeply involved in making war settlement payments. Wolo had promoted the war, and had been a brave warrior in the battles; now he had to make many payments, and those payments usually consisted of pigs.

The pigs in Wolo's household belonged to him, for it was the man who owned the pigs, but it was Meyong who did the work of raising them. She planted and weeded the sweet potato gardens, then dug the potatoes and carried them home. Every day she fed a portion of the potatoes to the pigs. During the day, the pigs scrounged for food in the woods and in deserted gardens, but in the evening after Meyong fed them potatoes, she shut them in the pig stalls inside her own hut. Meyong was an energetic worker, and because of this, her pigs prospered more than the pigs of her neighbors.

Meyong thought at least part of the meat from the pigs belonged to her because she had raised them. But Wolo did not even consider her rights. He had paid for his wife. Meyong and the pigs all belonged to him. He could do as he pleased.

The second child born to Meyong was a girl. Again, she

did not name her baby right away. She reasoned that the spirits would not want to cause the death of a baby by eating its spirit if that child were so unimportant that it did not even have a name. It was obvious to Meyong that her reasoning was correct, for the baby prospered and grew fat.

As the baby grew, she decided it was time to give her daughter a name; she chose *Togan-Wonem*. Literally that means "Every day another one disappears." In naming her daughter, Meyong was crying out in protest to her husband: "Every day you take another one of my pigs to make your war payments, and I never get to eat any of the meat."

4

More Wives—More Wealth

Meyong called to her son. "Come here. Take your baby sister and carry her around. I'm going to get some things ready for the evening meal." Kok-Me stood with his back to his mother while she placed the baby astraddle his shoulders. Reaching over his shoulders, he took each of her hands in his, balancing her so that she did not fall over backward. Her bare bottom slid down his back until her chin rested on top of his head. "Now be careful with her," Meyong said as she started off with her net bag full of greens.

Kok-Me walked around the village yard for some time. His sister was quite heavy for a boy his size, but he managed to keep his balance and keep walking. The baby was content to be carried. After a time, they came to the edge of the village yard where there was a cooking pit that had been used in a large feast some months before. The hole was now filled with water.

The boy squatted down and carefully slid his sister down his back to the ground. He eased a little closer to the hole, and his sister crawled up beside him. They both looked into the black, murky water. It reflected their images back to them like a mirror. This was the only kind of mirror they had ever seen, and they were fascinated to see the reflection of their faces.

Kok-Me moved back from the pool. He could still see the dark surface of the water, but now there was no baby in the pool. Crawling closer, he again saw the baby in the water. Again he moved back, and the baby was gone; but when he looked in closely, the baby reappeared.

The whole thing confused his small boy's mind. What sort of spirit was in the water? Suddenly he felt the urge to have his sister catch the baby in the pool. He gave her a little push, and she fell headfirst into the water.

The water was not very deep, and soon the baby's head surfaced. She began to sputter and then scream. Meyong heard the cries and came running to rescue her baby. She pulled her out of the water, turned her upside down and shook her by the feet. Water poured from her mouth, nose, and ears. Satisfied her baby would survive, Meyong sat Togan-Wonem on her hip and wiped the water from the baby's face with her hand.

"You bad boy! Look what you've done to your sister." Meyong shouted at her son and boxed his ears with several sharp blows. "Haven't you any sense at all?"

The baby's cries subsided and the incident was forgotten, until Togan-Wonem had grown and the family discovered that she was almost deaf. Then they remembered the incident of the cooking hole full of water. They were sure it was Kok-Me's fault that she could not hear. He had pushed his sister into the pool, and the water getting into her ears had made her deaf.*

One day Meyong noticed that her son did not go out and play with the other boys. He was content to sit in the house by the fire. That just was not like Kok-Me. Several days passed, and he still was not going outside. He was sick to his stomach, and his body was hot to her touch. He did not want the potatoes she cooked for him. All he asked for was sugar cane, which he chewed and sucked to get the juice. Ginger root tasted good, too. He took a piece, dipped it in some salt crumbled on a leaf, and nibbled on the spicy hot ginger. But he only picked at his potatoes—even the yellow mealy ones that were his favorite.

* The true cause of the deafness was probably an ear infection following a cold or pneumonia. But to the Damals, who never entered the water for either swimming or bathing, getting water in one's ear was traumatic and seemed the obvious cause of the little girl's loss of hearing.

The rays of the morning sun were shining through the door of the hut. Meyong looked more closely at her son. The whites of his eyes were yellow, and his dark skin had a yellowish cast. Kok-Me had *namang* sickness—infectious hepatitis. She was afraid her boy was going to die.

Meyong had to do something for her son. The food she fixed for him was of no help. The evil spirits were eating the spirit of life out of him. That was why he was so sick, and when the spirits had eaten all the seed of life, he would die.

Meyong set out for the jungle early the next morning. She went up and down on the mountainside, pushing her way through the tangle of vines and underbrush. Thorns tore at her net and her skin. Then she found it: a low tree with small, shiny green leaves. She plucked a handful of leaves, wrapped them carefully in another large leaf, and headed down the mountain.

Back home, Meyong crushed the leaves until they were pulverized and put them on a banana leaf, which served as a plate. She mashed a shoot of a mild asparaguslike vegetable and mixed it with the leaves. "Now eat this," she said to her son. "I've mixed the bitter leaves with a vegetable shoot so it won't taste too bad." Kok-Me managed to swallow a bit of the bitter potion, but spit out the rest.

Meyong put some of the leaves into her own mouth, and then, blowing and spitting, she spewed them into Kok-Me's face, on his chest, and under his arms. In a low voice, she spoke to the spirit. "Oh, spirit of the Beoga River, my son is not good to eat. He tastes very bitter. You won't like him. Don't eat him; don't make him sick; please don't kill him."

Meyong watched for improvement, but there was none. Days went by; still he lay listless by the fire. The yellow had gone from his eyes and skin, but he had no desire to go out and play with the other boys. Meyong knew she would have to call a man who knew how to appease the evil spirits, so they would go away and leave her boy alone. She had only one pig, and she would have to give that, for a man who performs sorcery always demands a pig.

When the spirit-man arrived, he said, "First I must have a pig." Meyong gave him her little one. He took the pig into the grass and killed it, saying the secret names of evil spirits over it. That was intended to entice the spirits to eat the spirit of the pig instead of the boy's spirit.

Then he took some red dirt and mixed it with water in a leaf. Again he said some magic words and ceremoniously dabbed the mud on Kok-Me's body. Finally, he took a string and fashioned a necklace for the boy, using two cowrie shells and the pig's tail. Taking the pig with him, the sorcerer went home to gorge on the meat. It was taboo for any woman or child to eat the pork used in spirit appeasement. Only the sorcerer and the men of his choosing could share in eating that meat.

Kok-Me began to feel better the next day, and soon he was out playing as usual. His mother made sure that he continued to wear the necklace with the pig's tail, for she was convinced that this charm had enticed the evil spirit to go away and leave her boy alone.

Meyong looked at her son and saw that he was getting tall. "Kok-Me," she said, "you are getting to be a big boy. It's time you slept in the men's house with your father, instead of with me and the other women who sleep in my house."

Kok-Me listened, but did not say anything. He felt so close to his mother. She was the one who had taken care of him when he was a baby. She had carried him, cooked his food, and nursed him when he was sick. He did not want to leave her loving influence—not yet, anyway.

Meyong sensed the indecision in her son's mind. "You know that sometimes the men have wild pig or jungle animals to eat. It's taboo for women to eat that meat. If you sleep in the men's house, you'll get wild pig to eat, too."

A half-smile appeared on Kok-Me's face. Soon he was sleeping in the men's house every night.

Meyong was pregnant again, and she was hungry—not for

sweet potatoes, because she was an energetic gardener and had enough potatoes—but she was hungry for meat. Her unborn child needed protein. Some protein was supplied from the sweet potato, and Meyong ate lots of those, but it was not enough. Her black hair soon took on a dingy, reddish cast from the deficiency, and she was always tired.

Although Meyong craved meat, there was none for her. Wolo used the family pigs in his business deals. He was making payments on a second wife. His allies from the war were still demanding indemnity payments. Sometimes Wolo ate pork, but he never shared any with Meyong. Culture demanded that he share meat with other men, but it was not necessary to share with his wife.

The third child was a boy. Meyong named him Na-Nonem, which means "I never eat pork." People would remember her plight every time they said his name.

Damal tradition was very firm that Meyong must remain true to her husband. Meyong belonged to Wolo, and he was ready to fight if there was any infringement on his property rights.

But for Wolo, it was a different story. He was free to marry as many wives as he wanted, provided he could make the payments. He was free to flirt with any single girl, and he could make approaches for marriage.

Wolo was attending the courtship sings quite frequently now. The night would be announced for a sing, and people gathered in the men's house. Girls of marriageable age and men looking for a wife took part in the sing. The men sat on one side of the fire, and the girls on the other. This was a time when eyes and hearts met, and emotions were aroused. Wolo had never sung to Meyong, for she had been too young to take part in a courtship sing when he married her. Now he sang to another woman.

Wolo aspired to become a leader. He had already made a name for himself in the war. The next step for a man of importance was to marry a second wife. Another wife would give him more sons; a man with sons increased his prestige in the community. His sons would bring their wives to live in his village, and more people would be under his leadership. More daughters would bring more bride price payments back into his family. Any Damal man of importance had at least two wives.

The pig was the keystone of the Damal economy. Every business deal involved pigs, whether for paying bride price, settling an offense before war began, paying war indemnity, securing the services of a spirit-appeasement man, or simply trading to increase one's assets. A second wife meant more pigs, because each wife tended her own sweet potato garden, fed the potatoes to her pigs, and thus increased the number of pigs a man owned.

There was still another reason why Wolo was taking a second wife. Meyong had a baby, and her life was filled with the care and feeding of that baby. She would nurse her son until he was at least three years old. The baby would begin to eat potatoes after a year, but no baby could survive on potatoes alone. Her milk meant life to him. Meyong knew that if she became pregnant, she would have no more milk for her baby. If she slept with her husband, her baby would die. It was as simple as that. That is why the men slept in a communal men's house, and each woman had her own hut, rather than husband and wife sleeping in the same house. They had no other way of family planning.

Meyong, like all Damal women, fiercely resisted any advances from her husband as long as her baby was small. Her emotional ties were stronger toward her baby than they were toward her husband. Wolo showed very little real love to his wife, and there was a different kind of love between Meyong and her baby—it was unbroken. She was never separated from her baby, even for a short time. The little one needed her, and that made her life worth living.

Wolo built a house for his second wife when she came to live in the village of Wung. His attentions were centered on his new wife, but Meyong did not mind. She had her baby.

The two women shared their lot of going to the garden day after day, and they became like sisters.

Through the years there were times when both women were seeking Wolo's attention and when each needed his help in digging a new garden or building a fence. When that happened they fought, but most of the time they shared the trials of a woman's life and were friends. Meyong's children called the second wife "mother," and the children of the second wife called Meyong "mother."

5

Lessons in Horticulture, Hunting, and *Hai*

Kok-Me squatted in the village yard, watching his father sharpen the point on his garden-digging stick. The stick was a sturdy piece of wood six feet long. Wolo held the handle of his ax close to the steel ax head. He chopped with short, quick strokes, turning the stick with his left hand. "There," Wolo said. "Tomorrow, when we go to the garden, it will be easier to dig with this sharpened stick. Go bring me the other digging stick so I can sharpen it, too."

Finishing the second stick, he laid it down. "When I was a boy your age, I had never seen a steel ax. All my father had was a stone ax—the same kind of stone ax that most people use today."

"My father," Kok-Me said, "you have the only steel ax in our village, and some villages don't even have one steel ax."

Wolo beamed with the pride of recognition that he *was* an outstanding businessman who owned a steel ax. "I remember when the first ax came into the Beoga," Wolo said. "I was in my mid teens."

"Tell me about it," Kok-Me begged. "Where do steel axes come from?"

Father and son squatted on the ground, enjoying the warmth of the sun. Wolo went on with his story. "Years ago, some Damal people who lived south of the big mountain range made a trip down into the lowlands. After traveling for many days, they came upon some stumps of trees that had been cut, but not with a stone ax. They snapped their gourds with their fingers in amazement and said, 'This is *hai*. We have found *hai*.'" (*Hai* is the Damal word that

64

describes something that is supernatural, has eternal life, and that promises the riches of earthly goods obtained by supernatural means—paradise.)

"The men went back to the mountains, but later returned in search of *hai*. In time, they contacted coastal tribespeople and began to trade their tobacco for steel ax heads. Although many Damal people died from malaria and other tropical diseases when they visited the lowlands, some returned to the mountains, bringing their *hai* axes with them.

"Later, the southern Damals traded steel axes over the mountains to the Beoga. A man paid a huge pig for an ax. There were only a few steel axes. Most villages had none. My father paid a good cowrie shell just to rent an ax for several days."

Kok-Me was still thinking about steel axes and *hai* as he watched his father get up and go into the men's hut.

The next morning, father and son started off for the garden. Kok-Me carried the two digging sticks, and Wolo balanced a roll of rattan tying vine on his head. When he reached the garden, Kok-Me saw that the ground had been planted sometime before, so they would not have to start from scratch and clear away trees or brush. Wolo took his digging stick with both hands, and, raising it partway over his shoulder, drove it into the ground. Then, with a prying motion, he loosened the dirt and broke it up into clods with the point of his stick. The ground was rocky—very rocky—having almost more rocks than soil. He threw the larger rocks in a row at his feet. This area would serve as a terrace between the sweet potato beddings.

Midmorning, Wolo said, "Let's rest awhile." The two squatted on the mountainside and took cold baked potatoes from their net bags. They ate in silence.

"My back aches," Kok-Me moaned. "I dug a lot of ground this morning."

"Well, you didn't dig all that much, but you'll improve with practice. You still have a lot of things to learn."

Wolo fished in his net bag and pulled out his fire-making stick. "I'm hungry for a smoke," he said as he took a piece of punk from his bag and placed it in the fork of the stick. Then he fitted a vine into the groove next to the punk and held the base of the stick on the ground between his toes. Bending over, he grasped the ends of the vine, one in each hand, and began a rapid sawing motion, pulling the vine back and forth on the stick to cause friction. Beads of sweat rose on Wolo's face as he worked. At last, a thin column of smoke began to rise. Bending to the ground, he blew vigorously on the punk.

From his armband he took a cigarette coil. Crushed tobacco was folded in this special dry leaf. He held the end of the cigarette to the punk, and it began to burn. He put the side of the cigarette into his mouth next to the burning end and inhaled. Squatting on the ground, Wolo enjoyed his smoke.

"Did you see those pandanas nut trees when we came up the mountain?" Kok-Me asked. "I think the nuts are almost ripe."

"Don't you get any ideas about stealing one of those nut clusters," Wolo cautioned. "The owner of the nut trees said the names of the spirits and put a hex on anyone who steals his nuts. If you steal them, you'll die. And I don't want you going into the gardens with another boy," Wolo continued. "If two of you are off by yourselves, you'll be tempted to steal. Do you hear me? You're not to steal."

After Wolo had finished smoking, they resumed their digging in the garden until early afternoon when it was time to head for home. "We'll go along the fence," Wolo said. "Somewhere there is a weak spot where the pigs have been getting into the garden."

Wolo found the place where the rattan tying vine had rotted, and the fence sticks were no longer evenly spaced. "Right here's the place," he said.

Taking a piece of rattan vine from the coil, he began splitting it with his teeth. He worked quickly until the entire vine was split right down the center. Kok-Me also took a piece of rattan and began splitting it, but his piece shredded off from the main vine, leaving only a short length. "Throw that piece away and try again," Wolo said. "You'll learn if you keep trying."

Wolo wrapped the long vine around and around the crosspiece of fencewood that held the stakes in place. After each wind, he put his right foot on the fence to brace it while he pulled back on the vine to cinch it tightly in place. "The pigs won't get in this garden anymore," Wolo remarked as he finished the job. He pointed with his chin to the black raincloud advancing from across the river and said, "The rain is coming. Let's go home."

An epidemic of dysentery had come to the village of Wung. Two babies had died, and men and women were sick, too. Wolo and two other men of importance conferred about the problem. The spirits must be appeased, or the sick ones might all die.

The next day, no one was allowed to leave the village. The women could not go to their gardens, and children could not go off to play. After the early morning chill had dissipated, Wolo began to call the villagers together. "You all gather. Everyone come and sit down here in the village yard." At first no one paid too much attention. Some of the men sat by the fire in the hut, and boys ran as they pleased. After more shouting and threats, people finally began to gather. The men squatted on their haunches, and the women sat cross-legged on the ground.

Wolo strung a rattan vine around the group. He and two other men were to perform the spirit appeasement. They took turns shouting in loud, angry voices at the people gathered. "Cover your eyes with your hands. Don't anyone peek. If you peek, you will see an evil spirit and then you will die."

The three men began to chase a pig around the outside of the circle. They were mumbling words, but no one could

hear them clearly. Their words were secret spirit words—
the name of an evil spirit. Wolo had paid a pig to learn that
spirit name from an old man who had a reputation for being
a successful spirit appeaser. All of a sudden, there was a
loud whack and the ear-splitting cry of a pig, as a man hit
the pig in the head with a club. More mumbling of words
and shouting of orders followed, as they completed the
killing of the pig.

"Keep your eyes closed," the men shouted. "We're going
to kill another pig."

The men began to chase the second pig around the circle.
Kok-Me decided he wanted to see what was going on. No
one would see him. He peeked through his fingers, and all
that he saw was the people seated around him, and the three
men chasing the pig. He saw no evil spirit, and he did not
die.

Again there was a thud and the scream of the pig. That
time they killed the pig on the opposite side of the circle.
The ceremony was over, and the group broke up.

That night in the house, the men were talking about the
spirit appeasement of the day. It was late, and Kok-Me had
already stretched out on his mat for the night. Perhaps they
thought he was asleep—but he was not.

"I think the evil spirits will leave us alone now, and no
one else will die," one man was saying. "We encircled
everyone in the village with our spirit worship ceremony.
The evil spirits should be happy with the pigs we gave them
and not eat any more of the spirits of our people."

"Well, I hope so," Wolo mused. "I hope so. I remember
when I was a boy—a little boy, not even as old as Kok-Me."

Kok-Me perked up his ears. He always liked to hear
stories that his father told. No one interrupted Wolo as he
went on with his story.

"There was a great sickness in our village. Everyone was
sick, and many people had died. The spirit-appeasement
men killed pigs and offered them to the evil spirits, but they
weren't satisfied. Other men came and offered more pigs,

but still, people were dying. The village men were afraid; they didn't know what to do. They were afraid that everyone was going to die.

"The men had built a short fence across the path that led into the village. On this fence they hung a whole pig, offering it to the spirits." (Usually the evil spirits were given only the tail of a pig, whereas the men ate all the meat.) "The stomach had been split open, inviting the spirits to come and eat, but they must not have been satisfied. The men decided they would have to sacrifice the spirit of a person to these evil spirits—only this would satisfy them.

"They discussed the problem night after night. 'A person has never been sacrificed to the spirits before,' they said. 'Is it really necessary? Who would be chosen for the sacrifice? How would it be done?'

"Finally, they agreed that they would sacrifice my cousin, Ambo. He was just a little boy. They didn't like giving one of their own family, but there was no other way, they decided. The men would say the spirit-appeasement ritual as they killed him, and then they would hang his body on the fence that crossed the path entering the village. The spirits coming into the village to harm the villagers would find the boy's body and be satisfied to eat his spirit instead of the spirits of those still alive in the village.

"Somehow a brother, just older than Ambo, heard what the men were planning. The two boys decided to run away. Never before had they traveled any distance from their home. They knew nothing about the trail to the distant Moni valley, nor anything about survival in the jungle. But run away they did—it meant life or death for Ambo. Even after the epidemic was over Ambo didn't return home. He was a grown man before he had courage enough to go back to his family and village."

Kok-Me shivered on his mat. Would the evil spirits be satisfied with the pigs that were sacrificed today? Would the sickness in the village come to an end? At last the talking of the men abated, and everyone slept.

The roof of the Wung men's hut leaked in two places, and the entire house had begun to lean a bit to one side. Wolo considered the problem, for he was obviously the head of the house. He was the only man of the five who boasted of having two wives. It was time to build a new house.

The men set out for the forest together. Wolo's steel ax was invaluable for the project. To use a blunt stone ax would have meant days of back-breaking labor, and the end result would have been extremely crude. With their steel ax, the men spent only a few hours felling selected trees and then began splitting boards in wedge-shaped pieces from the logs they had cut. That made the boards wide on one side, tapering down to a thin piece that came from the center of the log. It took two days' work in the forest to produce enough boards to build the house. Carrying the boards down to the village, the men sang with a resounding chant, so that everyone who heard them could share in the excitement of their community project.

The men dug and leveled the ground for the new house site, dancing round and round as they packed it firmly in place. Next, they sharpened one end of each board and drove the sharpened end into the ground in a circle, forming the interior wall of the house. Bending small saplings around the outside of the boards, they tied them together with rattan tying vine.

Another layer of boards was driven into the ground in a slightly larger circle. They were staggered in an attempt to cover the large cracks left between the first circle of boards. Now, between the two layers of boards, they stuffed grass and leaves to serve as insulation against the cold night wind.

The framework of the roof was built in a cone shape, and on top of the structure they laid sheets of bark stripped from a *tevat* evergreen tree. Over the bark they tied bundles of a long grass, and the thatching of the roof was completed.

To complete the inside of the house, a man was sent off to get a special type of clay to build the hearth. Around the hearth, a structure of small poles was laid on the ground, and over this reeds were placed side by side to make a floor. When the reeds had been laced together with rattan tying vine, Wolo said, "There's one more thing we must do. The spirits of our ancestors will be moving into this house with us. We must make them happy so they won't bother us or bring us sickness. We need to have an op feast, and we'll dedicate their spirits to our ancestors."

Addressing his son, Wolo said, "You and I will go hunting for ops. Before, when you cried to go with me, I never let you go. You were too young to go on a night hunt. But now I think you are growing up. In two days, the moon will be full, and we will go together."

Kok-Me felt good inside. His father had said he was becoming a man.

The day arrived for the hunt. Father and son were up with the first light of dawn. They put what potatoes they had in the ashes to bake and went off to a nearby garden to dig more. Returning home, each with a net bag of potatoes, they ate their breakfast.

Their net bags were packed, and Wolo checked off everything in his mind. In Wolo's net, he had a carefully wrapped cigarette roll, a bamboo knife, and his fire-making stick, with a roll of vine to use in starting fires. He had carefully wrapped some very dry leaves and bark inside other leaves. If everything were soaked in rain, he could get a fire started with that dry tinder. High up in the mountains, fire could mean the difference between life and death. Once they started a fire in their camp, they could keep it burning during their stay, but starting it the first time was critical.

Each of them had a rain cape, which would double as a sleeping mat, and a net bag of potatoes. Rations would be small, and they would be hungry, for a full three days' supply of sweet potatoes was too heavy to carry up the mountain. Kok-Me watched his father string his bow, swing a net bag on his back, lift the bow and arrows to his head with his right hand, and grasp the net bag band that went across his forehead with both hands, to help bear the weight. Kok-Me did the same.

In the first part of the journey, their path led past some villages, but soon they had entered the dense jungle. Although they were following the main trail, only the well-trained eye of a Damal could distinguish that there was any path at all. Fallen logs were strewn about, and sometimes the path led right up a log. A tangle of brush and vines caused them to stoop low and caught in their net bags. Mud holes and tricklets of water were always underfoot.

After two hours of hiking, they left the main trail to follow an even less defined path. It was little more than the line of least resistance through the jungle, but always going up. That path led nowhere—only deeper into the wilderness. Wolo led the way, and Kok-Me followed close behind. He was observing how his father picked out the signs that marked the trail. Tall trees rose on every side, and vines and foliage almost obscured any view of the sky. Kok-Me was glad he was with his father.

Wolo stopped in a little clearing and swung his net bag to the ground. Kok-Me could see the remains of a fire from another hunting party. "Here we are," Wolo said. "We'll build our shelter here. It may be getting dark soon, so we'd better hurry." (There is no way to tell, without a watch, whether the fading light is from the approach of night, or from a heavy cloud cover. And because all Damal country is so close to the equator, twilight is very brief.)

Wolo took his ax and started off with Kok-Me following behind him. He cut a small tree and used the poles to erect a pup-tentlike framework. For roofing he used some bark he had peeled from a large *tevat* evergreen tree. Leafy branches laid over the hut helped to hold the bark in place and completed the structure. Rain had begun to fall, and they were wearing their rain capes. Kok-Me shivered. It was much colder up in the mountains than it was at his village.

Wolo gave the job of chopping wood to his son while he started a fire. He got out his fire-making stick and the carefully wrapped tinder. It was dry, and that was good, because nothing else was dry. Rains were too frequent, and the hours of sunshine too few, to get anything dry once it was wet. Soon the fire was burning, and Wolo sat down to smoke.

Although the rain had stopped, the fire still felt very good as they roasted some potatoes in the coals. By the time a potato began to burn on the outside, the inside was still half raw. That did not matter to Wolo and Kok-Me. They were starved, and the potatoes tasted delicious, no matter how they were cooked.

The *dedel* beetles finally chirped their announcement of nightfall. Soon the moon rose in a sky speckled only by a few clouds. The moonlight falling on the foliage wet with raindrops created a glittering wonderland. Every drop of water sparkled like a diamond. But neither father nor son commented about what they saw as they picked up their bows and arrows and started into the jungle.

Perhaps their surroundings did not represent beauty to them, because Damal culture does not educate its people to appreciate the beauty of creation as Western culture does. The most common things are always valued the least. In the world of the Damal, there was no threat from man to mar creation in its natural state. The beauty in nature did not help sustain life. Beauty always surrounded them, so why take notice?

As they pressed through the undergrowth in the jungle, those sparkling diamonds of water felt like drops of ice on their naked bodies.

Op is a general Damal term used to describe the many small animals found in the mountains of Irian Jaya. Most *op*s are marsupials—the female carries her young in a pouch like the opossum or kangaroo—and are nocturnal. Despite the fact that there are vast jungle areas in Irian Jaya, there is relatively little game. Besides the marsupials, a small variety of anteater, the cassowary bird, and the wild pig are also hunted.

The man and boy moved through the forest, watching for the movement of an op in the trees. After what seemed like an endless time to Kok-Me, his father motioned to him to be still. Wolo drew his bow and waited. The arrow shot up into the tree in front of them, hitting its target. Kok-Me ran to retrieve the dark brown, furry animal that fell to the ground. "I'll take it back to camp," he said. "I'm too cold and sleepy to hunt anymore."

Wolo knew there was no point in trying to get his son to continue the hunt that night. "All right," he said. "You go back to camp and sleep. If I can find the op's trail, we'll build a blind, and tomorrow night we'll sit there and hunt."

Kok-Me stoked the fire, curled up on his mat, and was soon sound asleep. Once as he slept, he felt the movement of fur next to his body, and in his sleepy stupor thought it was a dog beside him. When he woke in the morning, he found that the fur he had felt was that of two more ops his father had killed and laid beside him.

When Wolo aroused, he said, "We'll eat the small animal and take the two bigger ones home." Wolo split the animals open with his bamboo knife, removed the intestines, and tied them back together with vine. He sent Kok-Me after a bundle of ferns, which he wrapped around the animals until there was no fur visible. Digging a shallow hole, he placed the two animals in it and covered them with sod. "This will keep the flies and bugs away from the meat until we can take it home."

"Last night I learned where the ops travel back and forth on a path," Wolo said. "Let's go and build a blind where we can hide tonight and shoot them." Wolo and Kok-Me went to the spot, and, taking several poles, they lashed them together to form a platform on which they could sit. Then they cut branches and covered their perch with the leafy boughs. Wolo was careful to leave a line of sight open where he expected the animal to come down the tree.

The long daylight hours were ideal for talking, and Wolo used the time to repeat again to his son the morals and teachings of their fathers. Kok-Me would soon be growing into manhood, and in order to be accepted into the Damal society as a mature man, he must know and follow the tribal teachings.

The moral concepts that Wolo taught his son may or may not have been repeated to him in a single afternoon, but they were taught in detail and with constant repetition. We do not know for how many generations of Damals those teachings were passed on from father to son. But we do know that they had no contact with the outside world or any teaching from missionaries. It is interesting to compare the Damal teachings with the Ten Commandments as they were given to Moses in Exodus 20:1-17 and those repeated by Jesus in Mark 10:17-29. It is also interesting to ponder the meaning of Romans 1, especially verses 19 and 20, in the light of those moral concepts.

Stealing is forbidden. Do not steal potatoes or other food from someone else's garden. And do not steal something large like a pig. Even if the owner does not find out that you were the thief, you will be punished.

If, when a man is sick, a theft is not confessed and paid back, he will die. If the owner of the stolen goods comes into the house where the thief is lying ill, the sick man will break out in a sweat, take an immediate turn for the worse, and die. Do not steal. A person who steals will die.

Do not give a false report. A person who says, "I will give you so-and-so" in a business deal, and then does not, has told a lie. That kind of person is known as a liar, and his word cannot be depended upon. Do not accuse another man falsely. If a man reports that a friend has killed and eaten someone else's pig, when the truth is that he has been hunting *ops* and eating them, that could even start a war.

Do not commit adultery with another man's wife. If you do, you are walking into fire. A person who has committed adultery will soon die in war or from sickness. Or the offended husband may come to shoot him, and war follows.

Even worse than adultery is incest. If you have relations

ﬥ who is called mother, sister, or aunt, or with
ﬥ your father's half of the tribe, then you must
die. If a man has commited incest, his gardens will not grow
and his pigs will die. And the same curse will be on his
extended family. In war, his arrows will become powerless,
and even if they hit an enemy, the man they hit will not die.
The entire clan will be defeated in war because of one
member's incest. The only remedy is to kill the offender, and
that will be done by his own brothers.

Do not become a man who kills other men. The tribe
looks down on a man who, in anger during an argument or
fight over payments, shoots and kills another. A man who
kills is always in danger of being killed himself. The sons of
the dead man will not forget who killed their father. Even
years later the sons may take revenge and kill the murderer.

Do not pile up unpaid debts. The person to whom you are
in debt will think evil thoughts about you, and you will die.
No one likes a man who has many debts.

Be quick to share everything you have with others.
Generosity is the highest virtue. When a stranger comes to
your village, welcome him into your house and feed him
well. Never eat a piece of meat by yourself. A generous man
always has many friends.

Listen to your father's words and you will prosper. Learn
how to dig a garden and make a fence the proper way.
People will praise you as a person if you follow the
instructions of your father. A woman does not want a man
for her husband who has not learned the ways of Damal
living. A son who obeys his parents' words will live to have
a gray beard.

A girl must learn from her mother all the Damal arts of
weaving a net, digging and weeding sweet potatoes,
cooking, and taking care of children and pigs. A daughter
who does not heed her mother's instructions will be passed
by when the desirable young men are looking for a wife.

"If you obey my instructions," Wolo warned, "you will
see *hai*. If you steal and lie, you won't see *hai*. You'll die."

"What is *hai*?" asked Kok-Me.

"*Hai* is a place of no death in the sky where there are lots of women and pigs. *Hai* is just *hai*. Our fathers said their children would see *hai*, but those children grew old and said to *their* children, 'You will see *hai*.' My father told me that in the third generation *hai* will come. He said war and killing and stealing will stop. My son, some day you will see *hai*."

Kok-Me did not really understand the definition of *hai*, but neither, for that matter, did Wolo. They had a vague feeling that it was paradise or pie-in-the-sky; all man's desires would be lavishly satisfied through supernatural means. Damals had no idea of scientific fact or logical proof. The spirit world was reality to them. When a formula to control or appease the spirits was carried out, but the desired results were not obtained, the Damals were not deterred in their practice. Next time, the desired end would be realized. Next time *hai* would come.

"Once our Damal people arrived at the place of *hai*," Wolo continued, "but they lost it again. This is the story that my father told me, and you can tell your sons.

"Two Damal men climbed up the roots of a tree which they found hanging down from the sky. They climbed until they crawled through a hole in the sky and found the place of *hai*. Many little people lived in this place where no one died. The men had many wives, and the wives bore them many children. The men wore large pig tusks in their noses, and there was much dancing with chanting. Sweet potatoes and *mo* were so plentiful that they rotted for lack of someone to eat them. The pigs were huge—more than the little people could eat. Every day the little people shared pork with the Damals. But the two Damals were greedy and decided to steal one of the pigs. They killed the pig, threw it down through the hole in the sky, and started down the tree root themselves. But the little people discovered that these earthly men had stolen a pig, so they cut the roots of the tree. Never again have earthly people been able to climb to the place of *hai*."

Wolo did not go on to make the analysis for his son that paradise was lost to the Damal through sin. He did not verbalize the fact that he and his people were completely helpless to keep the moral laws that were so carefully instilled in each generation. They knew that breaking the laws brought sorrow and death, but that knowledge gave them no power to keep those laws. Wolo needed no logical explanation to accept the Damal concept of *hai* or the moral commandments. The world of the supernatural was often more real than the physical world around him. *Hai* would come in the next generation.

The two hunters woke from their nap as the daylight began to fade into evening. "I'm hungry," Kok-Me said. "I'm going to cook some potatoes."

"No more potatoes now," Wolo said. "When you are hunting you can't eat your fill of potatoes. We didn't bring that many with us. Part of becoming a man and a hunter is to be tough and learn to keep on hunting, even though you are hungry."

Wolo sat smoking. "Do you want to smoke, too?" he asked.

Kok-Me did not. "Not right now," he said. He had had his first smoke the day his father told him he could go on the hunt. Smoking was part of being a man, Kok-Me had observed, but he found the taste of his first smoke bitter, and it made him sick. He had no choice about going without potatoes, but he could choose to wait a bit before he had another smoke.

Kok-Me broke the long silence with a question. "Will you climb up in the tall trees and hunt *ops* like some men do?" Some hunters shinny up the trunks of tall trees and climb up the branches to the top. During the day *ops* sleep in the treetops. The hunter has only to club the sleeping animal and it falls to the ground.

"Climbing tall trees is taboo for me," Wolo replied. "And that's that."

"Well, are we going to trap *ops*?" Kok-Me persisted. "I could help with that, because I know how to trap rats."

"No, not on this trip," Wolo answered. "We'd have to sleep up here six nights to make the trapping worthwhile. After you locate the paths that the *ops* follow, it takes a day to set your traps. Then you have to check your traps several days to make it pay. Not this time.

"Come on," Wolo said. "Let's go hunt *ops* from the blind that we built. We'll get some tonight."

The night's hunt was successful, and so was the next night's. In the three nights of hunting, they killed eleven *ops*. On the third night, they went back to their jungle shelter to get a couple of hours' sleep before starting for home.

Wolo woke with the singing of the birds. The moon was still shining, and he could detect no sign of morning light, but, hearing the birds, he knew that day was dawning. He roused his son. "Get up," he said. "We're going home. Cook these last potatoes in the fire, and we'll be ready to go."

Wolo dug up the *ops* that were stashed away under the cold earth and then packed them into the netbags. They ate their potatoes, and Wolo had his final smoke before they broke camp.

Down the mountain they jogged, slipping and jolting as they descended. The energy they were exerting to keep from falling, and also to carry their loads, helped a little to keep them warm, yet they felt the cold. No rays of sun reached them, and icy drops of water sprinkled on their bare skin as they pushed through the underbrush. Still, it was easier and much faster going downhill than it had been when they climbed up. Kok-Me was happy, too, for he was returning from his first hunting trip, and he had *ops* to show—even two he had shot himself.

The sun was just past the middle of the sky when they arrived at their village. The other men quickly appeared from their men's house. They were delighted to hear that Wolo and Kok-Me did bring *ops* for their house-christening feast. Everyone sprang into action. One man went off to his garden to dig some mo. Another went after sugar cane and greens. A third man went after more greens, and he also brought some ginger root.

The women were nowhere in sight. It was strictly taboo for a woman to eat even the tiniest piece of an op. Even the little girls who came to see what all the excitement was about were shooed away. No female could know anything of the spirit appeasement that would take place.

One of the men chopped some firewood and arranged rocks on the wood to heat for the cooking pit. Another man cleaned out the pit and lined it with banana leaves. Wolo busied himself skinning the ops. He carefully removed the fur pelts. One animal had a thick, rich, brown fur. This kind was not shot every day. He would make himself a fur headpiece from its pelt.

While the op meat steamed in the pit along with greens and mo, Wolo prepared for the spirit-appeasement ceremony. On his way down from the forest, he had cut a branch from a hevon tree, a special tree that the spirits respected. He stood the branch up in the corner of the house and carefully tied on the pelts. As he worked, he spoke to the spirits of his dead ancestors. He spoke with reverence and fear, for he knew that they were there. "Spirits of my fathers, we built this house for you. We have not forgotten you. These ops that I am hanging on this hevon tree are for you. Now be happy and don't molest us."

The pit was opened, and the men carried the steaming food on banana leaves into the new hut. A nice portion was placed in front of each man. Eating with their fingers, they sucked and slurped every drop of the strong-flavored juice from the meat; they gnawed and chewed on the bones until all the meat was gone. Then each man tucked his bones away carefully into his net bag. Later, in the leisure of the evening hours, the men would roast the bones in the fire until they were crisp, and devour every last bit of them.

When they had finished eating the cooked food, the man

who had brought the sugar cane handed out sticks to everyone. Each peeled the fibrous cane with his teeth. Holding the cane with his right hand, he bit a piece of fiber loose and hung on tightly with his teeth. Turning his head to the left, and pulling the cane to the right, he peeled off the strip of skin. When the cane was peeled, he chewed on the juicy center, slurping so that he would not lose a drop of the sweet juice.

Wolo pulled out a small, black, rocklike piece of salt from his net bag and passed it around. Each one scraped a bit of the salty charcoal onto a leaf. Taking a piece of ginger, he dipped the root in the salt and ate the spicy hot delicacy with relish. This, for the Damals, made a delicious dessert.

There was no dessert for Meyong. There was not any *op* or even *mo* for her to eat. All she had was sweet potatoes and greens from her own garden. Meyong was expecting again, and she craved good food—body-building food. Instead, she ate potatoes and more potatoes. Her black hair had grown even more scraggly and tinged with orange. At the same time, her body stored layers of fat so that she always had a large, protruding stomach. Her stomach muscles and her body chemistry never had a chance to return to normal. She nursed each child for three to five years—until she became pregnant again, and the cycle began all over.

It was Wolo's job to dig the ground for gardens and build the fences to keep out the pigs. But Wolo was not doing his work. He had two wives and, thus, two sets of gardens to dig. He had more important things to do than dig a garden—like hunting *ops*, trading shells, bargaining for bride price payment, fighting, demanding war indemnity payment, and performing spirit appeasement. He told Meyong that she would have to dig her own garden, and that in a thorny, rocky place. Meyong had no choice if she wanted to eat and feed her children, so she crossed the barrier of the traditional role of a woman and dug her own garden.

Meyong's fourth child was born—a boy—and she named him *In-a-Hilek*: "We women have to do it all!"

6
Who Is the Witch?

Many new moons came and went in the village of Wung, and all was well. The spirits were content. No one had been seriously ill for a long time. Life was ordered by its usual humdrum routine—at least for the women who went to the gardens every day to carry home a huge load of potatoes. Meyong's fourth child, In-a-Hilek, had been weaned and was off playing with the other little boys. Meyong knew that she was pregnant again. This was still her secret. She had no idea of counting moons to determine when her child would be born. She only knew that it would be a long time—even a long time before others could tell that she was pregnant.

Kok-Me walked across the village yard toward his mother's hut. He could tell by the smoke seeping through the grass thatch that she was cooking the evening meal. There would be plenty of food for him. Stooping low, he entered the tiny hut.

Meyong offered her son a leaf full of greens. "Have you heard about my big brother?" she asked. "He's very sick."

"What is his sickness? Have they performed spirit appeasement for him?"

"Yes, they have killed two pigs for the spirits, but every day he grows worse. He has the dreadful sickness of swelling."

For the Damal, everything that happened had its cause in the spirit world. Whether a person died from accident or disease, the reason was always the same. Life had been eaten out of the person by a spirit—an evil spirit, or the spirit of a living woman. If a bridge broke and a man fell into the river and drowned, a spirit caused his death. The proof of this was easy to see: another man fell into the river and survived. His spirit was not eaten. Two men were ill—one recovered and the other did not. An evil spirit caused the death of the one and not of the other.

Kok-Me clicked his gourd in amazement and said, "That is bad. And his wife died so recently. I must go and see my uncle."

When Kok-Me arrived at his uncle's village of Wang-Be, he found him sitting by the fire in the men's hut. Even after his eyes became accustomed to the dim light, he could hardly recognize his uncle's face—so distorted with swelling. This *was* the most dreaded disease of all.

Kok-Me was careful not to speak his uncle's name. If ever he should speak the name of his mother or her brothers, great disaster would come upon him. "My dear uncle," he said. "I see you are very sick. Why has this terrible disease come upon you?"

Wanin-Me made no response to his question but groaned and said, "It has been many sleeps since I could go out of my hut. They are preparing to do more spirit appeasement. They tell me they are building a spirit fence across the path to the village."

"Then I will go and help them," Kok-Me promised as he rose to leave.

Kok-Me found several young men who were heading for the forest to split boards, and he joined them. By the next day they had built a fence, not like the usual pig fences, but high like a fence that fortifies a village during war. The fence was twenty feet long, and cut across the path to the village so that no one could go in or out on the usual route.

The shaman knew that this time the evil spirits must be given more if they were to be appeased. Concerned relatives donated beads, a stone ax, net bag, cowrie shell purse, and a stone knife. The spirit men, chanting their secret formula, hung each item on the fence—never again were those items to be touched by human hands.

Without the sacrifice of a pig, spirit appeasement is

worthless. The relatives donated the required animal. Then, hidden in the tall grass outside the village, the shamen performed the ritual of killing the pig. This time they did not eat the meat themselves. They hung the butchered pig on the fence high above the reach of dogs or other pigs. Since the pork was for the spirits to eat, the villagers put up with the stench of the rotting meat and the added swarms of flies that bred there. Flies were everywhere, and no amount of shooing caused them to go away. The open sores of the children were black with sucking flies.

Everything that could be done to save the dying man had been done. Yet, expecting the inevitable, relatives came from far and near. The hut where he lay was crowded with men discussing his fate. No thought was given to comforting the patient.

"His stomach is swollen like that of a pregnant woman." "He's as good as dead." "What could be the cause of this sickness, since the spirits have not accepted the appeasement sacrifices?" "Surely he will die." Wanin-Me heard snatches of the constant conversation, and it added to the torture of his illness.

Meyong, too, had come to Wang-Be village. She had come to care for her beloved brother—this one who, in many ways, was closer to her than her husband. She tempted his appetite with mo and bananas. He would not touch a sweet potato, but he nibbled on ginger root with salt and sucked sugar cane.

Each time Meyong went to her brother, the hut seemed to be more crowded. She heard the talk of the men—all of them were her relatives, and she knew their thoughts. When her brother died, they would kill a woman as a witch, and she might be the one. She knew all that, yet the bond of affection for her brother kept her by his side. *Now is the time to run away,* she thought—*now, before he dies.* But she could not. She would not—even if it meant her death. She could not be separated from him while he lived.

Wanin-Me was dying from kidney failure, but, to the

Damal, he had the most dreaded of spirit diseases. Meyong was sitting by her brother when the end came. One of the men stepped out into the early morning sunshine and cried out in a strong voice, "*Me dilaga-tak-o.* The man has died. *Me dilaga-tak-o.*" Over and over again his call, which was almost a yodel, pierced the quiet of the morning until the mountains reverberated with the echo.

The next three days turned into a nightmare. Meyong began the death wail, and other women joined her. Their voices rose in a high-pitched cry that continued day and night. There was no comfort for them. Their loved one had gone forever to an outer darkness they did not know.

Men, women, and children poured into the village from far and near. Many brought pigs with them. The squealing of the pigs mingled with the angry voices of shouting men, the crying of distraught children, and the ever present wail coming from the hut where Wanin-Me's body lay. Men and women crowded into the hut to mourn, while children squeezed in simply out of curiosity.

Some men went off to the forest for wood for the funeral pyre. Other men talked in groups outside the village in the privacy of the tall grass. They had no difficulty in reaching the conclusion that Meyong was the witch responsible for their brother's death. The witch could not be either of Wanin-Me's wives, for they were already dead. Meyong was a strong-willed woman with opinions that she often expressed. She was the culprit!

When Wolo and the men of his family heard the talk, they rose to meet the men of Meyong's family head-on. "Don't you dare touch Meyong. We have paid you a good price for her, and she has borne us many sons. If you shoot her, we'll make war with you."

On the morning of the third day, they arranged the firewood in crisscross layers in the village yard. Then, amid shouting and wailing, the men carried the body uncer-emoniously to the funeral pyre, added more layers of wood, and set it ablaze. Women continued their agonizing wail, and the men spit and complained of the unbearable stench of burning flesh.

When the fire burned low, the men began to kill the pigs. The spirits of those pigs were offered to Wanin-Me to accompany him on his journey. The meat and fat was for everyone to eat, and not taboo to the women and children, as was spirit-appeasement pork. Eating pork seemed to assuage the grief of the mourners and quiet the anger of the men. By afternoon, many of the people had gone home.

Meyong slept better that night than she had for many nights. The intensity of her grief had lessened. But in its place there rose a new emotion—fear. Fearing that she would be killed as a witch, Meyong slipped from the village in the early morning light, **as if** she were going out to the weeds. Kok-Me saw her, picked up his bow and arrows, and followed. His spirit was one with his mother's, and he would defend her with his life.

They spent two nights in the forest protected only by the shelter of an overhanging cliff. Even if they had had a fire-making stick, they could not have used it, for smoke would have divulged their hiding place. They had nothing to eat, for had they stopped to dig potatoes, they would have given away their secret escape.

The bone-chilling cold and rain seemed unbearable to Meyong, who was exhausted from her long ordeal with death. Kok-Me tried to comfort his mother. "We can't stay here longer without food. I will take you back, and my father and I will protect you. We will not let them kill you." Finally convinced, Meyong went back to her village, to Wolo, and to a new daughter, for she was now to be the foster mother of Wanin-Me's only surviving child.

Kok-**Me** had a very close friend in Me-Tal, who was Meyong's younger brother. Me-Tal had been a baby when Wolo dragged Meyong off as his child bride. As young men, Me-Tal and Kok-Me were more like brothers than uncle and nephew, for they were only four years apart in age.

Kok-Me and Me-Tal sometimes crossed the Beoga River together to visit in the village of Kelandi. It was here that Kok-Me spotted a girl that attracted him. Aigik was from the Nduga tribe. Kok-Me, watching her from a distance, observed that she had a lot of fire in her, and he liked that. As the crush he had on her grew, he mused, "I would never marry a Dani girl, but Aigik is not a Dani; she is an Nduga, and that might be possible."

Kok-Me confided the secret of his love to Me-Tal. Both Kok-Me and Aigik were too young to take part in the courtship-sings. Nor did their culture permit him to talk to her either in public or in private. But there was a way to test her love for him. He would use a love-potion charm. Me-Tal could deliver the charm to Aigik.

Kok-Me went up into the forest in search of an *ail* bush. The leaves of that bush have a distinctive, pungent odor. When he found the bush, he plucked several leaves and tucked them away in his net bag. The next time there was pork to eat in his father's hut, he would be ready.

Kok-Me did not have long to wait. He took the portion of cooked pork gratefully. Slicing off a chunk of fat, he slipped it into his net bag. Later, in the privacy of the tall grass, he carefully crushed an *ail* leaf and inserted it into a slit in the chunk of fat. The next day Me-Tal carried the gift across the river and casually gave it to Aigik.

A love-potion leaf can be sent from a boy to a girl or from a girl to a boy. If an unattractive girl sends a love-potion leaf to a boy, the leaf is said to have no effect. But if the couple have possibilities for marriage, the leaf has a special charm that woos the heart of the recipient.

Kok-Me was dying to know Aigik's reaction. So Me-Tal went back to Kelandi and spoke quietly to Aigik. "Do you love my nephew, Kok-Me?"

"Yes, I do," she said. "I'll come to him in the future."

Kok-Me had his answer. The charm had worked.

Outside in the dark, the rain was pelting down. The men

of Wung village were crowded into Wolo's hut, listening to him recount the story of the recent defeat of the downriver village of Piloma.

At the end, a young man asked, "Have all the people fled from Piloma? Would it be safe to go and help ourselves to their gardens?"

"Yes," Wolo replied. "The people have all gone. The food will soon be rotting. Just go and get it."

"We'll go tomorrow. Everyone who wants to join us is welcome."

Kok-Me decided that he would go. Na-Nonem, his little brother, wanted to go, too, and Kok-Me agreed. He could carry a small load of food back.

The next afternoon the Wung villagers had their nets full, but they just could not resist digging one more mo root and picking one more squash before starting for home. Their loads were heavy as they picked their way down the steep mountain to the river. That was a very difficult path—one to be avoided except for pressing reasons. The mountains parted with steep cliffs on each side of the raging river. Just below that spot, the Wang-Be River joined the main Beoga River.

Most of the group sat down to rest and have a smoke. Kok-Me and Na-Nonem continued on. They came to a spot where there was no path, only bare rock on a steep incline. "Take my hand," Kok-Me shouted above the roar of the water at their feet. "This is a steep, slippery place, and your load is heavy."

"No, I'll be careful," Na-Nonem called back. They continued on—curling their toes around the outcroppings of the rock to secure their footing. Suddenly, Na-Nonem's foot slipped on a wet rock, and he fell into the foaming rapids below him. A cry rose in unison from Kok-Me and from the group seated downstream, for they had seen the whole thing happen. The men dashed to the water's edge in an effort to rescue the boy. Although the group searched for some time, they never caught a glimpse of his body. It was carried on to the Beoga River and then on to where—they did not know.

Almost as soon as the accident happened, the call was shouted up the mountain, "Na-Nonem has drowned." A man in his garden heard the call and relayed it on to Wung village, "Na-Nonem has drowned."

Wolo was the first to hear the news. In the heat of passion, his reaction was spontaneous. *This is witchcraft—a woman has eaten the spirit of life out of my son. Meyong has done this. Just four months ago she killed her brother, and now she has killed my son. She is a witch, and I will kill her before we all die.* He grabbed his bow and arrows and ran to find Meyong.

Meyong, too, had heard the call, and her heart was struck with agony. Before there was time to cry, she saw Wolo running toward her, and she knew why. She turned and ran toward the forest. Shooting arrows as he ran, Wolo called, "You pregnant witch, you killed my son. You'll never live to bear another child. I'm going to kill you." One arrow went into Meyong's arm, and a second one pierced her hip. The pain was like a shot of fire, but she managed to pull the arrows out and keep running. Wolo saw that he had hit her twice. *She'll die,* he thought, and gave up the chase.

Meyong kept on running. It was a matter of life and death for her, and she fled to the forest like a hunted animal. High up on the mountain she dropped, exhausted, to the ground, giving up her fight for life. Then she felt the child kicking in her womb and thought, *I will live and bear my child.*

Word traveled like wildfire across the mountaintops that Meyong had been shot as a witch. Men of Meyong's family grabbed their bows and arrows and flew over the trail to Wung. What right did Wolo have to shoot their sister? They would shoot him. When they could not find Wolo, they began shooting at Wolo's second wife. She ran for the forest, but she, too, was pregnant and made an easy target. When an arrow hit her, the men decided they had evened the score and stopped their pursuit.

Wolo heard what had happened and headed for the forest shouting as he went, "I'll kill Meyong! That witch is going to die." He found her tracks and followed them as they led up the mountain and then into a thicket of brush. There he found his wife huddled on the ground. She cried out as he drew his bow, and he saw that it was not Meyong but Novet, his second wife. Wolo abandoned his hunt for Meyong and helped Novet back to the village where he could care for her wound.

Rain came that night, along with a cold, mountain wind. Others might have died from exposure, but not Meyong. She was a woman with an indomitable spirit. She was no witch; she knew nothing of witchcraft. Neither Meyong nor any other Damal woman knew how to perform black magic. That was all an invention in the minds of the men. She mourned the death of her son. She knew not what spirit had taken his life, but she was determined that Wolo would not kill her and the unborn child.

After a second night in the jungle, Meyong started down the mountain. She was weak from hunger, but her wounds were beginning to heal. There was pain in her hip with every step she took, but it did not seem as great as the pain in her heart and in her stomach. Finding a stream, she followed it down a long way. Then she turned toward Wang-Be and the village of her younger brother. He would protect her.

In a few days, word reached Meyong that Wolo's anger had cooled and he wanted her to return. Meyong did return, but with a heavy heart because Na-Nonem was not there to welcome her back.

Talk of killing witches was not yet over. This time it was the men of Wolo's family who came demanding to kill both of Wolo's wives. "Where are those two witches?" they cried. "They will never bear their children. We'll kill them now."

"No!" Wolo shouted. "Don't touch my wives. Take their pigs if you will, but don't kill them."

The men grabbed the five pigs Meyong and Novet had been raising. That assuaged their anger, and they went away to gorge themselves on pork until they became sick.

Meyong and Novet were drawn closer together through their trials. They had both faced death from the hands of the men who were closest to them, and they had both survived. Each would bear her child—a child who offered the only purpose for living, and the only joy in life in a world that was ruled by the passions of men.

Meyong was first to deliver her baby, another boy. The name she gave him was a jibe at the men who had tried to take her life: Teme-Jagalek, "Who won't bear a child?" A few days later, Novet gave birth to her baby, also a boy. To add to the irony, she named him Taman-Jagalek, "Who said he wouldn't be born?"

7

Courting Days

Kok-Me slipped into his mother's hut for the evening meal. The hut seemed crowded to him. While slurping his greens, he gradually observed that besides the usual family members, there were two strangers: a woman and a girl. *Everyone seems to be drawn to my mother,* he thought. *She's a very generous person and is always accommodating guests.*

As he finished eating, he watched the girl out of the corner of his eye. She was a very pretty girl, although still very young and undeveloped. She had a clear, light complexion, he noticed. "Where is your home?" he asked her. Without raising her eyes, Delem replied, "My home is at Piloma." That was all that was said. Kok-Me returned to the men's house, and the next day Delem and her mother continued on their journey.

One afternoon Kok-Me heard the news that a group of Dani girls had arrived at Wang-Be from the Ilaga. There would be a courtship sing at Wang-Be that night. Kok-Me felt a surge of excitement that was new to him. He had attended these sings as an observer all his life, but tonight he decided he would go and sing to the girls himself.

He had to hurry and get ready. He removed his head net, rearranged the padding, and retied it carefully. Pig grease came next. He rubbed a new coat of grease over his entire body. From his net bag he took his makeup kit and got his friend to paint red and black stripes on his face. For a final touch, he unwrapped his most prized possession—the yellow plumes from a bird of paradise. Sticking the feathers into his head net he went outside to behold himself in a pool of water. He liked what he saw.

One final bit of preparation remained. He needed a supply of gifts for the girls he would sing to. In his net he placed several arm bands, a colorful woven belt, a string of black beads strung from the seeds of a tree, and a small cowrie shell. On his way to Wang-Be he picked a bunch of colored leaves and stuck them in the band on his upper arm.

After dark the sing finally got underway. A dozen brightly-painted young men were seated on one side of the fire, with a similar number of well-painted girls sitting opposite them. The hut was crowded with men, women, and children who served as chaperones and who had also come to enjoy the entertainment of the evening.

Kok-Me was attracted to one of the Dani girls who wore a fluffy skirt made of alternate rows of black and white grass tufts. She wore heavy strands of black and red beads over her breasts. His eye caught hers, and he began to sing. The words of his song were about a waterfall and some birds he had seen in the forest. As he waved his hand toward her in time to the chanting, she responded by waving her hand toward him. Their hands touched, and the first gift of the woven belt passed from him to her. Later, when someone else was carrying the melody of the chant, their eyes met again, their hands waved, and this time when they touched, Kok-Me took an arm band gift from her.

During the course of the evening Kok-Me sang to several different girls. He enjoyed this new-found emotion of warmth and desire for the opposite sex. He decided to attend the next courtship sing when it was announced.

Meyong had different ideas for her son. When they met the next morning, he could see she had fire in her eyes. She slapped his hands and said, "You're not old enough to go to a courtship sing. You don't even know how to farm and make fences yet. Stay here and dig my gardens for me instead of running off after the girls."

Kok-Me made no reply. Most people did not talk back to his mother, for she usually got what she wanted.

Some months had passed since the last sing in the Wung area. A group of Kok-Me's age-mates decided that if the girls did not come to them, they would go to the girls. Most of the young fellows were related to Kok-Me in some way, either through his father or his mother. All the fellows were single except his uncle, Me-Tal, who was Meyong's younger brother. Me-Tal was now a large, husky man and had recently married. Since he was attending the sings, Kok-Me wondered if he was thinking of taking a second wife so soon.

Me-Tal said, "Let's go across the Beoga River and sing to the Nduga girls at Kelanti. The next day you can help me dig garden at a plot I have upriver from there."

Word spread quickly of the arrival of the young men. Soon the whole village was buzzing with excitement about the courtship sing to be held that night. Unmarried girls from neighboring villages heard the news and "just happened" to appear at Kelanti that evening—greased and painted until their skin shone. Among the girls was Aigik, who had come to attend her first courtship sing.

Singing continued far into the night with the steady beat of the men's bass voices surging over the mountainside. When Kok-Me's turn came to sing, he described Wung village in his song to Aigik, for he hoped that she would some day come to live with him there. He sang of the river and the forest, the many pandanas nut trees, and the fertile ground that produced an abundance of food.

Kok-Me had given out his last gift to the girls when still another girl caught his eye asking for his attention. What could he do? In the emotion of the moment he slipped off the net band he wore across his chest. This was a special gift to him from his mother and was far more valuable than the usual trinkets exchanged, but he had nothing else. He rolled it up tightly and responded to the affection offered to him from across the fire. Finally, the last of the girls went home, and the men slept.

In the morning Kok-Me had a visitor. The father of Aigik called him off into the grass so they could talk. "I'd like you to marry my daughter and become my son-in-law. I'll have no one else." Before Kok-Me could reply, he called Aigik and asked her if she would agree. She nodded her assent. Their eyes met, and in that instant they agreed that they would marry.

The logistics of the bride-price in Damal culture were hidden from no one. But the starry eyes of youth did not worry about the problems that concerned their elders. Aigik's father had not given a moment's thought to her personal interests. Nor had he been attracted to Kok-Me as a person. He thought only of the fact that Wolo and his relatives were good businessmen, and he could extract a fine bride-price for his daughter.

The sun rose higher in the sky, and its warm rays had dried off much of the water left on the grass and bushes from the night's rain. "Let's go dig my garden," Me-Tal said. And the three young men, Kok-Me, Pagame, and Me-Tal started off for a hard day's work of breaking the soil of a new garden with their wooden digging sticks.

In the afternoon they set off for home, hungry and tired. Coming to a nettle bush beside the path, Me-Tal said, "My back aches so, it feels like it's crushed. I'm going to pick some nettle leaves so you can rub my back with them tonight. Wait up for me."

Me-Tal picked the nettles and then pushed deeper into the brush searching for ferns in which to wrap the stinging nettles. All of a sudden he shrieked in fear. "I've been bitten! A centipede bit me on my finger." (The centipede of the Beoga is a many-legged insect that grows up to five inches in length.)

The fear of death was written on Me-Tal's face as he came back to the path where the other two stood. Although Me-Tal could not see the spot on his finger where the centipede bit him, he felt a stinging sensation and knew from the

traditions of his fathers that any Damal bitten by a centipede
will die when the poison reaches his heart. Me-Tal did not
know that in truth there is not enough poison in the bite of a
centipede of that size to even cause the finger to swell.
Nothing at all happens to people of neighboring tribes who
are bitten by these same centipedes, for they have no
tradition of fear about them.

Me-Tal turned to Kok-Me. "Cut my arm. Cut it quickly
and let the poison out." Kok-Me took a bamboo knife from
his net bag. Beginning at the wrist he made a half dozen
slashes up the inside of Me-Tal's arm. Before he finished
cutting, blood covered his arm and then it began to spurt in
a rhythmic pulsation—splat, splat, splat onto the grass
along the side of the path. Blood was everywhere, and it
kept coming. Me-Tal felt faint and sat down.

Kok-Me ordered Pagame, "Find me a vine. Quick!" He
was soon back, and Kok-Me wrapped the vine round and
round the upper arm in a tourniquet, pulling it tight as he
worked. Still, the blood spurted in a pulsating jet. Me-Tal
grew weak and lay down on the ground in the pool of his
own blood.

"Go get help from the village," Kok-Me ordered. "We can't
carry him by ourselves." Pagame was off with a bound.

The blood came in weak spurts, and then it only trickled
from his arm. Me-Tal lay still, and he breathed no more.

The men came with two poles and vine to make a sort of
stretcher, but now that he was dead they tied Me-Tal's
lifeless body to a single pole. His corpse hung limp and his
head fell back at a rakish angle as the men bore their burden
back to the village.

Two men left at once to carry the news across the river
and up the mountain to Wang-Be village. Night fell, but they
pressed on. When they passed by Wung they called out the
news.

Meyong came out of her hut to hear what all the shouting
was about. Understanding what they said, she began to
wail. "My little brother is dead. The one whom I rocked in

my arms is dead. He's dead. He's dead."

Meyong's crying did not last long. She realized that soon the men would be after her as the witch who killed her brother. Plans were made. Meyong could not flee in the darkness alone. A visiting nephew agreed to go with her. Teme-Jagalek was weaned, so Novet, Wolo's other wife, could take care of her baby. Again pregnant, Meyong fled into the night from her menfolk, who would cry, "Witchcraft," and come to kill her.

The death wail rose again at Wang-Be village as the men carried Me-Tal's blood-stained body into the village yard. Above the wail of the other women, Me-Tal's young bride vented her emotions with shrieks of anguish. She ran to caress the lifeless form of her strong, young husband. Emotions of grief, anger, and frustration rose in the breasts of the men, but Damal men do not cry and wail like women. They wanted to strike back at this enemy, death—death, which held such complete power over their lives, and which they could not conquer. Someone shouted, "Let's go kill Meyong! She's the witch that caused the death of our younger brother."

"Let's go," came the response. Their voices changed from shouting to rhythmic hooting as they ran toward Wung village.

Wolo heard them coming and knew they were after Meyong. He met them with drawn bow. "You aren't going to kill my wife," he shouted. "We'll make war with you."

"Give us Meyong," they cried. "She's the witch that killed Me-Tal."

In the shouting and confusion that followed, Wolo shot four arrows that hit their mark and drew blood. He was not aiming to kill—only to protect his property. When the men were convinced that Meyong really was not there, they retreated back to Wang-Be. They did not want to start a war and, since no one was seriously hurt, the incident was considered a closed matter.

That same morning Nakal left her upriver home to visit her older sister, Meyong. Nakal's thoughts were happy ones as she hiked up and down the mountains that separated her home from her sister's. Meyong had invited her to come for a corn feast. Corn was a new food to the Damals of the Beoga. The seed had been traded into the Beoga from Moni country and points west. Meyong had corn to eat before anyone else did, and Nakal was going to share in eating the firstfruits.

Midmorning the path led Nakal close to the Beoga River where the bridge crosses to Kelanti village. She was surprised to see Dong, her cousin, coming toward her. "Where are you going?" he said. Before she could answer, he said in a rising voice, "I was coming to get you."

"Get me? What for?" she cried.

"Haven't you heard? Your brother, Me-Tal, died yesterday afternoon. It's good that you have come. I was coming to kill you, you witch!"

She stood petrified with fear for an instant. "My brother dead? Don't kill me. I'm not a witch. I didn't eat my brother's spirit."

But her pleas went unheeded. Dong raised his bow and shot her through. He shot another arrow, and another, shouting, "You witch, you killed my cousin. I'm going to kill you." He shot still another arrow into the crumpled, silent form that lay at his feet.

Exhausted from spent emotion, Dong laid down his bow and began to drag his cousin's body, still bristling with arrows, to the river. He heaved it into the foaming water with a grunt. "Now you won't eat any more men's spirits." His mission had been easier to fulfill than he had thought.

Life in the Beoga slipped back into a routine cog in the wheel of time. If a new war did not erupt, there were payments to be made from a war in the past. Perhaps fifteen years had come and gone since the war was fought over a man from Wang-Be who stole a Jugu man's wife. During those years there were a number of other wars, but none were considered as important because the number of people killed was less.

Damal tribal law required that payments be made to the family of each person killed in a battle. The indemnity payments did not come from the opposing side, which had killed the man. They came from the men related closely to the leader of the war, who had to make payments to their allies.

Wolo belonged to the same Komang clan as the wife-stealer who started the Jugu war. In the original war there had been no question as to whether or not the Komang clansmen would fight in defense of the wife-stealer. That was automatic. Men always acted in a group with the decision of the clan. Through the years Wolo had paid a number of pigs for different men who had died fighting for the Komangs. And now there was still another man, Omala, for whom payment must be made.

In life, Omala had been an important man, and after death, his clan built up his importance even more. His people had been agitating for payment from the Komang clan. If it did not come soon, they would make war.

Almost two years earlier a man related to the wife-stealer began arrangements for the war indemnity payments on Omala. He visited all the Komang men, arranging for certain pigs to be earmarked and raised for the payments. He also discussed and bargained for other cash items to be set aside. When the pigs were grown and he had a sufficient number of shell belts, individual shells, salt blocks and axes promised, he announced that in five more sleeps the war payments would be made.

The day before the payment was to be made, people and pigs began to converge on Wang-Be village. Everyone came—men, women, and children from far and wide— even if they had no actual part in the payments. Young men got a good look at all the eligible girls. Older men haggled over the bride-price of their daughters. Girls thinking about marriage took inventory of the handsome young men. Courtship singing would go on all night.

Daylight faded, the dedel beetles chirped their announcement of night, and to the delight of the young people, the usual evening rain did not fall. Instead, patches of sky opened through the clouds, and the evening star shone over the horizon. There was no moon to give its light, but that problem was quickly solved as several flaming torches appeared in the village courtyard.

A group of young men started to do the two-step dance. One man began the refrain of a chant and slapped the sole of his foot on the ground to help set the beat of the rhythm. Leading with his right foot he took two steps forward. The second time he slapped his right foot on the ground, he accented the beat even more by snapping his bow and arrows against his right leg. Then he took two steps back, and on the second step back, he again snapped his bow and arrows against his leg. By this time a group of men was dancing with him. A second group was facing him, dancing forward as he stepped back, and then retreating as he came forward again.

Soon the women and girls were dancing around the edge. Their dance step kept time with the men's chanting and stomping, but with a smooth walking-step forward and back, forward and back. Mature men danced with the youth and sometimes led a chant. Old women seemed to enjoy the dancing as much as the giggling girls who held hands as they danced. After a while, a second group of dancers started at the other end of the village.

Kok-Me eyed the girls that were dancing on the outer edge of his group. *Could that be Delem?* he thought. Yes, it was. Easing over to the edge by the girls, he said to her, "When did you become a young woman? The last time I saw you, you were still a girl."

After a time Delem responded, "I hear that you are going to marry an Nduga girl."

"Me? Marry an Nduga girl?" he replied. "I don't know

how to speak Nduga, or Dani either." Nothing more was said. Kok-Me eased himself back into the group of young men and kept on dancing.

In one of the men's huts an important council had convened. The Komang clan sponsors of the war indemnity payments were meeting with the clansmen of Omala. The men talked far into the night, deciding which man would receive which pigs, cowrie shells, or salt blocks. This was a complicated procedure, because closer relatives of Omala must receive larger payments and, at the same time, the more financially important men must be given more than the unimportant men. And Omala's sister and his "mother" must receive appropriate payments. His real mother was dead, but this younger woman was classified as a "mother," and in the Damal society she also deserved a payment.

All arrangements had to be made without the use of any system of writing or recording. The Komang clan knew the number of pigs that would be there, the size and value, and also the number of other items being presented and their relative values. Each decision had to come from the committee, although no formal vote was taken, and all arrangements were retained by memory. With the council completed, the men lay down to sleep. Others could dance all night, but their day would begin early tomorrow.

In the morning the air was rent by the ear-splitting cries of the pigs. Most of the pigs were medium-sized, and those were tied by their feet to poles. One end of each pole rested on a rack built three feet off the ground, and the other end lay on the ground. That left the pigs hanging upside down in midair. Neither the very large pigs nor the small ones could survive a day suspended from a pole in the hot sun, so they were tied by their legs to the display rack.

No one tried to count the pigs. Why should they? The important thing was that Omala's relatives be satisfied with the payments. It was enough to know that there were *very many* pigs.

All the Komang clansmen were painted and decorated in

their very best. It was important for everyone to see what generous and honest men they were in making this payment. Their leader wore the long black plumes of the cassowary bird fastened into a tall headpiece that swayed as he pranced back and forth.

He began to call out the names of the Komang men, who came up and stood by their pigs. Some also brought shell belts and precious blocks of black, native salt, processed and carried eight days by trail from Homeyo. Then he called out the name of Omala's brother, who came up to receive two large pigs, a valuable shell, and an ax, each presented to him by the donors.

This process continued, punctuated frequently by the shouts of men and the screaming of pigs. Toward noon, one recipient responded with shouts of anger when he received a pig. "This pig is just a runt," he shouted. "I am an important man, and the death of Omala was a deep loss to me. If this is all I get, I'll start a war." All of a sudden, he drew back his bow and shot an arrow up in the air. The crowd gasped and fell back. The arrow went up and over the crowd, falling into the weeds beyond them.

All at once men from both groups were running, shouting, and brandishing their bows and arrows. Through all this confusion the case was being tried. The decision rendered was that he did not deserve anything more. Gradually the excitement died down, and the rest of the payments were distributed.

Then Omala's brother began to call out, "We're satisfied with the payment you have given us for the death of our relative. You've paid us well." He ran into the center of the yard with all his clansmen following him. They began running in a circle, and their broken shouts blended into fast, rhythmic hooting, growing louder and louder. The dance slowed to a stop, and the mountains echoed back the hooting. Omala's death payment was finished.

The next day all the pigs were taken to the villages of their new owners. The female pigs and all the small ones would be raised and used in bride-price payment, given on another war indemnity payment, or used for spirit appeasement. The large male pigs were butchered, and all the villagers gorged themselves on the meat.

Kok-Me went to visit his mother. She had not returned to Wung, but was living at Piloma with relatives from her mother's side of the family. As soon as Meyong saw him, she said, "My son, I'm so glad you've come. I've been so lonely without any of my children. Stay here and make gardens for me." Kok-Me could not resist his mother's winsome urging, and he stayed.

Kok-Me was surprised to find Delem living with his mother. But then, wherever his mother went, she always attracted people to herself. As they saw each other daily, he found himself comparing Delem with Aigik, the Nduga girl from Kelandi. Delem was a Damal and Aigik was not. He felt more at ease with the prospects of marrying into a Damal family than having Ndugas as in-laws.

Both Kok-Me and Delem attended the courtship sings that were held now and again in the area, but he never chose to sing to her, although he sang to lots of other girls. Kok-Me came to realize that Delem's living with Meyong represented more than an interest in his mother. One afternoon Delem slipped him a bundle of trinkets she had received from other young men at the courtship sings. Kok-Me smiled and said nothing, but he was flattered to have her show interest in him this way.

Meyong's strong personality showed itself one day when she met a girl from Kelandi. Meyong looked closely at the man's chest-band that the girl had, and knew at once that it was the one she had woven for Kok-Me. "Give me that chest band," she demanded. "You stole it from my son." And with that, she snatched the chest band from the girl. The girl was startled, for she had received it as a gift at a courtship sing, but she made no reply. She realized that no one talks back to Meyong.

Meyong's role in life changed again quite abruptly. Her time of delivery had come, and she gave birth to her sixth and last child, a girl. Her world would again revolve around her baby, nursing, loving, protecting, and caring for it. She named her daughter Diamo. The name had a meaning in Meyong's life story, as did all the names of her children; but that one was not such a barbed jab at the men in her life. *Diamo* is the name of a broad-leafed plant that grows in the lower elevation of the river bottom near Piloma. It never grows on the high, cold mountain of Wung. Her baby was born in the lower country where the Diamo plant grows.

Shortly after the birth of her baby, Meyong returned to Wung to take up life again with her family.

8

Taganit Fights in the Beoga

Meyong watched the two women toiling up the trail to the village of Wung. Each carried a heavy load in her bulging net bag. As they came into the village, Meyong welcomed the visitors. "*Amolo,*" she said. "Where have you come from?"

"We have come from Kelandi, across the river," the older woman replied. Then Meyong recognized them. It was Aigik, the Nduga girl Kok-Me was to marry, and her mother. The mother continued, "We brought sweet potato vines to plant and also sugar cane and banana plants."

"Good," Meyong said. "I was just about to go to my garden. Come along with me, and we can plant them together."

From inside the men's hut Kok-Me watched them disappear over the fence. *Aigik hopes to be my wife,* he thought, *and eat those potatoes with me. I'll have to collect a lot more cowrie shells and pigs to add to the bride-price if that is going to happen by the time those potatoes are ready to dig.*

"Wem me motako," cried a runner entering the village. "The Taganit warriors have come from the Ilaga. They are at Wang-Be!" In an instant the ten men in the village of Wung grabbed their bows and arrows and were off in a trot for Wang-Be, hooting as they ran.

The words "Taganit warriors" struck fear into the hearts of the Wung people. Taganit was a Dani war chief who had come to the Ilaga from the North Baliem Valley. He was a

105

dynamic war general, the like of which the Damal tribe never produced. The Damals were a peace-loving, quiet people compared to the aggressive Danis, who seemed to thrive on war. Seven months earlier, fighting had broken out in the Ilaga, and the conflict soon became known as the "Taganit War."

One day when the Mudip clansmen were off working in their gardens, one of Taganit's nephews entered their village and stole several blocks of valuable salt. To get even, the Mudips burned houses in Taganit's village. Taganit rallied his clansmen, and the fight was on. As the battles continued, everyone in the Ilaga was drawn into one of the two sides. The Damals living in the upper part of the Ilaga Valley joined Taganit's forces, and the Damals living in the Mudip area were sucked into the opposing group. Danis of the Sinak Valley joined the Mudip group, and still they were not a match for the Taganit warriors. Men, women, and children were slaughtered on both sides—too many to keep track of—yet Taganit's forces were the victors. They drove the Mudips out of the Ilaga. People fled in every direction— to the Beoga, to the lower country of the Dem tribe, to the Sinak, and south to the Jila area.

Tensions were strong between the Danis and the Damals. About the year 1900, Dani traders from the North Baliem came to the Beoga to make salt from the salt springs near the headwaters of the Beoga River. On their way home, they passed through the Ilaga Valley, which was the home of a relatively small group of Damals. The traders were impressed with the virgin timberlands on the gently sloping mountains and with the fertile gardens of the Damals. The wild *kelam* plant, which the Damals ate as a vegetable something like spinach, grew much better there in the Ilaga than in the fields of the North Baliem.

Soon groups of Dani settlers moved to the Ilaga, gradually pushing the Damal people from the fertile flatlands up the slopes of the mountains. The Danis were a dominant, warring people in contrast to the easy-going, peaceful

Damals. The Dani people worked harder than the Damals, who did what they had to today, but would rather leave it for tomorrow. Danis had more neatly arranged gardens and kept them clean from weeds. As a result, they had more potatoes and pigs than did the Damals, who just did not like to work that much. Danis had more of a structured system of leadership, with recognized chiefs; each Damal tended to be a chief unto himself. Their languages were completely different, and so were many customs and taboos. Intermarriage helped to fuse some of the Damal people of the Ilaga with the Danis, but other Damals who wanted to maintain their tribal identity simply moved to the Beoga or across the 14,000-foot mountain range to the south. At the time of the Taganit War, the population of the Ilaga was three-fourths Dani and one-fourth Damal.

When Mudip Dani refugees fled to the Beoga, the Damals had mixed feelings about their coming. They knew all too well how Danis just move in and take over. That they did not want. The second emotion was one of pity for a people who had been driven from their homes in war. The Danis came asking for refuge, and the Damal tradition of hospitality and generosity prevailed. They opened their homes to them and shared all they had to eat. And once the Damal had invited the stranger in, he was bound to defend him as an ally if need be. That would not have been true of the Dani guests. They could have invited a man in to eat with them, and then turned and shot him as an enemy if circumstances directed. But the Damals were bound by their honor to keep an alliance—an honor passed on from father to son.

When the ten Wung men arrived at Wang-Be, they were greeted with a sight that overwhelmed them. Dani warriors were everywhere carrying bows and arrows and spears, shouting and dancing. Their faces were brightly painted, and they sported headdresses far more elaborate than the Damals ever wore. Kok-Me began to count the Dani warriors. By the time he got to fourteen he was saying, "Four on the second man's hands; five on the second man's hands; one on the second hand of the second man; two on the third man's hands. No, that's not right. There's too many for me to count." He sighed and gave up trying. There were very many.

The Ilaga Danis called out, "We're your friends. Come join our side of the war." That was wise strategy on the part of Taganit, because it gave him a firm foothold in a valley far from his home. The Wang-Be people were afraid to oppose the powerful aggressors, so they agreed to join Taganit's forces and fight against the rest of the Beoga people. However, that alliance did not stop them from warning women and children to run and hide out of the reach of the warriors.

Many of the Beoga women had huge goiters that bulged from their necks like two grapefruits. Inside their throats the goiters pressed hard against their windpipes so they could hardly breathe. One of the Beoga women with a goiter was trying to flee, but she could hardly walk, let alone run, as she struggled for every breath. The Danis shot her down just as they shot everyone else they could find.

One of the Mudip Danis who had fled earlier to the Beoga was killed in the fighting. Recognizing him as an important leader, the Taganit men chopped his body in pieces and hung parts of it on sticks along the path. Their brutality and passion to kill knew no bounds as they swept upriver. The Beoga people were stunned, for they were unable to kill any of Taganit's warriors in the fighting. It seemed to them that the Danis had supernatural power.

The barbarism of Taganit's men was more than Kok-Me could take. He quietly deserted the battle and went back to find his mother. All he found at Wung was the family sow in an otherwise deserted village. Glad to find at least that much, he led the pig to a place several hours' walk into the forest, and tethered her securely. Then he returned to dig a huge net bag of sweet potatoes and took them to the pig.

After more searching Kok-Me found his mother down by the Wang-Be River. Realizing that the warriors would soon be back, he escorted her and the children downriver to Piloma.

The next day word reached Kok-Me that Aigik was very sick. He decided he would go at once and see her. Stories that are passed along by word of mouth from one person to another can grow or change, but that one proved all too true. He found Aigik lying in her mother's hut. Women filled the hut, all talking about how sick Aigik was. "She is too young to die," they said. "But there is no hope. No one can help her, and there is nothing we can do for her."

Kok-Me learned from the women that Aigik had been sick for a week. It started with a sore throat, and then she lost her voice. She just lay on the floor of the hut refusing whatever they offered her to eat. All the time she was burning with fever. Kok-Me watched her. She was coughing, trying to expel the fluid that filled her lungs. Her nostrils flared out and then in, as she gasped for every breath. Her eyes were closed. *She doesn't even know I'm here,* he thought. *She's such a beautiful girl. It's not time for her to die. The potatoes she planted are not yet ready to dig.*

Kok-Me stepped out into the cool afternoon air. He was not prepared to face the question of death. To escape his thoughts, he joined the men in their hut, losing himself in their talk of war.

That night, Aigik did die, just as the women predicted.

By the time Taganit's forces arrived at Piloma, all the Wang-Be men had changed sides. Several of Taganit's warriors were killed at Piloma, which gave the Beoga people new courage. Kok-Me sped upriver with the news that many of the Ilaga people had been killed. Those men, who had seemed to be magically protected, were now dead! The news revived the upriver Damals. With their forces united, the Beoga people were able to drive out the invaders.

Part of the Danis crossed to the far side of the Beoga River and took refuge with the Ndugas who lived there. The larger part fled back over the trail out of Wang-Be, leaving behind them death and destruction, and taking with them any young women they could find—whether married or not—to be the second or third wives of their captors.

Kok-Me returned to look for his pig. She was still there and alive, although her potatoes were gone. He was delighted with his accomplishment. He had saved her both from the Danis and from going wild in the jungle as so many pigs did during a war. Wild, runaway pigs multiplied in the jungle, only to return and in a single night destroy the entire potato garden of a family.

The Beoga Damals were not willing to accept the encampment of Danis across the river. They sent a message, "Go home. Go back to the Ilaga."

"Never," was the reply. "We're going to kill you."

Kok-Me joined a group of men who were planning an attack to drive the Danis out. When they arrived at the village of Kelandi, Kok-Me remembered the last time he was there, when Aigik died. Now the village was surrounded by a high war fence. Inside the fence he recognized the man who would have been his father-in-law. He could not shoot. Instead, he called softly, "Flee. Go to Hitadipa with your family. Soon we will return, killing and burning."

The Damals did return and killed two men before the Dani warriors got organized. Then, recognizing the skill and ferocity of the seasoned Dani warriors, the Damals retreated back across the river. After talking around the fires at night, the Damals concluded they needed help to fight these Danis. They sent runners to the Sinak Valley where the main forces of the Mudip Danis were now living. The Mudips responded by sending a large group of warriors to help.

Plans were laid for a three-pronged attack against the Taganit Danis and their Nduga hosts. One group went upriver, crossed over, and came down, cutting off the trail of escape to Hitadipa. Another group descended upon them from the forest. A third group crossed the Beoga River at the usual point. Fighting as they came, the three groups converged on Kelandi. Some of the Ndugas and Taganit Danis were able to escape into the jungle, but many others were pushed into an area surrounded by enemies with no chance of escape. All the houses were burned and the Nduga side of the Beoga turned into a no-man's land. Five women and all the pigs that could be found were taken as the spoils of war. In tribal warfare it is a case of captors-keepers for both women and pigs. The woman becomes the property of the man who captures her, and she is his wife from then on, just as much as if he had paid full bride-price for her.

Encouraged by their victory across the river, the Beoga men began to talk of a reprisal attack on the Ilaga. Word was passed through the Beoga and everyone gathered at Wang-Be. Kok-Me was with them, ready to fight again. In the afternoon, someone got the idea of having an op hunt. The men, standing like fence posts around a garden, encircled an area of brush and small trees. Shouting and beating the grass and brush, the men began to move toward the center. Birds started to fly, but arrows soon brought them to the ground. The ops were startled and ran out of hiding to be shot. The men shouted and moved into the center until they had captured the last little furry creature. Kok-Me had in his net bag two ops and a bird. That night, when all the warriors ate op, they boasted, "We'll kill the Ilaga people like we killed these ops—many, many of them."

The party spent the night in the jungle and descended on the upper part of the Ilaga Valley early the next morning. Before they got into the populated area, an Ilaga man discovered their presence and sent out the cry, "Wem me motako. Warriors are coming." The Beoga warriors killed two men before the Ilaga people rallied and rushed on them like a herd of wild pigs. Beoga men were falling, and every man ran for his life. Kok-Me saw his cousin lying in the agony of death, but he could do nothing.

It was every man for himself on the return trip back over the mountain. When night fell, Kok-Me found dry leaves from the pandanas nut tree and lit a torch. He stumbled on through the night, cold, hungry, and depressed. Twenty some men who took part in the op hunt never returned over the mountain. The Beoga people had had their fill of war; that is, until the next time one man decided he wanted to fight, and the rest of his clansmen were obliged to join him.

9
The *Padagalo* Sky Beetle

One day Wolo informed Meyong, "You can stay at Wung if you please, but I am moving to Tingil, and my second wife, Novet, is moving with me."

"You never dig garden for me anyway!" Meyong retorted, "I will stay at Wung."

Kok-Me also moved to Tingil with his father, but at his mother's urging he promised, "I'll still come back to Wung and dig garden for you." Kok-Me now had the responsibility and privilege of having two mothers. He spent part of his time at Wung, helping his own mother, and part of his time at Tingil. He dug gardens for Novet, calling her mother, and she showed him the same affection and care that she gave to her own sons.

One morning the alert warning was sounded with hooting from men upriver. Kok-Me stepped out of his father's hut, still wondering what the danger could be. Then he heard it—a low rumbling sound. It was not thunder. Someone shouted "*padagalo*" and pointed to a tiny black speck up in the cloudless sky. No, it was not a bird; it really was a *padagalo*.

Kok-Me had seen a *padagalo* once before—when he was a very small boy. He was with his mother in their garden near Wung. Four of those strange objects flew across the sky in formation. Meyong's reaction was that of a mother hen protecting her young from a hawk. "Get down in the ditch," she commanded. "And cover your eyes with your hands." Raising her hands to the sky, Meyong called out like a man, "What wonder is this? It's a *padagalo*. Amazing! Amazing!"

And then the four whirring birds disappeared behind the horizon of the high mountains.

Those planes had no doubt been US Air Force planes. During the Second World War hundreds of them flew over the island of New Guinea. Although they avoided the high mountains when possible, still some had flown over the interior, and a number had even crashed in the highest peaks that divide the Damal tribe in half. Meyong knew nothing of the global war that was raging outside her secluded mountain home. She did not even know that there were people, flesh and blood beings, beyond her mountains.

During the years that Kok-Me was growing up he spent many long evenings by the fire listening to his father and other men repeat the story of the beginning of things. Man first came on earth from a hole in the ground somewhere to the east in the Baliem Valley. Out of the hole there came first *hi ki me*, a type of spirit, a white spirit. That *hi ki me* moved to the west—far to the west. It did not marry, or give birth to children, or die; yet it became many. The *hi ki me* built only rectangular houses with a gable roof, not round houses like the Beoga people.

The dog came next out of the hole in the ground and moved west. Finally the "real people," black mountain people who wear gourds and grass skirts, came out of the ground. They got so cold standing there that their teeth began to chatter. Thus chattering, each group began to speak a different language. And they moved toward the west.

The Damal story of creation really has no dimension of time—only that man appeared three or four generations before the oldest living men. They did not conceive of time going back any further than that.

Language is a living, growing thing. When the first airplane was seen by the Damals, an old man called it *padagalo*. The *padagalo* is a large whirring beetle that lives in the hot jungles of the lowlands. When the Damals had no word to describe that new wonder, they adapted a new meaning to a word chosen by one man. Kok-Me had never traveled to the lowland jungle or heard of a *padagalo* beetle. For him the only meaning of *padagalo* was this strange flying object that he now saw in the sky. "In a padagalo," the old men said, "travel the *hi ki me* spirits."

The *padagalo* flew downriver until it disappeared. *It's gone,* they thought, but after a time they again heard the whirring noise it made. This time it flew lower, and they could see what they thought was a man sitting on the tail of the *padagalo*. And what were those two things hanging down from the front of the creature? They must be two rocks to weight it down so that it did not blow away in the wind like a leaf. The *padagalo* flew over them and on upriver to Milavak where it turned around and flew downriver again, this time to disappear for good. The villagers wondered what the meaning of this *padagalo* could be, and the old men amplified the fable of the *hi ki me* spirits.

Kok-Me was in Tingil when he heard the news: "*Tuans* have arrived at Milavak. There are three of them, and they just arrived on the trail from Hitadipa."

For Kok-Me this day was just another nameless day in a succession of monotonous days one following another. But for the *tuans* (foreigners), Don Gibbons, Ken Troutman, and Gordon Larson, it was a red letter day: April 12, 1956. They had come to build an airstrip and open a mission station in the Damal tribe. Ken Troutman was the senior of the three and field leader for the mission, the Christian and Missionary Alliance. Don Gibbons and Gordon Larson had teamed up to open the work in the Beoga Valley. They would start building an airstrip and pick out sites on which to build their houses. Their wives and families would follow after the strip was completed.

On March 27 the dream that Don had cherished for fifteen months was fulfilled when pilot Ed Ulrich flew Ken Troutman and Don on a survey flight of the Beoga and Ilaga valleys. The single engine Cessna 180 flew the men on a two-hour survey flight, and they discovered one possible

at Milavak in the Beoga and another site in the
_____ ve carriers were not willing to guide the
missionaries to the Ilaga, but they were willing to take them
to the Beoga. The air survey had opened the possibility of
missionary families' entering this distant tribe. Only three
days later the men left their wives at Enarotali and began the
two-week trek to the Beoga Valley.

Rounding a bend in the trail near the village of Milavak,
the missionaries were startled to meet a woman screaming
and crying out in pain. She had blood streaming out of a
deep gash on her head. They could not understand her
anguished words, but the Moni-Damal bilinguals with them
explained that she and her husband had been fighting, and
he had settled it by clubbing her with his large garden-
digging stick.

As they came up over the last hill, the men looked down
on the site they had seen from the air. The sloping ground
was covered with gardens, trees, boulders, and thick clumps
of reeds and brush.

This was their destination. They walked on up past the
village and set up their tent beside some evergreen trees.
The trees would serve as an aerial pole for the two-way
radio.

Through the crackle of the static Ken Troutman's voice
came into the room at Enarotali where I was glued to the
radio. "This is C and M A Advance calling C and M A
Enarotali." After Ken took care of some mission business he
turned the microphone over to my husband. In his usual
easy way Don told me they were camped beside the Beoga
airstrip site. He had already looked over the area and felt
sure he could make it into an airstrip. The Damals were all
friendly and eager to help. Kathy, our three-year-old
daughter, said hello to her daddy, and then Don's voice said,
"This is C and M A Advance over and out."

Kok-Me was up early the next morning and on his way to
see those *tuans* for himself. He found the area full of Damals

who had come from everywhere, like he had, to see these strange, white beings. The women and younger children stayed back a safe distance, but the men and boys crowded around the missionaries.

The *tuans* were about to eat something. The three of them were seated on metal boxes in front of their tent. They bowed their heads, closed their eyes, and one of them talked in a strange language. Kok-Me poked the man next to him. "They must be doing spirit appeasement," he said. "Strange, isn't it?"

The *tuans* picked up metal bowls and began to eat something with a spoon. And they were drinking black mud from a metal cup. Kok-Me was not interested in their strange food, but he *was* interested in their metal dishes and spoons.

Later he found Ken Troutman doing some sort of white man's spirit worship connected with the evergreen trees. That made sense to him because spirits do live in certain trees. Actually Ken was taking his turn cranking the army surplus generator. To charge their battery for their fifteen-minute radio contact each day it took an hour of stiff cranking. Ken might have turned the job over to a carrier, but none of the tribesmen had the technical skill to turn a handcrank with rhythm and force. The generator was compact, and in order to give it a steady base Ken had lashed it to a tree. Thus Kok-Me connected the strange humming sound of the generator with the trees. Spirit worship for sure!

Gordon Larson, highly trained in the science of linguistics, was seated with a group of men involved in an earnest conversation. Coming closer Kok-Me observed that this *tuan* was saying a word in the Moni language and his informant would give that word back to him in Damal. Then the *tuan* loudly repeated the word. What Kok-Me did not observe, for he had no background to understand it, was that Gordon, using the phonetic alphabet, was writing all he heard in a notebook.

Kok-Me found Don Gibbons walking over a piece of land and talking to the men about buying it. He understood that the *tuan* was paying three steel ax heads to the men who owned this land so that he could make a resting place for a *padagalo,* and that he was paying blue beads and cowrie shells for the sweet potato gardens on the land. What the coming of a *padagalo* would mean Kok-Me did not know, but the *tuan* seemed to know, and he was determined to bring it to pass. The *tuan* was also bargaining for boards from two deserted houses that he wanted torn down to build a Damal hut for himself.

In the days that followed work began on the clearing and leveling of the airstrip. The workers were Damal men and older boys, and their only tools were their familiar garden-digging sticks. The missionaries had only two axes and two machetes with them, and those were used to keep the digging sticks sharpened. With one hundred men working on the strip, it soon began to take on a new form. The men dug around the roots of the trees. Then, tying a rattan vine twenty feet up on the trunk of each tree, they pulled it over. The roots were torn out of the ground as it fell.

The five-gallon kerosine cans that had served as carrying tins for supplies on the trip were emptied and used to carry dirt from one area to another as the ground was leveled. Another crew worked at digging and prying loose the thick clumps of reeds that grew in some spots. Those they dragged off to the edge and threw into the streams that flowed on both sides of the strip.

One day Kok-Me sat down with a hundred others to listen while Gordon Larson spoke in Moni and a Beoga man who also knew Moni translated for him. Kok-Me understood the words; they were spoken in his mother tongue. The *tuan* was saying, "A heavenly man named Jesus came to earth to take away the punishment for all the bad deeds of earthly people. Even though those who follow Jesus will die, they will come to life again."

What talk is this? Kok-Me thought. *These are amazing*

words, but I don't believe them. Never mind about the talk of these tuans. *I'm interested in their axes and knives.*

"The *padagalo* is coming. It's coming." The cry went up from a man on the airstrip, and the little side valley of Milavak echoed and reechoed with everyone's shouting.

The missionaries were expecting a free drop of powdered milk and bread as pilot Ed Ulrich flew on his way from Sentani to the Lakes. Ken Troutman had radio contact with Ed. "I'm over the strip and releasing your drop," Ed said. "Watch for it." All the *tuans* and the Damals were watching, but no one saw anything. The little plane disappeared behind the high mountains and was gone. And everyone went back to work on the strip.

A letter that I wrote to my parents on April 24, 1956, best tells the next turn of events.

Dear Mother and Dad,

Last week was the first week since we came to New Guinea that I could have sent you a letter and didn't. I just didn't have what it takes to write—not even to you. I'll try to start from the beginning.

On April 12 the men arrived on the site that Ed Ulrich had picked out for an airstrip in the Beoga Valley. Their reception from the Damals was very good, and the site looked promising from the ground. Don surveyed it and found it was 1,700 feet long with an average grade of 12 percent—all very good.

On Monday, still camped there, Ken Troutman called an executive committee meeting on the radio. The plan was to make the strip right away, and Don was going to stay at the site to work on it. Ken felt there was no danger to Don in being alone, and the executive committee agreed. I was thrilled beyond words with the prospect of someday soon going to the Damals.

Don built a native style house for himself and the Damals were cooperating well in working on the strip. Plans were made for a drop of supplies. Ed Ulrich was flying across the field on Tuesday, so he made the drop on his way.

Well, the drop was lost. The high mountain tops around

had clouds on them, so he did not go down into the valley. The plane was flying at 12,500 feet, and the strip is at 5,600.

By Tuesday Ed wasn't so confident about the strip site, and on Wednesday he completely reversed his decision saying that plans to build an airstrip in the Beoga should be canceled.

Ken started home on Thursday, Gordon started on Saturday, and Don will be starting home next Saturday. I felt and still do feel that Satan won a real victory in this. Do not misunderstand. I'm not saying that Ed was out of touch with God's plan; I do not have any feeling toward him but love. The defeat had nothing to do with him personally. I had planned to write a letter of rejoicing Wednesday night, and when it turned to defeat I couldn't bring myself to write anything at all. I think Don took this better than I did on first word of it, and I'm OK now too.

Don continued to work on the strip during his remaining days in the Beoga Valley. Damals came from far and near, and excitement was running high. One night by the light of a full moon twenty-five men worked all night chanting their rhythmic songs as they dug the ground.

The Saturday deadline was coming, and Don prepared to leave. He had a can of cowrie shells, which he buried in the ground inside his hut, and he also left a trail tin and a few other things in the house. He told the people, "I'm leaving my heart with you. I *will* return."

At Don's invitation, Kok-Me and two other young men decided to accompany him back to Enarotali. Don felt they could be used to teach us the Damal languge. The three went with Don to the top of the Beoga Valley and had started into the forest when they became fearful and decided to turn back. The Taganit War was still in progress. What if some Danis were in the Moni's valley over the mountain? They might be killed. So they turned back—back to their life as their ancestors had known it.

10

War, A Wedding, and Witches

"Men are stealing!" the Milavak chief called out. "They are stealing the *tuan's* goods." People came running to see, and sure enough what the chief had said was true. Kok-Me and five of his buddies were trying to untie the rattan vines that secured the door of the *tuan's* hut.

Several months after the airdrop was made to the missionaries, a Damal had found the bundle way up in the forest. He brought it back to the village, where the people held a council. They decided to place it in the *tuan's* hut to await his return.

"What are you doing?" the chief now demanded of Kok-Me.

"We wanted the tin cans to give to the girls tonight at a courtship sing."

"You leave that hut alone! You're not going to steal those tin cans. They belong to the *tuan.*"

Hanging their heads, Kok-Me and his friends left without the prized *hai* tins that would have really won the hearts of the girls.

Months had passed since the disastrous battle in the upper Ilaga, but time had not healed the wounds of grief and anger over the loss of so many clansmen. The open sores from Taganit's victory continued to fester with hatred and revenge. Nothing could satisfy that burning passion except killing—brutal killing of any men, women, or children from the group allied with Taganit. Revenge! Life must be taken. Blood must be spilled to avenge their losses.

121

All over the Beoga that passion was growing. It must grow, and they must be united in a single spirit to retaliate. The attack had come upon them as a unit of people, and they must strike back as one.

To give them success in battle, spirit appeasement was being performed all over the valley. At Wang-Be the women and children were herded out of the village. No woman should see or hear anything of spirit appeasement. If she did, all her future offspring would die.

A man climbed up on the thatching of the men's hut carrying a writhing, squealing pig under his arm. Carefully he balanced himself at the peak of the conical roof. Stretching an arm toward the sky he cried out, "Spirits of these mountains, listen. Spirits of our ancestors, hear me." He listed the names of spirits and then the names of the dead, men who had been leaders and successful in war. "Help us," he cried. "Ancestors, help us so we won't all die and your village of Wang-Be become a deserted place with no people." Taking a knife he cried, "I'm cutting this pig's ear for you. I offer it to you. Give us courage. Give us success. Help us kill many of the enemy."

The Sinak warriors kept their rendezvous with the Beoga men. They spent the night in the cold rain just a few hundred feet from the village of Tovegi. In the pitch blackness they could see nothing except an occasional flicker from the fire in one of the huts. They did not need to see Tovegi village. They knew what was there. This was the flat lower end of the Ilaga Valley, quite unlike the steep mountains the Beoga people farmed. Here the Mudip Danis had lived and been driven out by Taganit some months earlier. The victors had moved in, taking over the lush gardens. They built new houses—a half dozen men's houses with all the women's huts to go with them—because the Mudip houses were all burned.

There was no moon, only deep, black darkness and pelting rain. The men sat shivering under their rain mats. Hunger gnawed at their stomachs. But no one thought about the cold and rain. As one man they were waiting to kill, to avenge the death of their father, their sister, their uncle, their brother. And kill they would.

The rain had stopped, and soon the first bird would announce the coming of morning. It was time to begin. The men carried rolls of rattan tying vine and pandanas leaf torches they had painstakingly shielded from the rain through the night. They fanned out in groups to each of the huts. With quick, practiced movements they tied the doors shut, lashing them securely in place.

From the upstairs sleeping floor a man heard the sound of movement and called out, "Are you warriors?"

Chief Kawa hesitated a moment and then replied, "I'm looking for Me-Ki," a well-known Damal man who had been killed in a recent battle. "Is he there?"

Terrified, the Dani cried out, "Warriors! They are attacking us!"

A warrior entered a woman's hut and snatched up a burning piece of wood to light the torches. The startled woman cried out, "What are you doing here? Are you an enemy?"

Running in every direction, they set the houses on fire, lighting the dry grass under the eaves of the thatched roofs. A great cry of terror rose from the village. Flames ignited, spread across the hut, and leaped into the air. The sky was lighted from the flames, only to be darkened again with the heavy fog that lay over the village.

The Sinak and Beoga men were following their well-laid plans. The Danis had encircled the village and kept guard with their drawn bows and arrows while the Damals ignited the huts.

Women shrieked and then were silent. Men clawed and hacked at the walls of their burning prisons. When some did escape, crying with the pain of their burns, the Danis were ready with their bows and arrows. The silhouette of a burning hut looked at first like a giant incandescent light bulb, and then the structure crumbled to the earth. The air was full of the stench of burning flesh, the cries of babies, the pleas for mercy from men, the shrieks of agony from women, the shouts of triumph from the victors.

The light of a new day looked down upon a scene of devastation—charred bodies lying in the smoldering ruins of Tovegi village. A shroud of fog still kept the secret of revenge from neighboring villages. Intoxicated by their victory, the warriors were reluctant to leave. *Let the enemy come. We can conquer the whole Ilaga. The spirits are helping us.*

When the fog did lift and men from other villages saw what had happened at Tovegi, they came with the fury of a wild pig wounded in a hunt. The Beoga and Sinak people were exhausted from being up all night and having little to eat, but they prepared to fight and win.

All of a sudden the arrows of the enemy began to hit their mark. First one man fell, and then another. If the wounded man could not get up and run, he was left for dead. There was no thought of trying to carry a wounded comrade back behind the lines to safety. When the enemy found him he quickly finished him off, for the whole point of the fighting was to kill. Those men who fell were brave men, seasoned warriors. Although there were only five who fell, it seemed to the Beoga men that everyone was being killed. Their courage left them, and a cry to flee arose from all directions.

Kok-Me ran with the others as fast as his legs could carry him over the rough terrain. He was headed for the bridge that crossed the Ilaga River to the side that led to home and safety from the Taganit warriors. When he reached the bridge he found it was crowded with men trying to get across.

No Damal knew how to swim, for there were no waters suitable for swimming in all of their tribal area. This was the time to learn. With the shouting of warriors behind them men waded into the river, taking their chances with the water rather than with the Taganit Danis. Men were half-wading, half-thrashing in the swift, churning water of the river, but they were emerging downstream on the far bank.

Kok-Me took in the scene with a glance and decided to press for a place on the bridge. Crossing the bridge was like crossing a tight rope with a dozen other men walking the rope with him. The core of vines bound together to serve as footing bounced and swayed and gave a little with the weight of so many. Kok-Me carried his bow and arrows in one hand over his head. The other hand followed the single strand of vine that served as a handrail to help in that balancing act.

Meyong searched the faces of the returning warriors for her son. "Have you seen Kok-Me?" she queried. But they had not. They told of the great number they had killed, embellishing the story on every side. But Meyong found little comfort. All the other men from the nearby villages had come home, and Kok-Me had not.

At evening the tragedy struck her full force. She went out and plastered herself with mud and began the death wail. "I'm going to the Ilaga and kill a Dani with my own hands," she cried. "They killed my son." And she began to wail again.

Emerging on the Beoga side of the bridge, Kok-Me looked up and saw his good friend Jenin. "Let's travel together," Kok-Me said. "We don't dare travel on the regular trail. The Danis might ambush us." Jenin agreed, and they headed up into the jungle. Their plan was to follow the basic direction of the trail by the river. But they had not counted on all the cliffs and dead-end places they came to. They discovered there was a good reason why the main trail hugged the river bottom. It was almost impossible to travel in this rugged terrain.

Two days later they emerged in home territory. How good it was to sleep in a hut beside a fire and eat sweet potatoes and greens once again. After a night of rest, Kok-Me headed for Wung.

When he saw his mother's mud-covered face and body he knew she was in mourning over his presumed death. The expression on her face changed very quickly from disbelief, to relief that he was alive—and then to anger.

"You crazy son," she cried. "Always going here and there to fight. You never stay home to make gardens for me. I told you not to go off to fight, but you wouldn't listen."

After her anger cooled a bit, Meyong went out to wash off the mud. She sat and listened to the story her son had to tell, and her emotions changed once again, this time to admiration and love.

Delem was sitting alone in her mother's hut when her father came in. "I want to talk to you about something," he said. "I need some cowrie shells, and I'm going to take them as payment for you. There is a man who has a beautiful indo shell that I want very much."

Delem continued to draw lines in the ashes with a stick. After a silence she said, "Go ahead and take the indo shell from that man if you want to, but whoever he is, I won't go to him. I want to marry Kok-Me. I don't want anyone else."

"Kok-Me? Why do you want to marry him? Does he have lots of good shells?"

"Kok-Me helped cremate my brother's body when he died. I couldn't even go to see my brother because there was witch talk. They accused me of killing him. But Kok-Me, out of love, went to the forest and got wood for the cremation. I'll have no one else for my husband."

"Well, then, I'll go and see Kok-Me. I'll see if he wants to marry you and if he has enough cowrie shells and pigs."

Light in the men's hut grew dim as a man's figure stepped through the low doorway. Kok-Me recognized Delem's father, who was now seating himself across the fire.

"I have come to talk about Delem," her father said. "I want to collect cowrie shells in exchange for her, and she says she won't marry anyone else but you. Has she given you any love-potion leaves?"

Kok-Me blushed at the mention of love-potion leaves. "No, she hasn't given me any leaves," he said. "But if you will go to the village of Tingil with me you can see what shells my father has."

Delem's father agreed to accept the shells they offered. The three shell-belts and twenty individual shells, each wrapped in its own little cocoon case, would do as a down payment on his daughter.

Rumblings of war talk again swept through the Beoga. The seed of that talk came from the Damals in the Ilaga Valley. There had been no communication between the two valleys for many months now. The Wang-Be trail was "sewed up tight," as the Damals say, and so was the river trail that followed the Ilaga River as it flowed around the bend to the Beoga. One man did get through on the river trail with word inviting the Beoga people to come and join the Ilaga Damals. They would switch sides and together the Damals would drive the Danis out of the Ilaga Valley. Another bit of news was that *tuans* had come to the Ilaga and were digging ground, which was in some way connected with *tuan* magic and the *padagalo*.

The talk of war was relayed up the Beoga Valley. In all of the major villages shamans performed divination ceremonies to determine if the spirits would give them success in this battle. The shaman chose a secluded spot away from all women and prepared a pit quite like the cooking pits Damals use for the steaming of food. He heated rocks and wrapped them in leaves, but instead of cooking food he placed bundles of grass around the edge of the pit. The bunches of grass were separated by sticks, and each stick represented a specific evil spirit or the spirit of an ancestor. After the pit had steamed a reasonable length of time it was opened, and the grass carefully examined. If any of the grass was partially uncooked then the shaman knew that the particular spirit represented was offended and would not give success in the Ilaga battle.

All up and down the Beoga the verdict was unanimous— they would have much success, eat the Danis' pigs, and be conquerors. So it was that the Beoga warriors joined for the third time to attack the Ilaga. Kok-Me joined the others at Ogam where they hiked up and over the 10,000-foot mountain that divides the two valleys.

They spent the night on the top of the mountain not far from the place where there was a steep drop into the Ilaga. In the morning they descended toward the barren, sandy area, the traditional battleground for fighting.

Something was very different about the whole place. A long, smooth piece of ground was visible, with ditches and piles of mud along the edges. *This must be the tuan's ground,* Kok-Me thought, *but where are the Ilaga Damals who were to join us in fighting the Danis?*

It was just after noon when they crossed the airstrip and headed down toward the first villages, still hoping to be joined by their allies. Pressing on, they heard the lone cry, "*Wem me motako.* Warriors are coming," but paid no heed because they knew that their enemies lived across the valley.

Suddenly Taganit warriors appeared from nowhere, raining arrows upon them. Before a single Ilaga man was hit, two of the Beoga men were shot down. Word was called out, and the Beoga people began to retreat. But the Dani warriors were more than a match for them. Some circled up and behind the Beoga men, making the fight for their lives even more desperate. One Dani was hit with a Damal arrow, but his comrades were able to move him on a stretcher back to the village. Several days later he did die—the only death from the Ilaga.

The Beoga men and the Sinak Mudips who fought with them were not so fortunate. Numbers of them were wounded, and their bodies lay where they fell. Some were close to the villages. Others fell on the airstrip itself, and even more were hit while up in the forest in their desperate attempt to fend off their enemy as they fled for home. Once a man was down and could not run, he was left to die. There was no one to carry him back home and nurse him. He was as good as dead when he fell.

Kok-Me missed being hit by the Dani arrows. He fled, not
on the trail but into the trackless expanse of the forest. For
two days he fought his way through the tangle of the jungle
and up and over the rugged mountain. He tried to eat some
leaves and grass, but that was no food. He was desperate for
food, for it had been three days since he had eaten a decent
meal of sweet potatoes. He had now had his fill of war and
all that it meant. He promised himself he would listen to the
earnest pleas and angry outbursts of his mother as she
begged him not to go off to war again.

Kok-Me heard a rumor from Piloma. Delem's father was
taking bride-price payment on her from another man—an
older man who already had a wife. Kok-Me lost no time in
hiking downriver to Piloma. Confronting Delem's father, he
soon found that the rumor was true. The older man had an
indo shell—a very valuable one, which he had given to
Delem's father.

"Can you match this shell?" the father demanded.

"No," he replied. "Just give me back all the shells I paid
you, and I'll buy another girl."

Kok-Me took the shells and was satisfied that they were
all there.

Later Delem asked Kok-Me, "Why have you taken back all
the shells you paid for me?"

"Your father is taking payment to marry you to another
man. That's how it is."

"I see," Delem said, and quietly walked away.

Kok-Me was depressed. His disappointment was far
deeper than he cared to show to others. He had planned to
marry Delem shortly, and now the marriage was all off. He
looked for something to release his pent emotions and
decided to spend some of the shells returned to him from
the bride price. First he bargained for a new bow and
arrows. He needed new ones after the last battle in the Ilaga.
Then he bought a large red fruit that belongs to the
pandanas nut family. A red, oily pulp covers hundreds of

nonedible kernels on this fruit. After it is cooked, the red fruit is kneaded into a puree and collected in a wooden trough. If the Damals had any type of alcoholic drink Kok-Me would have sought that, but in its absence he buried his sorrows by gorging on the red, oily puree from the pandanas fruit.

At that point one of Kok-Me's uncles came along and listened to his story of disappointment. "Delem isn't the only girl in the world," he countered. "There is a courtship sing tonight. Why not pick out another girl to marry? I'll come along to help you."

Kok-Me spent the night singing to the girls. And just as his uncle had suggested, he did find another girl who he decided to marry.

In the morning Kok-Me was greeted by Delem's father with a drawn bow pointed at him. "What do you mean by accepting the shells back and then running off with my daughter?" the man demanded.

"I don't know anything about your daughter," Kok-Me replied. "I spent the night at the courtship sing, and I'm going to marry another girl."

"Well, if you didn't steal her, then she's run off somewhere by herself. She didn't spend the night in any of the houses in the village, and no one saw her leave." The father took one of his sons, and the two of them started off to look for Delem at Ogam, one day's walk downriver.

The afternoon before, when Delem had heard the news about her father's decision, her reaction was immediate. *I'm going to marry Kok-Me,* she thought. *I don't want that old man who already has another wife, no matter how much my father likes his shells.*

Delem watched for her chance, and when no one was looking she slipped out of the village under the cover of evening dusk. Her path led upriver but was always well away from any people who might discover her presence and report her flight to her father. All night she stumbled on, even though the rain shower chilled her and the bushes and thorns tore at her skin. She was not going to be married to that man as a second wife.

In the light of dawn Delem reached the Wang-Be River, followed along the wet, slippery rocks that skirted the river's edge—the place where Na-Nonem had drowned—and then climbed up the steep mountain to the village of Wung.

"Greetings, my daughter," Meyong said as Delem appeared in the doorway of her hut. "Come in. Why, you've been out all night in the rain! What has happened? Why have you come here?"

"I have come here permanently to live with you," Delem blurted out. "I'm not going to marry that old man who already has a wife. I want to marry Kok-Me."

Meyong understood the whole story at once. "My daughter," she said, "you may stay with me always. Here, have these potatoes I just cooked. You must be hungry." Delem relaxed in the warmth and hospitality of Meyong's hut.

When Delem's father returned from his fruitless search downriver, he learned that his daughter had run away to Kok-Me's mother. There was no point in trying to get Delem to marry the man with the indo shell. She was a strong-willed girl and would never stay with the old man.

So he went upriver to negotiate the bride price with Kok-Me, Wolo, and their other male relatives. After much bargaining, threats, and angry outbursts the price was settled upon: five pigs, six shell-belts, a number of individual shells, and an indo shell that Wolo finally agreed to part with. Everyone understood that with his payment Kok-Me could marry Delem, but more payments would be demanded in the years to come.

Delem did not go back to her home in Piloma. She stayed with Meyong until the bride price was paid, and then Kok-Me took her upriver to Tingil. Here Wolo's second wife welcomed Delem into her home just as if she were her own daughter, and Kok-Me stayed in his father's hut. Life fell quickly into the routine of garden work for Delem, but now

she worked with her mother-in-law instead of with her own
mother. Life was also much the same as before for Kok-Me
except that he had lost his interst in attending courtship
sings and concentrated his efforts on wooing his bride to a
rendezvous in the woods.

The Ilaga battle and crushing defeat of the Beoga people
was now a month behind them. Still there was no sign of an
upriver chieftain, Nanol, or of his brother Nil. On the day of
the battle at the Ilaga airstrip the brothers were seen as they
fled up into the forest. The Beoga people at first concluded
that they had fled across the central range of mountains to
the southern Damal valleys. But as the days passed without
their return or word of their whereabouts, talk began to
change. The inevitable conclusion was accepted. They had
been killed in the fighting after they entered the forest.
Upriver at Kelma the sister, mother, and other relatives of the
two men began to mourn their death.

In Wang-Be six young warriors started to talk of witchcraft
being involved in the death of Nanol and Nil. They headed
for Tingil and added Kok-Me and Dulal to their number.
The more they talked the more they were sure that Nanol's
spirit must have been eaten by a woman. The killing of two
important men like Nanol and his brother could not be
overlooked. The witch must be killed. The Wang-Be youths
knew that Nanol had a large mo garden, and concluded that
he had not given his sister enough of the mo. They were sure
that her resentful thoughts had gone to the Ilaga and she had
eaten the spirit of her brother.

The party of young men headed upriver, painted for war
and brandishing their bows and arrows and a machete.
They found Imi, the sister, mourning the death of her two
brothers. Entering the village yard, they demanded in loud,
angry tones, "Imi, come out of the house. We are going to
kill you for being a witch." Imi's son-in-law was in the
house with her. He with other young men who looked on
Imi as their mother or aunt heard the threat and imme-

diately came to fight in defense of their "mother." Imi did not come out of the hut, so three men went inside to kill her with the machete. As they were scuffling with her son-in-law in the dim light, they cut Imi's throat, and she fell to the floor, acting as if she were dead.

Outside the hut their companions were now engaged in a battle with sons and nephews of Imi. The group retreated to an open field better suited for warfare, where each side could arch arrows into the enemy group and then run for cover. After some time of that game of war, Dulal fell to the ground. It was time to call a truce for the day. Kok-Me and the others came to Dulal's aid. He was not dead, but he lay unconscious on the ground. What could have happened to him? There was no arrow beside him. Carrying Dulal back downriver, they carefully examined his body for an arrow wound, but found nothing, not even in his hair. Their conclusion was that an arrow did not cause Dulal's unconsciousness. That fact was very important. If Dulal should die from an arrow wound, then a full-scale war would begin.

The next day Kok-Me and his friends received the taunting news that Imi was not dead. She was very much alive. The machete had cut her throat but had not killed her. Kok-Me's party added a number of young warriors to their group and headed upvalley, determined to dispatch this killer of men who refused to be killed herself.

They found Imi with her elderly mother crying over the loss of the two brothers. This time they would not be thwarted in their purpose. When the two women stepped into the village yard the men shot them at close range with their arrows. Even after they fell they continued to shoot until the bodies of the two women looked like pin cushions. Satisfied with their deed, they turned and fled downriver.

That closed the incident. Two witches had been killed in retribution for the death of Nanol and Nil, and that evened the score. Although Dulal had regained consciousness and was able to talk, his body was paralyzed from the waist down. Had they known the truth, discovered by a Dutch surgeon some years later, war would have continued and more people would have died. They did not know at the time that an arrow tip lay imbedded in Dulal's spine, causing his paralysis.

This story of war and witchcraft, killing and spirit appeasement, birth, marriage, and death could go on without end. Who knows how long it had been going on, repeating itself over and over in an endless cycle. Time and the rest of the world had forgotten the Damal people.

But no! Not all of the world had forgotten the Damals, nor had God forgotten them. For some years members of the Christian and Missionary Alliance churches of North America had been praying for the Damal tribespeople, who were then known as Uhundunis. Soon my husband and I would walk into the Beoga Valley, and the lives of the Damal people would be dramatically changed. When the killing of Imi and her mother took place, the events had already begun that would bring us to the Beoga.

PART 2

11
Two Steps Forward
And One Step Back

Just before dawn on August 8, 1956, the Ekari women on Lake Paniai turned their canoes and paddled toward their village of Enarotali. The women had been out all night fishing on the lake, not for fish—for there were no fish in the lake—but for freshwater shrimp. Their canoes were only logs hollowed out first with fire and then with an ax. The ends of the canoes were blunt, which made their progress very slow.

Life in the village of Enarotali had changed drastically during their lifetime. Indeed it was changing for all the Ekari living around the three sister lakes—the larger Lake Paniai and the smaller lakes of Tage and Tigi. The outside world had burst in upon the "stone age" Ekari, and the hands of time could not be turned back.

The western half of the island of New Guinea was under the administrative control of the Netherlands. For a hundred years the Dutch government had administered all of the coastal areas around the island, but the mountainous interior had been ignored until October of 1936, when a Dutch oil company plane discovered the three lakes. The pilot, F. J. Wissel, was flying from the north coast to the south over a route that took him high into the mountains.

Suddenly below him he saw a large lake. He dived down to take a better look and discovered there were canoes on the lake and gardens and villages surrounding it.

That was the first time the outside world learned of the existence of the Ekari people, and that was the Ekaris' first hint that they were not the only people in the world. Following their discovery, the lakes were drawn in on the map and named the Wissel Lakes. A year later the Dutch government sent an overland patrol to explore the area, and that led to the opening of a government post at the village of Enarotali.

The Christian and Missionary Alliance was close behind the Dutch government when in January 1939 they sent Walter Post and Russel Deibler over the trail from the south coast to begin missionary work. The Second World War interrupted that pioneer venture, but missionaries returned to the Wissel Lakes in October of 1946.

The government post of Enarotali was built on a hill rising steeply from the lake's edge, affording a gorgeous view of Lake Paniai and the surrounding mountains. In 1956 the government community included offices and residences for their personnel in the civil government, police post, agricultural station, post office, hostel for the occasional traveler, and hospital with doctor and nurses. Beyond the government buildings was a Roman Catholic church and compound; and above them the Alliance missionaries had their homes with four families and three single ladies in residence, a Bible school and dormitory, an elementary school for the Ekaris, and a church. Still farther up the hill there was a group of Ekari houses and a cemetery. That was Enarotali in 1956—the only government post in the vast mountainous interior of Netherlands New Guinea.

On that particular morning shortly before dawn kerosine lamps were lit in two of the missionaries' log cabins. Don Gibbons and Gordon Larson were preparing to leave on their third trip together with the aim of opening a mission station far to the east. Their destination was the Ilaga Valley. One month earlier the executive committee of the mission had met and appointed Gordon and Peggy Larson to the Dani tribe to reduce the Dani language to writing and eventually translate the Bible. Don and I were appointed to the Damal tribe in the Ilaga. With the appointment a promise came by cable from our New York headquarters that two couples would be sent in 1957 to reinforce our planned outreach. One couple would come for linguistic work in the Damal tribe and the other for general missionary work among the Danis.

Gordon Larson grew up attending an Alliance church in Jamestown, New York, and often heard the plea for missionary recruits. However, he did not believe the Lord was leading him to the foreign field until his years in the army at the time of World War II. Gordon was stationed in Washington, D.C., and played the clarinet in the United States Army Band. It was there also that Gordon met attractive, blond Peggy Bowman, who was employed as a secretary in the Pentagon. Peggy had felt God's call to missionary service through a Youth for Christ meeting before they met.

When Gordon's term of service in the army was over they were married and he began his college education, which led to a master's degree in linguistics and anthropology. Gordon and Peggy Larson left for Netherlands New Guinea in the fall of 1952. Their immediate call was to work with an unwritten language, reduce it to writing, and then translate the New Testament.

Don grew up in a large family with eight brothers and sisters and three cousins, whose mother had died. Through the depression years they lived in poverty, but Don never resented the lack of material things in his home. Because of that background he adjusted easily to a life-style of pioneering when he came to New Guinea. His mother was a faithful Christian, and she reared her son in the church. Don cannot remember a time when he did not love the Lord with all of his heart.

In high school Don's goal was to become a dairy farmer, but the Lord had other plans for him. He enrolled at Northwest Bible Institute and there, through a missionary message, God called him to foreign missionary work. After graduation Don started a Sunday school in a small, rural community on Whidby Island, Washington, with the hope of later building a church where there was none. He supported himself by working in a small sawmill.

I grew up in a Christian family very active in the Christian and Missionary Alliance church in Glendale, California. I heard the Lord's call to be a missionary while I was still in high school. Simpson Bible Institute in Seattle, Washington, was the school of my choice for missionary training.

My call to be a missionary was not dramatic. It was a still small, inner voice saying, "I want you to fulfill My biblical command and go as a foreign missionary." I was not a "spiritual giant," and am still not. From high school I took one *small* step at a time as the doors opened.

A major test came to me at the end of my first year in Bible school, although the open door did not seem critical at the time. The call was given for volunteers to teach vacation Bible school in small churches. I had never even taught a Sunday school class—how could I help lead a whole school? My church ministry was only at the piano and organ. But the Lord seemed to say, "You had better start learning to teach children if you are going to be a missionary."

I had other excuses too. A good summer job was waiting for me at home, and I needed the money for school. This was my first time away from home, and I was homesick. And I did not want to miss attending the Bible camp where I had heard God's call on my life two summers earlier. That year Darlene Deibler Rose from Dutch New Guinea was the missionary speaker, and I did so want to hear her.

But, putting all those reasons aside, I took one more step along the path of God's leading. My second vacation Bible school was on Whidby Island, and it was there that I met

Don Gibbons and our friendship began. A year later Don enrolled at Simpson Bible Institute as a senior. We graduated together in June, 1951, and were married that same month.

The Alliance requires its missionary candidates to fulfill two years of practical training in the States before going overseas. We served under Village Missions in a rural area in eastern Oregon. Our assignment was to start a church in a small ranching and lumbering community. Paulina, Oregon proved to be an excellent training ground for both of us.

We went to Paulina after a week's honeymoon. Our friends and family had set us up for housekeeping with carefully selected wedding presents. Among them were a toaster and iron, and I also had my sewing machine, which I planned to use a lot. We found Paulina at the end of a fifty-six mile dirt road: a general store with a half dozen houses and no electricity!

Having been raised in the city, I had a few things to learn about country living. I learned how to cook on a wood stove, use a Coleman lantern for light, not just on camping trips, and carry water in a bucket from a hand pump in the yard. When Don said, "We'll have to get sadirons to do the ironing," I thought he was joking; but he was not! I learned to heat four cast-iron sadirons on the wood range and rotate them to do my ironing. I am still using sadirons and find that they really work quite well.

Don faced the challenge of church planting from the ground up, for there had never been a church in Paulina. The community we served had less than three hundred people living in an area twenty by eighty miles. Many of the roads were only passable to Jeeps and logging trucks and our old 1937 Plymouth. Where could a better training ground have been found for both of us? When we left Paulina after two years there was a church building, converted from an abandoned school house, and several Christian families who have continued to serve the Lord through the years.

We applied for foreign missionary service under the
Christian and Missionary Alliance, not to a specific country,
but to any one of the twenty-two countries in which the
Alliance worked at that time. God's choice for us through
the mission board was Dutch New Guinea, and we set sail
on a freighter in 1953.

In the early morning light two missionary wives were
down at the boat landing at Enarotali to wish their husbands
God's blessing on their journey. Peggy Larson with her three
children, eight-year-old Marlene, six-year-old Romaine, and
two-month-old Daniel were there to say good-bye to
Gordon. And I was there with our two girls, four-year-old
Kathy and fifteen-month-old Joyce, to send Don on his way.
There were no parting kisses on the dock, because such a
display of affection in public between husband and wife
would seem vulgar to Ekaris. Respecting that cultural
difference was one of the many things we had changed in
our life-style in order to win the friendship and understanding of those primitive people.

The mission boat was bobbing gently at the side of the
dock as the Ekari carriers swung their thirty-five pound
loads aboard and climbed in themselves, followed by the
two missionaries. Don pulled the starter rope on the
outboard motor. It sputtered and then took hold. Slowly the
boat turned and headed out on the shimmering smooth
lake. Everybody waved, and they were on their way.

Three weeks earlier Don had started out for the Ilaga by
himself. I had come to the dock and waved him off just as I
did this morning, but four days out on the trail his radio
transceiver stopped working. The agreement was that he
could not go on without a radio, for it would be essential in
arranging airdrops once he got to the Ilaga. He had no
choice but to return to Enarotali.

When Don returned I wrote to my parents:

> The fact that Don had to turn back is quite a discourage-
> ment to me, because we have been waiting to go to the

Damals for over two and one-half years. However, on our day of prayer on Friday the Lord encouraged my heart by saying, "Faithful is He that calleth you, who also will do it" (1 Thess. 5:24). I really needed this encouragement; and when it had accomplished its purpose, the Lord showed me the phrase in the same book—"but Satan hindered us"—concerning Paul's desire to visit the church. I feel this is the balance of the truth. First He is faithful; but we must also win the battle in prayer, for Satan is a very strong foe.

Don is home now but plans to start again in a week—as soon as the plane brings another radio. My hope is that the next time I see Don will be when I fly to the Ilaga and land on the airstrip he is going to build.

The plane did not come with a radio. But Ken Troutman, our field leader, gave Don and Gordon the Enarotali station radio saying, "You take this radio and be on your way. We'll get along without one until a replacement arrives."

The next hindrance was a rumor that three Ekari traders had been killed in the Ilaga. The fifty Ekaris who had been vying to carry the twenty loads suddenly vanished. Word reached us by radio from the missionaries at Homeyo that the rumor was false, but that made no difference to the Ekaris. Twelve men from Lake Tigi, including several Christians, signed up to carry loads; but the day before the men were to leave, word came that they too were afraid and would not go.

Don and Gordon started out that morning with only six carriers, hoping to add twelve more on the way. Their boat moved slowly across the lake to the mouth of the Agabu River and then began to find its way upstream through a flat, swampy area. Nearing the rendezvous point, they saw that there were carriers waiting for them. When they got closer, however, they observed that the men were smeared with mud—a sign of mourning. They explained to Don that their sister was dying and that they could not carry his things for him.

The two missionaries in the boat, although quite different in their backgrounds, made a good team. Gordon was a scholar with a compelling interest in reducing an unwritten language to writing and giving the people the New Testament in their own language. He also had the ability to stay at his desk working patiently with language informants for countless hours, and he was meticulous in the details necessary to produce a good Bible translation.

Don was an outdoor man who loved people and found it challenging and enjoyable to hike the New Guinea trails, explore the land, and share the food and hospitality of the native people. He had never taken a college-level language course, but he had a natural gift for learning languages—not from a textbook, but by living with the people who spoke the language. Because of his interest in people as individuals he also quickly understood their culture and thought patterns. He was not schooled in the traditional methods used by missionaries in similar tribal cultures. Don was a radical in terms of breaking tradition but a conservative in believing that the Bible had a pertinent answer for every question in any culture—an answer directly out of Scripture that did not need to be transmitted through Western culture.

Both Gordon and Don were called of God to take the good news of salvation through Jesus Christ to tribal people who had never heard. They had met for the first time in this very boat traveling on the same river. Don had just arrived as a new missionary, and Gordon had hiked out from Homeyo on a short business trip. Don ferried the boat upriver to meet Gordon and bring him back to Enarotali.

On that trip Gordon shared with Don his burden and insights into four distinct tribes that lived to the east of the Homeyo mission station. Natives from the east came regularly to Homeyo to make salt at the best salt spring in all of the interior. Here Gordon met the travelers and through the Moni language was able to do some basic language analysis in Damal, Dani, Nduga, and Wolani. On that day Don first learned of the Damal tribe, and from that small seed his desire to reach the Damals with the message of

Christ had increased. Now Gordon and Don had teamed up for the third time in an effort to open a mission station among the Danis and Damals.

The river narrowed as they wound farther upstream. It took careful maneuvering to get the boat around the bends without catching grass or debris on the propeller as it passed close to the riverbank. Midmorning the village of Komopa came into sight. Above that point the river channel was too shallow to operate the outboard motor. Carriers were to meet them in Komopa, too, but only one man showed up. Rearranging their loads to include only the barest essentials, Don and Gordon decided to go on anyway. They could secure Moni carriers at the Homeyo mission station two days' walk on their way to the east.

Gordon knew the Homeyo trail better than Don did, for he and his wife, Peggy, had been stationed at Homeyo for over two years working among the Moni people. All food, household supplies, and even their wood range had to go upriver in the mission boat and be carried over the trail to Homeyo. When Peggy and the girls went along the journey took three days, but Don and Gordon managed it in two. They used walking sticks and wore hobnail boots to make it easier to move at a reasonable speed over the moss-covered logs and slippery rocks, through the mud, and always climbing up or jolting down over the obstacle course that is called "the trail."

At Homeyo, Don and Gordon were welcomed by the Moni missionaries, Bill and Grace Cutts, Leona St. John, and Rosali Fenton. Don was anxious to be on his way, so he planned to start out with his Ekari carriers, and Gordon would recruit Moni carriers and follow in a couple of days. The next morning Don arose to find that five of the Ekaris had deserted during the night. All he had left was Andy, a young man from Lake Tigi, and one other Ekari. Plans were changed again. In two days Gordon started out with six Moni carriers, and Don planned to follow when more could be recruited.

Several days later Don arrived at Gordon's camp, but there were no more carriers. In fact, half of the carriers who had come that far were not willing to go on. It was one thing to travel the five days up the Kemandoga Valley, through Moni villages where food could be purchased for the party and the carriers could sleep in a men's hut each night, but it was quite another thing to think of starting out on the five-day hike over the high plateau to the Ilaga. On the plateau there were no gardens, no villages, no people.

Carriers were afraid to go on because of rumors of war in the Ilaga, which came from every direction. Often they appeared to be new versions of the same story. None of the rumors were specific, because the tribal people never tell such stories in a factual way. Even if a man has observed an incident, when he tells the story he will embellish it and tell it in veiled language so that no one really knows what he is saying. Pass the same story on through a number of people, and the facts may be completely lost. The implication of the rumors was that Moni and Ekari carriers would be in danger; even the lives of the *tuans* could be threatened.

Don and Gordon could not deny the fact that they had been raided two years earlier in the Ilaga. Most of their food and equipment had been stolen, and they had fled for their lives. There had been forewarnings then, too. The missionaries did not know at that time that the basis for the rumors was the Taganit War, the largest war in the memory of any tribal man, in which hundreds of people were killed in the Ilaga, Beoga, and Sinak valleys. The Taganit War was still continuing, and no one knew when and where the next battle would be fought.

Whatever evaluation Don and Gordon gave to the rumors, the fact remained that they could not go on without carriers. Gordon decided to continue upriver to the last village in the Kemandoga Valley. Ugimba was a Dani-Moni village established on the trade route to the Homeyo salt springs. Five hiking days out of Ilaga the Danis made Ugimba a stopover before hiking the next five days to Homeyo. Here Gordon found Ilaga Danis who also spoke Moni, an ideal situation for a Moni-speaking linguist newly appointed to Dani language reduction work.

Gordon set up his two-man puptent, blew up his air mattress, unrolled his sleeping bag, and was at home. He had no table, and his only chair was a carrying tin used for his supplies. By that time much of the food was gone, and he had to depend on the vegetables the people brought him—sweet potatoes, squash, greens, cucumbers, and more sweet potatoes. But the lack of the comforts of home was of little import to Gordon. He was determined to hold the ground gained thus far in reaching the Ilaga. In the meantime he buried himself **in his** language work.

Gordon kept the transceiver **ra**dio with him, but it did him little good. (Those were the days before the transistor radio.) The thirty-pound radio was temperamental, objected to being jostled over New Guinea trails, and required frequent tuning. The generator for recharging the battery was a hand-crank model called the Gibson Girl, salvaged from World War II surplus. Gordon was able to charge the battery enough so that he could hear the mission's broadcasts, but Homeyo never heard his attempts to transmit from Ugimba. When he found a man traveling downriver he sent a letter back to Homeyo, informing them that all was well with him, but that the radio would not transmit.

Don turned around and retraced his steps back to Homeyo. He used the long legs of his six-foot-two-inch frame to good advantage on the trail. He could cover the distance back to Homeyo in two days when he was in a hurry—the same distance that took most men three days of trekking. Although Don was faster on the trail than some, that fact offered him little comfort. Hiking any trail is hot, dirty, exhausting work. He was discouraged going back over the same trail on which he had come. One month earlier he had done exactly the same thing—retraced his steps four days to Enarotali because his radio had failed. Where was all his effort leading? Was it God's plan for him to reach the Damals with the gospel?

That evening after he arrived at a village where he would sleep, Don went off to a secluded spot to wrestle with God in prayer. He wrote in his diary:

> Friday, August 17, 1956. Partly through the disappointment of having to return to Homeyo and partly through other things, the Lord has broken me before Himself. I have not been as faithful in my prayer life as I should be. Today I vowed to spend an hour in prayer and Bible reading each morning before the work of the day. The Lord was very precious to me and assured me that this present expedition *will* reach the Ilaga.

Don had returned to Homeyo in order to gather carriers, but the news that greeted him was anything but encouraging. Because of the war rumors, none of the Monis around Homeyo wanted to carry. Only three Ekaris were willing to come from the Lakes—not enough to be of any help.

While Don waited, he spent his days working on the airstrip being built at Homeyo. The Homeyo station had been opened before World War II by Einar Michelson. Ken and Vida Troutman reopened the work after the war. In all that time the missionaries and all their supplies had had to travel over the Homeyo trail from the Lakes. Now the Alliance had a Cessna 180 plane, which opened the possibility of supplying Homeyo directly by flights.

Until the arrival of the Cessna, the only air link to the Lakes had been by pontoon plane. The site chosen for the new airstrip was at Obano—an hour and a half across the lake from Enarotali by motorboat. The Obano strip had added a new dimension to the missionaries' lifeline of supplies, at least most of the time.

On August 21 the Cessna was scheduled to make a drop of food supplies to Gordon at Ugimba. The plane was to fly the three hundred miles from Sentani (the airstrip that served the government capital and harbor) to Obano with mission supplies. Then at Obano it would load and take on a pusher to make a drop to Gordon. At the last minute the flight was canceled because the Obano strip was too muddy, and Gordon got no food. It seemed no progress was being made toward reaching the Ilaga. If we took two steps forward, we slipped back one.

12

Over the Top

Standard pay for a man carrying a thirty-five pound pack the thirteen hiking days from Enarotali to Ilaga was two steel ax heads and 240 blue, porcelain beads the size of peas. The steel axes were valuable because the demand for steel to replace stone was very great, both in the tribes to the east and in the distant parts of the Ekari tribe. A man's wages working around the mission station for a month was one ax. The blue beads had become a type of currency comparable to the cowrie shell. Most carriers purchased a pig in the east and brought it back home—another rewarding part of the trip. Wages were not the problem. No offer of pay was big enough to induce heathen men to brave the unknown rumors of war and danger in the Ilaga.

Don had waited ten days at Homeyo, and there was still no sign of getting carriers anywhere. Then the missionaries at Enarotali presented the need to the men studying in Bible school. Six of them accepted the challenge to take Don and Gordon to the Ilaga during their vacation from school.

In 1956 there was only a handful of Christians around Enarotali, consisting mostly of Bible school men, grade school children, and women. However, in Bomo village on Lake Tigi the majority of the people, including the village elders, had burned their fetishes five years earlier. It was from among those Christians that eight carriers finally came to augment the Bible school volunteers.

On September 4 Don was working on the Homeyo airstrip as usual when the plane flew over on its way upriver to make a drop to Gordon at Ugimba. But in a few minutes it was back over the Homeyo strip. Don saw the open door of the plane, and then someone shoved the load that was intended to go to Gordon out the door; the parachute opened and floated to the ground. Don learned later that the weather had been cloudy at Ugimba, and once again Gordon had not got his drop of supplies.

The next day the Ekari carriers from the Lake, arrived at Homeyo. Don spent the afternoon and far into the night repacking the loads. There was rice, corned beef, and mackerel; oatmeal, cheese, and cooking oil—all in cans; powdered milk, salt, and sugar; and a large tin of pancake mix that I had made. Trading items included ax heads, knives, blue beads, and cowrie shells needed for buying food for the party as they traveled.

Everything had to be packed into carrying tins—some larger and some smaller, but no load more than thirty-five pounds. Each carrier was given the load that would be his to carry for the trip. The little man who weighed only a hundred pounds got a smaller tin. A trustworthy man got the load with the trading items because those were most important of all to survival. Don had learned by experience not to give the load with his sleeping bag, water canteen, and cooking kit to a fast man who might be an hour's walk ahead of him when it was time to make camp for the night. The new six-volt storage battery made a load in itself. It was filled with battery acid and was fully charged. The carrier had to balance that battery on his shoulder without spilling any acid even once. To spill the acid would mean cutting the life line of radio contact.

Each carrier took a piece of rattan tying vine and, splitting it with his teeth, made it pliable like a rope. With that he began to tie his tin, forming a handle of vine which he would wear over his head to help support the weight of the load on his back. Excitement ran high that night as they finished the last details of packing. The Ilaga was now only ten days away—or so they thought.

On the morning of September 9 the party was nearing the village of Ugimba when who should come running to greet them but Andy, the young Ekari from Tigi. Andy cried and hugged his "father," as he affectionately called Don, and was elated to greet other Ekaris from his home at Lake Tigi. Don returned his greeting with warm affection.

Gordon, too, was delighted to see Don with the party of Ekari carriers. He had spent twenty-three days alone at Ugimba, been seriously ill, received neither of the attempted drops of food supplies, and for the most part had had no radio contact. During that lonely vigil God encouraged Gordon with the assurance that this expedition *would* reach the Ilaga. His radio was not working now, and he did not even know that Don had started out from Homeyo. The new battery carried from Enarotali solved the problem for the radio, and at 4:00 that afternoon they made contact with two excited wives—Peggy Larson and me.

The news at Ugimba was not encouraging. Rumors of danger and war in the Ilaga were everywhere. They had enough Ekari carriers to take them over the plateau, but without Dani guides they could not find their way. Obviously the Danis did not want to escort them. After three days of evasive talk the Danis said the party must not go until they received word from the Ilaga about the war.

One man started for the Ilaga with the promise to return in ten days with word. Two days later he was back with a load of jungle nuts. On his way he had met a party of Danis hunting the nuts, and that had proved more attractive to him than helping the *tuans* reach their destination. Now the Danis said, "In two more days someone will start for the Ilaga."

Don and Gordon had no choice but to play the Danis' game. It would be sheer folly to start out on the high plateau without a guide. They could easily get lost and die of exposure. Moreover, they needed Danis with them when they entered the Ilaga to assure the people that they were friends coming in peace and not a war party.

In one of the daily talk sessions with the Danis, Don got a new idea. "If you don't take us in three or four days," Don said, "we just won't go to the Ilaga. We will cross over to the Dugindoga Valley and build our homes there." That did the trick. The Danis agreed to leave in three days and escort the party to the Ilaga.

Jimbitu, an influential Dani man, said, "I will start for the Ilaga tomorrow. I'll announce your coming so there will be no trouble. But the weather has been bad for many days. Pray that the weather will be good for my trip."

Don, Gordon, and the Christian Ekaris accepted the challenge and prayed. The next day was a beautiful, clear day. It was Sunday, and after a church service the Danis announced they were ready to leave the very next day. Jimbitu and two others left Sunday noon as he had promised.

On Monday five Danis carried loads, and others went along as escorts. Three Dani women were also in the group. Their presence would indicate that the party was coming in peace and not for war.

If hiking through the Kemandoga Valley was difficult, hiking in this high, cold country was twice as hard. The trail out of Ugimba led up through forest until the trees became short and stunted. At 11,000 feet elevation the foliage changed to brush and grass with an occasional clump of stunted trees. The vivid green that is everywhere in lower regions had turned to shades of yellow, tan, and brown. Even on the equator, it frosts on a clear night at this elevation. When clouds were not hanging on the Puncak Jaya peaks, the beauty of their snow-capped tops was dazzling. It seemed to the men that they could almost reach out and touch the snow, but to actually hike there would have been another matter.

The trail now led through relatively flat, open country. The advantages that offered were lost to the problems of hiking in the thin cold air. At times they sloshed for an hour or two through a spongy marsh. Then they walked on rocky clay covered with short grass. Rain began to fall by noon, and for the carriers without the protection of Western clothing that meant being chilled to the bone. Without watches they could not tell that the darkening light was only from the low-hanging clouds and not from the approach of evening. The *tuans* urged them on, for they knew that if the party made camp too soon they would not reach the Ilaga in five days, and they did not have enough food for an extra day.

In the late afternoon the party came upon two A-frame huts left by an earlier group of travelers. Finding the roofs in ill-repair, the men stripped off slabs of bark from nearby trees and set about mending them. They chopped a good supply of firewood, too, in order to ward off the sharp chill of the night air. The men had to keep the fire blazing all night, and even then the side of the man's body away from the fire froze while the side next to the fire roasted.

After the second night out on the plateau Don was told that several of the Ekaris were sick and wanted to turn back. He thought that sounded suspicious and found that a Dani chief with the party had done a lot of talking about war during the night and the Ekaris were frightened. In fact, only the faithful insistence of an Ekari Bible school student had prevented their deserting during the night. After prayer and reasoning they all decided to go on. "Truly the Lord has helped us," Don wrote in his diary that day.

The third evening they set up camp in cold, drenching rain. After dark the rain stopped and the sky cleared, giving them a beautiful view in the moonlight of the snow-capped mountains. In the morning there was frost and ice all around. The plastic tarp the men used for their shelter was stiff with ice. Don worked carefully over the fire to thaw the ice enough to fold it for the carrier's load. That evening at 5:00 when he unfolded the tarp he found pieces of ice that had not thawed even though the sun had shone all day.

The next morning their Dani guides chose an alternate trail—one that led even higher, climbing to an elevation of 12,500 feet. The regular trail led into the Ilaga on the side of the valley where the Danis lived. The alternate trail led into the Damal side of the valley. The fear of the Danis to enter the Ilaga Valley with such a large party was genuine. They reasoned that the best entrance would be through the Damal villages where the people were less warlike.

At noon on the fifth day Don and Gordon got their first view of the Ilaga Valley. It was beautiful to them. The wide, bowl shape of the valley below them was quite different from the steep mountainsides of the Kemandoga. The Ilaga was checkered with the green of sweet potato gardens, the brown of newly dug potato beddings, and the dark green of trees. Smoke rose from several points where men were burning brush before digging a new garden. The Ilaga River flowed down through the valley and disappeared as it turned to the left at the far end of the bowl. Mountains covered with the dark green of the forest ringed the valley. To the left the mountains rose in jagged peaks that looked like the teeth of a giant saw. And in the background *Kela Bo*, the Forbidden Peak, with its cap of white rock, rose majestically to 14,000 feet.

It was September 22, 1956. Five more hours of stiff hiking lay before them, but they would reach the Ilaga Valley with its Dani and Damal people before the sun set.

13

Chief Den Welcomes the Missionary

Pen-Me continued to help his father break up the ground in their new garden plot on the edge of the forest. It was late afternoon and still the rain had not come, so the group of Damal villagers continued their work. Pen-Me heard a shout and looked up to see a string of men coming out of the forest—black men carrying shiny loads on their backs and in the group two white men. *Tuans* they must be, although he had never seen one before. Pen-Me's first thought was to run and hide. He carried only bird arrows—he could not defend himself like a man. But none of the travelers readied his bow to shoot, so Pen-Me continued to watch, frozen in wonder.

"*Amolo, amolo,*" the *tuans* called out. Pen-Me found his voice and returned the greeting. The taller of the *tuans* handed his canteen to Pen-Me and said, "Would you carry my water gourd for me?" Taken aback by the disarming request of the foreigner, he took it and followed along. Pen-Me was just one of the hundreds of Damals stepping into Don's life who would be known and loved as individuals through the coming years.

There was bedlam in the village when they all arrived. Everyone was greeting everyone else with a handshake of snapping fingers twice and then clasping hands. The Dani carriers passed the word on to the Damals that the *tuans* had come to build themselves houses and live in the Ilaga.

Don and Gordon were delighted with the reception and decided to set up camp for the night. With ten hours of trekking behind them they were dead tired. But the Dani guides had another plan. "We must go on," they said, "to a Dani village a half hour's walk further." They gave their usual vague reasons of "war is coming" and "danger." Perhaps the Danis only wanted to sleep in a Dani village themselves. Whatever the reason, the missionaries agreed to go on even though it meant setting up camp after dark, but first they must make radio contact with Enarotali. They were in the Ilaga. That was what really mattered.

The missionaries quickly unpacked the radio and sent an Ekari up a tree to secure the aerial. It was already five o'clock, and with darkness radio reception would become unreadable. The radio cracked. "This is C and M A Ilaga calling Enarotali. Do you read?"

"Roger, roger, we read you," came the reply.

"We have arrived in the Ilaga, and the people all seem friendly. Praise the Lord!"

Ken Troutman had news for them, too. Tomorrow the plane would be making a drop of supplies to them. With that good news the party moved on to spend the night in the Dani village.

Saturday dawned a beautiful day. The airdrop was to take place across the valley in an area below the location chosen for the airstrip. Don and Gordon packed up their equipment and escorted it across the Ilaga River and up to the drop site. They dared not let the carrying tins out of their sight for a moment lest they be stolen. On each end of the drop area they built a fire so the rising smoke would mark it for the pilot.

Then they heard it, the faint buzz of the single engine Cessna 180. Bill Paul, the new Alliance pilot, had never flown to the Ilaga before, but Ken Troutman was in the plane to guide Bill through the maze of mountains and rivers to their destination. The door had been removed before take-off, and one can imagine how cold the two men were after their forty-five-minute flight from Obano. The plane circled low over the drop site, not far above the treetops, for this was a free drop—without parachutes. Ken pushed the packs out the open door. All 170 pounds were out on the third round. Bill Paul dipped his wings in salute to Don and Gordon, and the Cessna headed for home.

Everything landed in good condition, which is not always the case. Canned goods were packed in rice and tied securely in burlap bags. The ax heads were also tied in bags. Nothing would be wasted from the drop. When the food was eaten the can would become the prized possession of a Damal woman in exchange for a bundle of greens. The axes would buy ground for the two mission stations, the airstrip, and wood to build temporary houses. The burlap bags became "vehicles" to transport mud and dirt in building the strip.

Two hundred fifty men gathered to watch the drop. They cocked their heads and clicked their thumbnails against their gourds to express their amazement. Neither they nor the six thousand other people of the valley could really comprehend what they saw. Some described it as "a bird expelling little things which became big, so big they had to be tied to a pole for two men to carry." No one understood that there were men in the plane. The Danis and Damals had nothing in their background with which the phenomenon could be compared. Thus they concluded it was a supernatural happening in some way connected with those two white beings who had entered their valley.

After the excitement of the drop was over the men rented a Dani hut and stored their equipment. They left Andy to cook dinner and watch everything while they hiked up to the site selected for the airstrip. The entire area was relatively flat and free from trees. The white, sandy soil looked like it would be good and hard for a strip. Ditches must be made and clearing and leveling must be done, but it would not take too long to complete. Don paced the length and found it was fifteen hundred feet long.

One question remained in their minds. This was the traditional battleground for wars in the Ilaga. Would the men, both Danis and Damals and also the women, be willing to come here and work on the strip? The Ekari carriers were even afraid to come to this side of the valley. The two missionaries might have been even more concerned had they known the extent of the Taganit War, which still had no settlement in sight.

In the afternoon Don went back across the river to the Dani village where the carriers were camped. He spent the evening in a men's hut. One of the Dani's wives was a Damal. When she found out that Don wanted to learn to speak Damal, she decided to teach him in one easy lesson. Although she did not succeed that night, it was a start. Being a very talkative person, when Don found himself in a situation where he could not speak to anyone in English, or even in Ekari, Indonesian, or his faltering Moni, he passed the time by learning words and phrases. He did not do so in the scientific fashion his linguist friend Gordon used, but learned simply by repeating, guessing at a meaning, and trying to use what he had heard.

Don had a keen memory, which had been developed in the seventh and eighth grades where he was assigned every week to memorize large blocks of poetry. Don also had a natural ability to fill in the rest of the thoughts in a sentence even when he only understood part of the words. He might guess wrong, but he always guessed. If he was wrong, the Damals corrected him, and he kept right on learning.

That night was Don's first night to sleep in an Ilaga hut. He was familiar with the men's houses in Moni and Ekari country where the house was rectangular in shape and the men slept on the drafty floor by the fire. In the Ilaga it was much colder at night because they were almost 8000 feet above sea level. Because of the cold the people had learned to build round houses without any cracks. On the ground level the house had the usual fire in the center of the hut. For sleeping at night it had a second story with a reed floor just under the grass-thatched roof.

When the men were tired of talking and ready to sleep, they put out the fire downstairs and built a very small fire in the center of the upstairs sleeping floor. They all slept like spokes in a wheel with their heads under the eaves and their feet next to the fire. Don found it to be quite an acceptable arrangement. The house stayed warm all night with only a small fire, which meant less smoke. Most of the smoke rose into the center of the cone and found its way up through the grass thatching.

Sunday morning Don had a church service for the Ekari carriers in the corner of the village yard. During the service he observed that the Danis were doing something special too, and of course it had nothing to do with its being Sunday. Numerous pigs, of various sizes but all with deafening squeals, were brought into the village yard. Crowds of people came all painted and feathered for this special occasion. Don learned that it was a settlement payment for a man killed in a past war.

At one point an elaborate dance was the center of attention, including four men dressed in special gourds that extended to their chins. Their hair, which is usually tied up in a net, was let down, and long ringlets of black, greasy hair bobbed on their shoulders. Ten dancing women were painted in red and black pig grease with colorful nets draped over their heads and hanging down their backs almost to the ground. Don did not understand anything that was going on. He simply watched, and the Danis in the excitement of the occasion paid no attention to him.

Later in the day, a boy of perhaps fifteen years approached Don and greeted him in the Indonesian language. What a surprise it was to find an Indonesian speaker in the midst of the babel of Dani and Damal. Sam, as he was later named, had been taken by Roman Catholics to a school near Enarotali. He had a keen mind, and during his two years at the school he learned to speak conversational Indonesian. When he returned to the Ilaga for what was intended to be a visit, he determined he would never go back to school at the Lakes.

Sam brought a message from his father, Den, a very

important chief among the Damals. Would Don please come to visit him at his village of Kunga? Don could hardly believe his ears. Of course he would go right away and meet Den. Had Don been able to communicate with the Damals, he would have inquired as to who was their chief and sought the man out in order to pay him respect. Now Den had invited Don to come, and his own son could translate for them through the Indonesian language.

Don found Den, who was perhaps fifty-five years of age, to be a man with quiet dignity—quite different from most chiefs, who were loud and boisterous. He had a large frame with shoulders as broad as many *tuans* have, although he was not as tall. Den spoke in a deep resonant voice while Sam translated for his father. "Greetings and welcome to my village," he began. "I am glad that you have come. Let us be friends. You should come and live here with us. I have chosen a site that I will give you to build your house on. Let us make a reciprocal friendship agreement."

Don replied with a heart full of joy. "I would like to become your special friend. I am happy to accept your invitation to build my house here. Let's go and see the place you have picked out."

They walked just a few hundred feet from the village to a site on a hill overlooking the entire valley. *Kela-Bo*, the mountain with a hundred moods, stood majestically in the background. The airstrip site lay across the valley at the same elevation, separated by an hour's hike down to the river and up again. Kunga was the closest Damal village to the airstrip. Den had chosen that site for the Damal mission station because he saw a good political move in establishing a friendship for trading with the *tuan*. At that time he did not know that it all was really God's choice and not his own.

Den was a man of genuine political stature among the Damals, but he was not a war chief. He was tired of all the fighting the Danis brought to the Ilaga; there seemed to be no end to the Taganit War.

In his lifetime the Danis had spread from a small corner

of the valley until now they occupied most of the Ilaga. The Damals were ever being pushed up the rim of the valley and forced to make new gardens in the forest. Den was fed up with their aggression. He had made plans to move south of the Puncak Jaya mountain range to Damal country where there were no Danis. Already gardens were planted south to prepare for his move—an exodus that was never to take place.

Don and Gordon moved up to the airstrip site on Monday morning. First they needed someplace to sleep. There were no villages closer than a half hour's walk, so this time sleeping in a men's hut was not an option. They were able to buy some used hand split boards from a deserted native hut. Using the boards for siding and Don's plastic tarp for a roof, their helpers tied it all together with rattan vine. All their supplies were stored in the hut, where Don slept. Gordon continued to sleep in his little pup tent.

The men staked out the airstrip to mark its exact boundaries. Don surveyed the grade on the strip, using a hundred-foot tape measure and a carpenter's level. It proved to have a 6 percent slope that could be made into a strip one hundred feet wide and fifteen hundred feet long. Gordon checked by radio with the pilot, Ed Ulrich, and he agreed that the site was satisfactory. By the second day they had a group of 50 men working on the strip. Word got around that the tuans were paying the fabulous price of a cowrie shell to everyone who worked a day for them. The next day 150 showed up to work, and then 400 came, making real progress on clearing the ground. Stripping the grass off revealed that the mud was much deeper than they had anticipated. But, given time and manpower, the mud could be cleaned off and a fill made with hard sand.

With crowds like that Don realized the cowrie shells would soon be gone. He asked for a drop of shells and beads, knowing the plane was coming across to the Lakes. He learned that the plane was to make its first landing at Homeyo on Monday. The plane would make a drop in the

A typical Damal hut, with people seated outside

Don Gibbons baptizing a young believer with the help of a Damal witness man

Net bags worn on the back are used by Damals to carry everything from babies to food. Here, a young Damal girl returns from her garden

Chief Den in his garden. The large leaves are of the mo plant, a specialty food.

A Damal man dressed in his woven war jacket and war paint

Two Damal men discuss a business transaction. Shells and pigs are part of the exchange currency in the Damal culture.

Sweet potatoes are scrubbed with bundles of grass before being taken to the hut to be steam-baked and eaten.

A Damal witness family returns to the Beoga Valley in the Mission Aviation Fellowship airplane

Kathy, seven, after flying home from school in Sentani for the first time in 1960. This group of Damal girls and Lori greeted her, and one of the girls gave her own beads to Kathy.

The Gibbons family, January 1981 — Don and Alice Gibbons, (1-r) Lori and Helen in college, Darlene in sixth grade. Not pictured are Kathy and Joyce, who are both married with their own families.

Ilaga on Wednesday on the way back to Sentani.

On Monday at Homeyo excitement was running high. The Monis had worked on the airstrip for many months and now the promised airplane was going to land. For the missionaries it meant they could forget the Homeyo trail with all of its aches, blisters, and exhaustion. Ken Troutman had hiked to Homeyo to check the strip for the first landing. He found it smooth and hard, ready for the plane.

Ed Ulrich took off from Obano with one passenger on board, a government man who would inspect the airstrip and give permission for regular landings. In fifteen minutes the plane was over Homeyo. Below them was the airstrip, a tiny shelf on the side of a huge mountain. The plane touched down and taxied up the strip. As the pilot braked hard, the wheels broke through the top crust and dug into the soft earth below. The plane flipped completely over and came to rest upside down.

Ed and the inspector unfastened their seat belts and crawled out of the plane. The Monis watching the event did not know that anything was wrong. They assumed that that was the way planes always land!

No one was hurt, but the propeller and both wings on the plane were damaged. It looked as though the plane would never fly again. *Parts could be salvaged,* the pilot thought, *but it can not be repaired at this remote spot,* so a new plane was ordered with the insurance money. The Homeyo trail was *not yet* abandoned by the missionaries—Ed Ulrich got his introduction to New Guinea trails when he hiked out to Enarotali.

In the Ilaga, Monday was the best day yet for work on the strip. Six hundred people turned out. Before the missionaries finished paying that crew, their cowrie shells were gone, and Don had to give out slips of paper which were to be redeemed with a shell when their drop came. The next morning they learned of the accident at Homeyo. There would be no drop for some time. Less than a hundred workers came each day now that there were no shells to pay them.

Those who did come began the mountainous job of removing a one- to three-foot layer of mud that covered much of the strip. Everything had to be done by hand. The men used garden-digging sticks to break up the ground. Then others balanced the chunks of dirt on their shoulders and carried them off to the side. A few used burlap bags for carriers. Two poles were fitted down the sides of each sack, making a stretcher. With a pile of dirt in the center two men carried it off and dumped it. The work was slow. They needed picks and shovels and more burlap bags, but there were none.

Life in the Ilaga may have been discouraging at times, but it was never routine. One day a man threatened to burn the missionaries' hut down because he had not received the ax owed to him. Another time a Dani man went berserk, threatening the crowd with his spear. Men chased him back and forth, finally knocking him to the ground and disarming him. The Damals were frightened and wanted to leave, but they finally agreed to finish the day. Another afternoon the Danis tried to steal several burlap bags and two machetes. It was only after Don and Gordon made a big fuss that the missing items were returned.

Sunday was a day of rest from strip work. Since no one lived near the strip, Don and Gordon took turns visiting the people in their villages. They could not both leave the camp at the same time lest everything be stolen. When Gordon went down to a Dani village a crowd would soon gather to watch this strange, white foreigner. Using a bilingual Dani to translate from Moni, Gordon would tell them a story of Jesus. On one occasion when both Damals and Danis were present, he told them of the future resurrection of the dead. The Danis laughed at that story, whereas the Damals listened eagerly. Each tribe was comparing what they heard with the traditions passed down by their fathers. To the

Danis this story of Christ was ridiculous; to the Damals it was amazing yet credible.

When Don left the camp he went to visit Den and the Damals at Kunga. Since he would spend the night there, he took two things with him, a canteen with boiled drinking water and a native rain cape. The pandanas leaf cape the Damals used so much was a very practical item. He wore it as protection from the drizzling rain as he hiked across the valley by day, and at night it became his sleeping mat.

Den received his visitor with a warm welcome. When he learned that Don was planning to spend the night with them, he sent a young man to the garden to dig some mo tubers to serve to his guest. Mo is a specialty food. If the sweet potato is bread to a Damal, then mo is cake. Don enjoyed that treat, for it tasted more like bread than anything else the Damals eat.

The roundhouse was full of men. Besides the usual residents, others had come in from a nearby village. Don was able to eat with them in a completely natural situation and share at least the beginnings of why he had come to make his home with the Damals. These were the people that Don wanted to reach first—the chief and other men who led their community.

Around Lake Paniai Don had observed that most of the converts were young people, grade school children and women. The men, who were the village leaders, were noticeably absent in the groups that gathered for church on Sundays. If teaching the young people occupied most of the missionaries' time, then how would the men be reached? In a tribal society, the mature men never followed the women or young people in any matter important to the community. If the adult men were first won to Christ, would not the women and children follow naturally? He found the following directive in the policy statement of the Christian and Missionary Alliance: "As a mission our primary calling is to win adults to Christ by a direct approach through the Spirit-filled ministry of the Word of God." That became Don's goal as he worked with the Damals.

While Don was seeking ways to win the friendship of the Damals, they were also sizing him up. Was he a ki me, a real person, as they classified all interior tribal people? Or was he a supernatural being who possessed a magic eternal life? The older men tended toward the second conclusion. They explained the white man in their creation story. He came out of the ground in the Baliem at the same time ki me appeared. The tuans then traveled far to the west and disappeared underground. Now they were coming back.

Don heard there was to be a mo feast at Kunga. Very few were coming to help work on the strip, so he decided to attend the feast. He found a large crowd of people already gathered when he arrived. During the morning men ran here and there shouting orders to groups bringing rocks and firewood, while others sang and danced. Through that organized confusion piles of rocks were heated, the mo tubors were scraped, and then the mo was placed in pits lined with hot rocks and covered over to bake.

About noon two groups of warriors fought a mock battle outside the village and then, uniting into one group, entered the village shouting and circle-dancing in the center of the yard. Everyone sat down on the ground. Suddenly all was quiet. Two men ran alternately into the center of the village carrying a bundle of uncooked mo in each hand. As each of them laid a bundle down he called out the name of an important man—leaders from all over the Ilaga Valley. Then the man who had been called ran out to pick up his gift and returned to his seat. The last two names to be called at the end of this hour-long ceremony were "Kibi" and "Lato." Don recognized that Dani-Damal version of "Gibbons" and "Larson" and ran out to the center to pick up the two bundles of mo.

Once again the scene erupted into pandemonium. The pits were opened and an aroma filled the air—as good as the smell of fresh-baked bread. Teams of young men ran carrying steaming mo to the women, who were seated in groups.

There was not enough to serve everyone, but the men who had grown the mo and sponsored the feast knew that. They were following the traditional courtesy of serving the cooked mo to the women. The men could have what was left along with sweet potatoes that had also been steaming in the pits.

As the crowd was breaking up to go home, Don chanced to meet an important man—Kip, the second Damal chief of the Ilaga. Don noted in his diary, "Kip is an influential man from the Damal area two hours' walk from Kunga. He seems quite friendly, and I want to establish a real personal friendship with him."

14

"My Times Are in Thy Hand"

Life at Enarotali had settled into a routine that, without Don, had become very lonely for me. Sunday seemed to be an especially long day—a day of rest from the activities with which I tried to fill my time of waiting. Sunday mornings the Ekaris around the mission station took a bath, and all who owned western clothes donned them to attend the service at the church. I too attended church with my two little girls, squeezing into the building and perching on a pole along with all the Ekaris. On Sunday evenings we missionaries had an English church service, and the two men left on the station took turns speaking.

For Kathy, Sunday was the best day of the week. She had passed her fourth birthday not long after her daddy went away, and she was growing up. Sunday meant school to Kathy—Sunday school. The older Troutman and Larson children had school each weekday, studying correspondence courses with their mothers as teachers. But for Kathy school was only on Sunday. After I braided her long blond hair into French braids, she put on her Sunday dress and shoes and was off to Sunday school.

The five children and I as their teacher gathered in the Troutman's living room one October morning. We sang choruses with the children doing the actions as I played the little pump organ. I used a Sunday school quarterly written for primary age children—a choice that was a compromise between the span of their ages. Our lesson was on the Philippian jailer. In the application I asked the question, "Are you a Christian?" and gave each child a piece of paper

166

with different answers that people give to that question—answers like, "yes," "no," and "I hope so." I gave Kathy the "no" answer, thinking it would be easy to remember. After she gave her answer she began to cry, sobbing through the rest of the lesson. Later she told me through her tears, "I don't want a no answer; I want a yes answer, because I love Jesus." That was Kathy's testimony of trusting Jesus as her Savior. In all the years that have followed she has never turned aside from loving Him.

Joyce was also special to me during those long months of waiting. She was my brown-eyed brunette. At eighteen months she was full of mischief and into everything. We lived in the large log house, which we shared with three single ladies who were Aunt Vonnie, Aunt Marion, and Aunt Elze to my girls. There were two rooms downstairs for our kitchen and living room, and one of the four bedrooms upstairs was ours. The big house, as we called it, was rather like Grand Central Station for all the missionaries because one of the rooms also served as mission office, and there were any number of Ekaris who went in and out with their duties. The outside door was left open more often than not, and Joyce never missed a chance to escape.

Outside there was mud everywhere—mud puddles in the yard and deep, slimy mud in the drain ditches around the buildings. An adult could avoid most of the mud, but not Joyce. Mud magnetized her. Besides that hazard there were high banks all around created when the hillside was terraced for the buildings.

To meet the problem I hired a teenage Ekari girl to watch Joyce when I was busy in school. Maria followed Joyce around outside or sat on the bamboo floor inside and talked and played with her. Sometimes she carried her around on her shoulders.

Joyce loved Maria and the Ekari boys who worked in the kitchen. She understood everything they said to her in Ekari and was completely at home with them, squatting on the floor and sharing their sweet potatoes. They taught her to jump in rhythm to their chanting, which she especially enjoyed.

Joyce had been born in our log cabin home at Enarotali— the first white baby to be born in the mountains of what was then Dutch New Guinea. Her life began in a bilingual setting of English and Ekari. It must have confused her, for the only word she said at eighteen months was *mama. Mama* means "mother" in Ekari just as it does in English.

The Bible school students who had carried loads to the Ilaga returned, and it was time to start school again. I had been teaching in the school, but I thought it would not be good to leave my classes in the middle of the three-month term, so I told Mr. Post, the head of the school, that I had decided not to teach. In his fatherly way he said, "Now, Alice, what if there are more delays than you expect and then you aren't teaching?" So I taught my classes again: the gospel of John, reading, and Scripture memorization, and sewing for the wives. I also continued teaching a group of village people to read Ekari, and I served as storekeeper. All the basic food supplies arrived at Enarotali in case lots, and I filled the orders of the missionaries and national workers and made out the bills. It was good to have something to do to help fill the weeks and months of waiting.

Every fourth day it was my turn to talk to Don on the radio for ten minutes. Usually the time was filled with a list of supplies they needed and then word about work on the airstrip. After the plane accident at Homeyo their food went down until all they had was rice, salt, and two small cans of cheese. Don did tell me that the Ilaga was a garden paradise compared to Enarotali, and he enjoyed wild raspberries, corn, beans, and peas. He said his speciality dish was creamed mushrooms on fried *mo.* Although Don did not speak of his personal feelings over the radio, I could tell that when their food supplies were gone and they had no cowrie shells to attract people to work on the strip, he was discouraged and lonely.

Then their little hand crank generator broke. After that they used their radio as little as possible, stretching the minutes of charge left in the battery. On the last transmission Don was speaking to Ken Troutman. Ken heard that someone was sick with a fever, but the battery went dead before he understood whether it was Don or Gordon who was sick.

Mission Aviation Fellowship (MAF) pilot Dave Steiger agreed to make a drop to the men in the Ilaga from the Piper Pacer, the only local mission plane flying at that time. Supplies of food, axes, and cowrie shells were packed for a free drop. Their weight was limited to 280 pounds, for that was all the Piper Pacer could haul with a second man on board to push out the load.

Dave Steiger took off for the Ilaga 250 miles to the southeast, although he had never been there before. In the maze of cloud-capped mountains and winding rivers he tried one valley and then another but found nothing. Finally his fuel was running low, and he turned back. The clouds had built up on one of the mountain passes which lay between the Pacer and Sentani. He circled again and again trying to gain altitude, but still the "mighty" Piper Pacer could not top the clouds. "One more round," Dave said, "and if we don't make it this time we'll have to dump our load to the natives who live down there." That time the plane rolled over the ridge, and they got back to Sentani.

The next day, armed with more information about the location of the Ilaga and a full tank of gas, the drop was made successfully. Dave saw both Don and Gordon on the ground, so we still wondered who had been ill.

Some might call Don and Gordon brave men because they had pressed so far into the interior of New Guinea with only a tiny thread of lifeline connecting them to the world from which they came. But they were not the only heroes in taking the good news. The pilots who flew those little planes were also very brave.

Dr. Louis L. King, who was then our Foreign Secretary from New York headquarters, planned to visit the field. Excitement ran high among the missionaries at Enarotali. We hoped he would visit us at the Lakes. In the end Dr. King's arrival in Sentani was delayed, which gave him only one day in Sentani, one in the Baliem Valley, and the third day he was to take part in a drop to the Ilaga on his way to Enarotali. On Wednesday morning as planned, the Piper Pacer took off with the door removed and Dr. King on board as passenger and pusher. Even though the weather was poor, Dave Steiger found the Ilaga. Dr. King pushed the bicycle battery charger out the open door. On the second time around he waved to Don and Gordon as he pushed out a bundle of clothes and letters.

The weather grew worse as they flew west, making it impossible to go on to the Lakes—the only airstrip on the western end of the island. Dave diverted the little Piper Pacer north toward the ocean to the island of Biak, which was over two hundred miles from the Ilaga. Dr. King missed his stop at the Lakes but made his connection with the international flight out of the country.

By four o'clock that afternoon Gordon had charged the battery and was on the radio. The news he gave was that Don was still sick. His fever had gone down, but he continued to have nausea and vomiting and was exhausted. But word about the strip was encouraging. Since the drop with cowrie shells, people by the hundreds were back again to work.

I paid a call on the government doctor at Enarotali to ask him for advice concerning Don's illness. After hearing the symptoms he said, "It is either infectious hepatitis, a viral infection of the liver, or fatigue. If his skin turns yellow in a few days we will know for sure." Four days later Don's skin did turn a sickly yellow. The doctor's response was, "There is no known medication for hepatitis. He should have complete bed rest for three weeks, and his diet must include lots of sugar with no fats. It is important to get the proper rest and diet because permanent liver damage can result from infectious hepatitis."

As I left the doctor's house I longed all the more to be in the Ilaga where I could care for my husband. I knew that several missionaries in the Lakes area had recovered from hepatitis with bed rest and proper diet. Ed Maxey, a fellow missionary, had just been flown from the Baliem to the coast where he could get proper care for the same disease. I could do nothing but commit Don into the Lord's hands.

I told Don what the doctor had said about bed rest, a proper diet, and the possibility of serious complications. I knew he would try to follow the doctor's orders, but how could he when his bed consisted of a sleeping bag spread on a pile of grass? He had no pillow and nothing to read. Flies were such pests, and when the wind blew with rain there was hardly a dry spot in the hut. For food he had local vegetables supplemented with canned meat and fruit, oatmeal, and powdered milk.

During the time that Don was sick, word reached the Ilaga that the strip would have to be eighteen hundred feet long— three hundred feet more than what they had been told before. After the accident at Homeyo, requirements were being tightened. The Ilaga strip was 7,600 feet above sea level, and at that elevation the plane needed a longer strip for safe operation. Gordon surveyed the lower end of the strip site and found that if they made some cuts of six feet and similar fills they could squeeze out three hundred more feet for the strip.

On October 22 the new Alliance plane—a Cessna 180— arrived in Sentani. That was really good news. We again had a plane to serve us. Four days later it made a drop of supplies to the men in the Ilaga. I could not send anything special to Don since the plane had come from Sentani, but I was able to arrange for a pillow and some magazines and books to be dropped to him.

By the end of the week Don had more good news for me.

He said work was really going well on the strip and that he hoped it would be ready for the first landing in twelve days. I knew better than to start counting the days, but still the end was in sight. We would be settled in the Ilaga before Christmas. He also told me that the Damals were collecting building materials for our first temporary house. They had the poles for the framework all cut and enough slabs of bark for the siding and roof.

The very day after our radio contact with the Ilaga, Ed Ulrich came on the radio, saying he had had further word about the strip. Civil aviation had informed him that a government inspector must walk to the Ilaga and inspect the strip from the ground before the first landing could be made, and that would not be until December or January. I knew from Don's response that the world had just fallen out from under him. He was still sick with hepatitis, and the news was hard to take. A dozen questions flooded our minds. Would an inspector, not called of God, be willing to walk that long trail? Could they find carriers? Maybe the strip would never be opened.

After they finished talking I called Ilaga again to share with Don the verse that the Lord had flashed into my mind: "My times are in thy hand (Psalm 31:15)." Although we could see no end in sight, we could trust the Lord and keep on walking in faith. That was a memory verse from one of the vacation Bible school lessons I taught during the summer I met Don. Perhaps those junior boys and girls had forgotten that lesson, but I had not. We turned the radio off; Don went back to his hut to read and pray, and I went back to our two little girls.

Monday was our birthday. Both Don and I were born on October 29. We talked on the radio, but there was not much to be said. Don had a birthday card from me, which he opened that morning, but there was no way for any mail to be sent out from the Ilaga. I told him that I had a surprise for him for his birthday. It would be dropped to him when the new Cessna flew there from Obano on Saturday.

Saturday became the focus of activities for everyone at Enarotali. The new Cessna was coming to bring Mr. Robert Chrisman, our Area Secretary from mission headquarters in New York. For two weeks now the plane had been flying into the Baliem Valley, and Mr. Chrisman had visited all the missionaries there. Plans were made to have the dedication of the new plane at Obano when Mr. Chrisman arrived.

Everyone wanted to go, so we decided to make the day into a special outing. We planned a picnic lunch and swimming at the Sandy Beach on our way back from Obano. The five missionary children could hardly wait. The Sandy Beach was the only spot around the lake with any sand for swimming or wading, and we had not been there for a long time.

I was busy fixing things to drop to Don. I made a birthday cake using dates and walnuts from home that I had hoarded for the occasion. The cake, along with some fudge, I packed tightly in a tin, sure that it would arrive in good condition. I made a large batch of pancake mix and also packed two birthday books and all our recent mail. Besides other food for the drop there were the even more important ax heads, beads, cowrie shells, trench shovels, and other tools for working on the strip.

Saturday morning the usual sunshine was missing. Low clouds and fog hung all around the lake. Vida Troutman decided to stay home with her baby and the Larson baby, but the rest of us were eager to go anyway. Nine missionaries and six children, counting Joyce, set off on the two-hour boat ride across the lake. At Obano the boat went a little way up the river, and then we all climbed out on the muddy bank. I had expected to get some Obano boys to carry Kathy and Joyce the mile walk to the airstrip, but no one was around. The sweet potato gardens were deserted. One of the boys who came with us in the boat carried Joyce, but Kathy had to slosh through the mud by herself, trying to keep up with the adults.

In recent months Obano had become quite a center of

mission activity. When the mission decided to use a small wheel plane instead of an amphibian plane landing on the lake, Obano was chosen. Here the ground was a little higher than most ground around the lake, and the valley was wide, giving room for the plane to maneuver.

Mr. and Mrs. Lesnusa, Indonesian school teachers with the mission, had lived in Obano for some time. They conducted a school for Ekari children in grades one to three. Mr. Lesnusa had also built up an Ekari congregation and served as their pastor. Just six weeks earlier, Elze Stringer, a missionary from Holland, had moved to Obano. She was teaching fourth, fifth, and sixth grade subjects to sixty boarding students who had graduated from the six primary mission schools in the Ekari tribe.

Already there were seven mission buildings at Obano, including a three-room school. Two carpenters had been hired, and they were building dormitories for the boarding students. A house for Elze Stringer was the next building to go up. She was living temporarily in one of the classrooms. I was impressed that day with all of the buildings. It looked like Obano would soon become a second Enarotali.

When we arrived at the airstrip there was no Cessna in sight. We wondered if it had turned back due to the clouds. Nothing was ever sure in New Guinea until it had happened. Then we heard it—the faint drone of a single engine. The sound grew louder and louder until the beautiful new Cessna touched down on the strip. Ed Ulrich was the pilot, and Mr. Chrisman was with him! They had made it through even though the weather was touch-and-go all the way. Mr. Chrisman brought greetings to all of us, and we felt as if we really had not been forgotten after all.

Ed told Ken that the weather was too bad today for a drop in the Ilaga. He would make the drop on Monday, so the men stowed the things for the drop inside the plane. Don's birthday cake would have to wait two more days. I felt sorry for Don, lonely and sick, so far away.

Ken Troutman announced that the dedication service

would begin at once. I looked around at the group gathered and was surprised to note the absence of many Obano village people. Ekaris usually gathered in large numbers to see an airplane. The schoolchildren were there, the Lesnusas and another Indonesian teacher couple from Okeitadi, the Teteleptas, the two carpenters, and of course the missionaries. Two policemen stood at attention with their guns at their sides. They had come to watch the plane over the weekend lest any inquisitive hands damage it in their investigation of this strange new bird.

Just as the service began it started to rain. We crowded under the shelter of the wings of the plane and listened. Mr. Chrisman spoke of the Christians in America who had given sacrificially to buy this Cessna. The plane was given to the glory of God for only one purpose—to bring the message of salvation to the many tribespeople locked away in the mountains of New Guinea.

Ken Troutman had been observing the black rain clouds closing in—most unusual before noon—and he announced that there would be no picnic today at the Sandy Beach. We would eat an early lunch in Elze Stringer's house and start back across the lake.

Our group was larger by three as we returned. We were joined by Mr. Chrisman, Ed Ulrich, and Elze Stringer, who took the opportunity to spend the weekend with the other single ladies at Enarotali. We squeezed into the boat and shared the ponchos that kept off some of the rain. Joyce slept in my arms. As we passed the Sandy Beach five pairs of sad eyes peered at it in silence from beneath their rain gear. They too were learning to accept disappointment like their elders.

15

Tragedy At Obano

Saturday's events were good to break the routine of life for me, but Sunday was normal again. We had Sunday school for the children and then attended the Ekari church service. After a lonely dinner with my two girls we all lay down for a nap.

All of a sudden I realized that something was going on below my bedroom window. I heard the panting voice of an Ekari man talking to Ken Troutman. It was the pastor from a church an hour's walk away. He had run the distance in a fraction of that time. "We saw billows of smoke at Obano and then mirror flashes. There are mirror flashes coming from Okeitadi too." Ken knew that someone was calling for help with the mirror signals. The line of sight between Enarotali and Obano is broken by a little island near Obano called Goat Island. The Ekari pastor knew that and had come running to Enarotali with news of the signals.

Ken Troutman called the other three missionary men, and they headed for the lake. On the way down the hill they stopped at the police station, told them about the mirror signals and the smoke at Obano, and asked to borrow the 25 horsepower police motor. With that motor and a light load they sped across the lake. Just at Goat Island they met an Ekari boatload of people fleeing from Obano. Coming alongside of the boat, they saw the people were all smeared with mud, the mud of mourning. "Everyone is dead at Obano— the schoolteachers, the carpenters, the police—everybody was killed. The mission buildings are burned and the plane is chopped to pieces."

It was obvious to Ken that the friendly Ekaris were fleeing for their lives; he dared not go any closer. Ken turned his boat toward Goat Island, where they landed and climbed up the hill to get a better view of Obano. They saw through binoculars that all the Ekaris had said was true. With heavy hearts the men returned home. What could all of that mean?

The quiet routine of a Sunday at Enarotali was shattered. Everyone moved into the big house—a group of thirteen missionaries and eight children. Those who did not already live there came bringing mattresses and bedding and bread and vegetables to augment the food of the hastily set up community kitchen. The police had ordered us all into the one house with the words, "We may move you all down to a government building. The head government officer has gone to Obano. When he returns we will assess the situation and let you know."

After dark a group of schoolboys who were Elze Stringer's students arrived from Obano. They were quite shaken up, but this is the story that we pieced together from their account and that of other eyewitnesses, who arrived later:

A group of mature Ekari men had banded together to rid their land of all foreigners, their laws and police actions, schools, and religious teachings. The Ekari young people were being drawn away from their tribal traditions to become preachers, policemen, and schoolteachers. It appeared that Obano would soon become another Enarotali. The final straw came in the epidemic among their pigs. The pig was the Ekari's most important possession—the center of all economy with an intrinsic value far greater than the meat it provided. It seemed obvious to the Ekari that the cause of the pig sickness was supernatural—the result of foreign influences intruding on their Ekari traditions.

Plans were made to make the initial attack at Obano on Sunday morning after church when all the foreigners and Christians would be gathered in one place. Saturday morning when the mission plane and the missionaries appeared suddenly, word was passed to the warriors, "Come quickly! The foreigners have all come and we will kill them today." In God's providence it did not happen that way, for He sent the rain—unusual morning rain. That rain slowed down the Ekari warriors and sent the missionaries scurrying for home.

Sunday morning was a beautiful day at Obano. The schoolchildren and other village people took their baths as usual and gathered at the church about ten o'clock. The two policemen joined the other worshipers, leaving their guns behind, for no one took a weapon inside the church—whether it was a bow and arrow or a gun. Mr. Lesnusa preached in Ekari that morning as he always did. Although the Lesnusas taught school as a means of support, their first calling was to missionary work among the Ekaris.

As the congregation filed out of the church the warriors who were gathered outside began to chant and dance. The Lesnusas knew this was the war dance, and the drawn bows could mean only one thing. They ran to their house with the two Indonesian children who boarded with them and locked the door. Outside the dancing and chanting increased in fury until they were ready to kill. The warriors then broke the windows and filled Mr. Lesnusa's body with arrows. Mrs. Lesnusa and the two Indonesian children were next. There was no mercy for any foreigner. The Biak policeman was killed, but they allowed the Ekari policeman to flee into the jungle. Still chanting and dancing, they looted Elze Stringer's house, taking whatever was of interest to them, and then set fire to all the mission buildings. The plane was next. Their axes quickly chopped through the thin aluminum covering, and to their delight they found all the cowrie shells, beads, axes, and other tools ready to be dropped in the Ilaga.

Before the Lesnusa house was burned, the war leaders chopped fingers from Mr. Lesnusa's body and sent them with runners in every direction. Any group who received a finger pledged to fight. Some groups refused the finger, saying they would protect the foreigners, others were passive, and a few areas joined the Obano men and were ready to fight. One of those areas was Timida, only an hour's walk behind Enarotali.

The schoolboys told us they had tried to protect the Lesnusas, but there was nothing they could do. The warriors threatened to kill them if they resisted, so they ran to the lakeshore and hid until they found a boat for escape.

The hours wore on, and still there was no word from the government officer. We three mothers decided to put our children to bed. As he was getting ready for bed, eight-year-old Kenny Troutman asked his mother some questions that none of the adults had dared to put into words. Robby Paksoal had been Kenny's friend and playmate until two months earlier when he had moved to Obano to attend the new school. "Mama, why did they kill Robby? Will they try to kill us, too?"

"I can't answer all of your questions, Kenny," Vida Troutman told her son. "Only God knows why He took Robby home to be with Him. But I do know that God protected us all when we were at Obano yesterday, and we can continue to trust Him."

Then Vida read the first five verses of Psalm 91:

> He that dwelleth in the secret place of the most High shall abide under the shadow of the Almighty. I will say of the Lord, He is my refuge and my fortress: my God; in him will I trust. Surely he shall deliver thee from the snare of the fowler, and from the noisome pestilence. He shall cover thee with his feathers, and under his wings shalt thou trust: his truth shall be thy shield and buckler. Thou shalt not be afraid for the terror by night; nor for the arrow that flieth by day.

"Kenny, we don't need to be afraid, for God will protect us just like the mother hen protects her little chicks under her wings."

It was almost midnight when the government officer returned. "Our police party was attacked," he said. "It took us two hours of crawling in the ditches to travel the mile

ssion buildings to the lake." He confirmed the
the schoolboys and added, "You can all sleep
here in the big house tonight. Tomorrow we'll consider
further steps to be taken."

Monday morning Don came on the radio with a weather
report from Ilaga. He was expecting to hear my voice, but
instead Ken Troutman answered and gave a brief report of
the raid and massacre at Obano. The new plane had been
hacked to pieces, and for the second time in a month the
Alliance mission was left without any plane service for
three growing works: the Lakes, the Ilaga, and the Baliem.

Ken did not spell out further details, but Don knew what
that meant for them in the Ilaga. Work on the strip would
stop because they were out of trade goods to pay the
workers. Their food was almost gone, so they would have to
live on the sweet potatoes and other vegetables raised by the
native people. Don decided he would leave the airstrip and
move across to Kunga to start building a cabin for his family.

On Monday morning I started my washing as usual. What
else could I do when all of our clothes were dirty, including
a pile of diapers? Before the job was finished a large navy
plane landed on the lake with Dutch marines. Then word
came that the Timida people from the area behind Enarotali
were coming to attack. They had already killed the two
Catholic teachers there and burned the buildings. We were
ordered to go at once to the government hotel, a building the
size of a large house, where the few police could stand
guard more easily. And so began a week of alerts, running to
the government post, trying to feed everyone under very
crowded conditions, caring for our children in all the confusion and danger.

We really did not know where we stood with the Ekaris
who were everywhere around us at Enarotali. We dared not
trust them, although we could not do anything else. Word
came from Obano that it was Mr. Lesnusa's best friend who
had killed him. That Ekari had been sitting in the front of

the church Sunday morning, and had promised to protect the Lesnusas if trouble came. The schoolboys said he was the first to shoot an arrow.

Someone got the idea of giving out strips of rolled bandage to every Ekari who pledged loyalty to the government and the missionaries. Each Ekari wore this band of white around his head day and night and was never separated from his bow and arrows. Many of the Ekaris who wore the white band were not Christians, but all of them were showing friendship as we had never seen it before. The men were exhausted from standing guard day and night, but still they would do anything to help us. Women came to hug us and pledge their allegiance. "Don't be afraid," they said. "God is with all of us." Had these closest village people turned against us, there would have been little hope left. Instead they warned us and fought for us, even though some of their houses were burned by the enemy, one man was killed, and others were wounded.

We spent Tuesday sitting in the government hotel. In the afternoon we were told that all the missionaries would have to sleep in a nearby government house. What confusion we had trying to feed and prepare sleeping places on cement floors for twenty-three people. Ekari watchmen reported that the hills around Enarotali were covered with enemy warriors. All the friendly Ekaris were sent to the villages for the night lest friend and foe be confused in the darkness. We prayed, committed ourselves to the Lord, and lay down to sleep. Knowing that a heavy rain would stop the warriors, we had prayed for a downpour, but none came. God held the attackers back without it. Christian Ekaris told us the next morning they had prayed all night.

Wednesday morning we were allowed to dash home, change our clothes, and collect more food for the day. I talked to Don on the radio, telling him of the danger to our lives. Until now he only knew of the tragedy at Obano. Being locked away in the Ilaga and still sick with infectious hepatitis, there was nothing Don could do except pray and commit us to the Lord.

Again the cry rang out, "The enemy is coming," and this time it was true. The police and hundreds of friendly Ekaris went out to meet them. In two hours they were back doing a victory dance in front of the house where we were confined. The village Ekaris danced with their bows and arrows and the Ekari policemen danced with their guns. After fifteen minutes the cry came again, "The enemy is coming," and they all ran off to fight. There was a spirit akin to a football game, where half of the sport is the cheering. The players fight a bit, then dance a bit, then fight some more.

The Dutch marines who had gone to Obano found that fighting an Ekari war was quite different from any warfare they had ever known. Arrows could arch up from a ditch and when enough were shot, some would find their target. Bullets could not follow that pattern. The Ekaris were as agile as gazelles when fighting in their home territory, while the marines were bogged down in the mud and rough terrain with their heavy gear. The hills around Obano rang in defiance with the chanting and dancing of the Ekaris. The chanting warriors took advantage of the tall grass and ditches and moved right up to the edge of the marine encampment, pelting them with arrows. When the soldiers moved out to counterattack, the Ekaris vanished. For the marines it was like trying to catch a large balloon; when their hands made contact, the "balloon" bounced away.

Almost a week passed before coffins were made and it was possible to bring the bodies out of Obano. Even then one of the policemen carrying a coffin was shot in the arm. At Enarotali the procession wound up the hill to the church for a funeral service, and then farther up the hill to the cemetery. The two families of the children had come from their posts on Lake Tigi and the eight-year-old son of the Lesnusas was there. He had been at Enarotali the whole time attending school.

At the graveside just before Mr. Paksoal laid his son's body to rest he led in singing "When the Roll is Called Up Yonder," first in his own tongue of Indonesian and then in the language of his son's slayers. For us who were Christians it was a real challenge to dedicate our lives in living service to the Ekari even as these had given their lives in death. Many Ekaris who heard that father sing his song of victory did not know Jesus in a personal way. We prayed that through this sacrifice they, and many thousands of others, might come to Christ.

With the arrival of police reinforcements we were once again allowed to sleep in our own houses. Sometimes the enemy advanced right to the edge of Enarotali, but they were no match for the police with their guns coupled with the Ekaris who fought on our side.

At Obano the marines brought in morters, but those were of little value. The Ekaris continued to shoot arrows at the marines and police, but the many rounds of ammunition shot back caused little damage. The marines were very frustrated shooting at an enemy who never showed himself. Surrender finally came in late December after a group of a thousand warriors came from the Christian areas around Lake Tigi. Those men fought the Obano people in their own style with bows and arrows, and that is what finally brought peace to the land.

The formal peace was made in Ekari style, even as the war had been fought and won according to their rules. A single line of defeated warriors came running down the hill into Enarotali, through the settlement, and up the opposite hill to the house of the government officer. To the accompaniment of their rhythmic hooting they danced in a circle. That was the Ekari way of signing a peace treaty. Then the Ekaris who fought on the side of the government came running and waving branches. They too did a circle dance, and with that the war was ended.

16

Talking Leaves

Don picked up another big sheet of bark and fitted it into place on the wall of the building that was to be his second honeymoon cabin. Although Don was not a carpenter either by training or natural ability, he was highly motivated as he worked on building this temporary house. He daydreamed as he worked. The house would be finished before too long; the strip was nearly ready for landing, and then the girls and I would be there with him. Those months of being a bachelor were not for him. Maybe some men could manage, but he could not take it much longer. Still dreaming as he nailed, Don thought of Christmas with his family. It would be the best ever in our little bark cabin.

Progress had been good during those two weeks of building. The pole framework was up, the bark roof was on, and the rough boards were on the downstairs floor. Now the siding was going on the outside walls. Large sheets of bark had been peeled from a tree similar to a cedar. Each sheet was approximately three by five feet in size, although no two were alike.

Don hammered nails through the bark while his Damal helper held the other end of the sheet in place. One day, as he was reaching for another nail in the can, Don realized that he did not have enough nails to put on the rest of the bark. He turned to the young man who was helping him and said, "I want you to go over to Larson and get me something I need to finish building this house."

Digging in his gear Don found a scrap of paper and penciled a note to Gordon, asking him for a few more nails. "Here," Don said, "Take this leaf to Larson." Since the

Damals had never seen paper before, they coined a new word for it, *ogolal*, which comes from the word *leaf*. A leaf is the closest thing to paper that a Damal had ever seen.

The Damal man looked at the *ogolal* and frowned. "Tell me what I'm to get from Larson," he said. "I don't want to go clear across the valley for nothing."

Don smiled. "This is a 'talking leaf.' You just give it to Larson, and he'll give you what I want."

The man shook his head. "Leaves can't talk."

"All right," Don replied, "I'll tell you what I want." Picking up a nail, he continued. "I want some nails like this one. But don't you say anything to Larson. Just give him my 'talking leaf' and see what he gives you."

In an hour the man was back. He could hardly contain himself because of his excitement. "Here are your nails, and I didn't tell Larson a thing! He just looked at your talking leaf and gave them to me."

That night in the men's house the chief topic of discussion was the "talking leaf." The story was repeated over and over of how Gibbons made a few marks on an *ogolal* and Larson saw it and understood what Gibbons was saying.

Living at Kunga with the Damals was a pleasant change for Don from supervising strip work, where most of the contact with the people was with Danis, acting as a foreman over a crew of workers. He found he slept better on the upstairs sleeping floor of a men's hut at Kunga than he did with his sleeping bag in his own crude shelter at the airstrip. Almost all of his food supplies were gone, so he had no choice but to eat native food, and that was much more tasty steamed in a pit or baked in the ashes rather than being boiled in a pot.

Bonds of friendship began to grow between Don and certain men. Den, the chief, was an industrious person who was always busy working in his gardens rather than sitting around talking. Kugum was a quiet young man, very faithful in helping with menial tasks like cutting wood. Mewi was a flashy dresser, intelligent and progressive. Those and many

more Don learned to appreciate and pray for by name. He
longed to explain the way of salvation to them, but his
growing language ability would not stretch that far. For now
he prayed that they might see the love of Christ expressed to
them through him.

Tita had a winsome personality and was always ready
with a smile and a joke. He had lost one eye in an accident
with a bow and arrow, but that was no handicap to him. Had
he lived in a Western society he would have been a business
executive; in Damal society he was headed toward becoming a chief in a few more years.

Sizing up a man from another culture was not a one-way
street. Tita wondered what Don ate that made him so big.
But seeing Don eat potatoes and greens with the Damals,
sleep in the men's house, and try to speak their language he
had to conclude that possibly this white being *was* a man
just like the Damals. When Tita corrected something that
Don had tried to express in Damal, Don would make some
marks on his "talking leaf," and then he did not make that
same mistake the next time. Tita was amazed.

One morning Tita found Don sitting alone on a rock
reading his Bible. "What are you doing?" Tita asked.

That's not an easy question to answer, Don thought, *but it
gives me a chance to use my new Damal word for God.* The
Damals had no concept of a supreme being; they knew only
evil spirits to be appeased. Following the same pattern the
missionaries had used in the Ekari language, Don found the
Damal word for *make, form,* or *create.* Adding the word
person he formed the new term, *Unkangam Me,* the person
who creates, or *creator.* From that base the Damals would
have to be taught the meaning and concept of God.

"Tita, these leaves here have the Creator's words written
on them. This is talk from God written here. I look at this
book, these leaves, and I hear God's words speaking to me.
Do you understand what I'm saying?"

"Yes, I think I understand. Your little black book must be
very important to you, for I have seen you looking at it many
times."

Don knew that Tita could not fully understand at this point, yet he sensed that the beginning of understanding was there because Tita had a genuine desire to learn.

The Damals had no concept of dividing time into weeks, months, or years. The idea of setting aside one day in seven for God was completely new. One Sunday a large crew of men came to work on the airstrip. Don felt frustrated in sending them home because he could not communicate to them the message of Sunday as the day that Jesus rose from the dead. Instead they must have gone away feeling that Sunday was simply a taboo day for the foreigner.

Don chose to designate Sunday by its Indonesian name, *hari minggu*. When the Damals had learned the meaning of *hari minggu*, the word became so much a part of their language that years later some Damals studying the Indonesian language were startled to find that the word for *Sunday* was *hari minggu* in Indonesian. They said, "Isn't it strange that the Indonesians have taken our word for Sunday?"

The Damals at Kunga were cooperative in everything that Don suggested to them, and gathering on Sunday morning was no exception. Thus it was that each Sunday morning, when the fog had dissipated and the sun had warmed the air, people gathered in the village yard to hear what the *tuan* had to say. Men sat in the center of the group and the women and girls sat on the edges of the circle.

Church began with the singing of a hymn—a Damal chant tune with simple words. Instead of following the usual missionary pattern of setting native words to Western chorus tunes like "Jesus Loves Me" or "The Wise Man Built His House upon the Rock," Don believed the Damals should have church music using their own native tunes. He had observed in Ekari country that only young children could learn to sing the scale of our Western music, and the adult Ekaris ended up with a cacophony of sound when they tried to sing Western hymn tunes. Here are the words to that first Damal hymn.

Jesus, wa-e
He was in heaven, wa-e
He came to earth, wa-e
He brought the new words, wa-e
Men killed him, wa-e
Having died he rose again, wa-e
He returned to heaven, wa-e
He will come again, wa-e
He will come for us, wa-e
We will go with him, wa-e
Heaven is a beautiful place, wa-e
In heaven there is no sickness or sores, wa-e
In heaven no one dies, there is no war, wa-e
There is no sin in heaven, wa-e
We will remain with Jesus, wa-e
Jesus, wa-e

With no foreign music, even the old people could understand the message of this song as it was sung by Damal men who had memorized the words.

After a simple prayer Don began his Bible story—usually taken from the gospels. He spoke in Indonesian; Sam, the chief's son, translated it into Damal; and then Den repeated it in Dani for the Danis who were present. Don was able to follow Sam's Damal, and he listened carefully in order to correct any errors. Den had to grasp everything that was being said in Damal in order to translate it into Dani. If it was not clear to him, he asked Don to explain. And so the Damals began to hear the stories of the Bible in their own tongue.

Whenever Don and Gordon were together for a leisure hour of talking, their conversation usually gravitated to one theme: learning to know the Danis and Damals better, understanding new aspects of their culture, and considering methods to use in reaching them for Christ. Gordon came with his background of formal studies in anthropology and the delight of a scientist being set down in a tribe untouched by foreign government, commerce, or religion.

Don came with a mind open to new ideas, always learning from the people around him. He had the firm belief that no culture was evil in itself—only those practices within the culture that directly conflicted with the teachings of the Bible were wrong.

Three books came into Don's hands that greatly influenced his thinking at that time. *The Christ of the Korean Heart* by Arch Campbell was a personal gift from Dr. A. C. Sneed, the Foreign Secretary of the Christian & Missionary Alliance, to all missionaries serving overseas. This little book told of how the Presbyterian mission in Korea had seen many thousands of Koreans come to Christ in large groups and how they had been discipled into strong, indigenous churches.

The second book was *Behind the Ranges*. Mrs. Howard Taylor told the story of how God used O. J. Fraser to bring thousands of the Lisu tribespeople to Christ. The Lisu were a simple people living high up in the mountains of China, yet they turned to Christ by whole villages and served him fervently.

Dr. Donald A. McGavran had just written *The Bridges of God*, his first book on missionary strategy. He proposed that the long-used "mission station approach" of winning converts one by one was not nearly as effective as using the natural bridges of kinship and culture to reach many people in a mass movement coupled with systematic teaching of the Bible to ground each convert. After reading those three books Don was challenged to believe that God could also cause the Damal people to turn to him by the thousands.

On his third day in the valley Don had made the friendship of Den, the Damal chief from Kunga. The other important Damal chief in the valley was Kip. Don had met Kip once at a *mo* feast, but he felt it was now time to work on building a permanent friendship. So Don started off on the two-hour walk to Kip's village.

On the way he met two of his friends, who were taking part in a garden-digging party. The garden owner had

invited a number of men to spend the day digging a new
garden for him, and in the afternoon he provided a special
pit-cooked meal for all the workers. Having no family
responsibilities, Don was almost as free from a schedule as
the Damals themselves, so he joined the men in digging and
then enjoyed the meal with them before going on to visit
Kip. He spent the night with Kip, and felt a stone had been
laid toward building a tower of friendship. In the morning
Kip took Don out to his special *mo* garden and gave him a
section as a gift to be delivered when the tubers were
mature.

Although Don did not enjoy carpenter work, he did enjoy
gardening and animal husbandry. While he worked on the
house he hired a man to dig ground to plant a vegetable
garden. Since the Ilaga is only four degrees south of the
equator there are no seasons. Planting and harvesting can be
done year-round. Always there was plenty of rain—sometimes too much—but a rainy season could not be predicted
by the calendar. At Kunga the elevation was almost 8000
feet, which made the air chilly. All of that affected what
could be grown.

During his years at the Lakes Don had experimented with
planting various vegetables to see which ones grew best.
Now he chose to plant pole beans, tomatoes, cabbage,
carrots, and squash. He put the seeds into the ground with
special loving care, for this garden was for his Alice, Kathy,
and Joyce. As Don worked in the soil with his hands, his
emotions ranged from despair that the hindrances would be
endless and we would never come, to hopes that the strip
would soon be finished, the weather dry, and we would be
in the Ilaga before Christmas. Each seed was put into the
dark, wet ground with hope and faith that God would bring
it to fruition in due time. Don continued to trust that God
would bring his family to him in the Ilaga, and that together
they would see Damals come to know and serve the Lord.

The bark cabin was not finished, but there were no more

nails, so Don moved back to the airstrip. With no cowrie shells or beads to pay the workers, very few came to help on the strip. One afternoon when all the people had gone back to their villages except one lone Dani man, Don was sitting in his hut writing. The Dani spied Don's mirror and motioned that he wanted to look at his face. Since the man had never seen his face in a mirror before, Don allowed him the pleasure. Becoming engrossed in his writing, Don forgot the Dani, and when he looked up both the Dani and the mirror had vanished.

That Dani thinks he has outsmarted me, Don thought. *He thinks that I would never recognize him again among hundreds of men who all look alike. But he had an unusual scar on his chest, and I will know him when I see him again.*

Sure enough, two months later Don saw that same scar on the chest of a man working on the airstrip. He grabbed him and hung on. "Bring me back my mirror," he demanded, "and I'll let you go." Men came running and shouting to help in the argument. The Dani kept repeating, "I don't know what you're talking about. I didn't take your mirror." But Don hung on and shouted back, "I recognize you by the scar on your chest. Send someone after the mirror, and when I get it back I'll let you go." Struggling and shouting they waited until a Dani came running with the mirror. That time the *tuan* had won a battle of wits with the Danis in their practiced art of thievery.

Another day the Danis won the contest. People had not arrived to work on the strip until almost ten o'clock, for the morning was typically foggy and cold. Just after noon it began to rain. Don and Gordon decided that they could not let the people go home after only two hours of work, so no one was to be paid until late afternoon. In the cold rain the people huddled under their rain capes and tried to crowd into the hut of the missionaries. It was very nerve-racking for the *tuans* to have the noisy men push in about them until they could not even move, but this day they took pity on the shivering people and let them in. That turned out to be the last time they were allowed inside, for someone stole an ax, and the loss was not discovered until everyone had gone home for the night. There was no way to put group pressure on the thief to return the ax, so the Danis won that round.

In late November the Mission Aviation Fellowship received a new Cessna 180, and soon it came to the Ilaga and dropped food, trade goods, and nails to the stranded men. Now that a new supply of shells and beads was available, the number of men and women working daily on the strip increased to several hundred. Even the extra three hundred feet at the bottom of the strip was taking shape, and Don was sure the strip would be ready for landing before Christmas.

But the pilots were not so sure. When they made a free drop from just a few feet above the strip, mud splashed up onto their plane. Don and Gordon assured them that the mud was only on the surface and that the ground under it was solid, but after their experience with the plane's turning over at Homeyo they were quite cautious.

Neither the pilots nor the government inspectors seemed to be able to make up their minds as to what the exact requirements were for a first landing. At one point the government said that a soil inspector must walk into the Ilaga and inspect the strip, but no inspector was willing to walk that long trail, so after some weeks they said that soil samples could be sent out by trail for analysis. But, before the soil samples ever reached the government office, word came from the pilots that someone would have to walk in and inspect the strip before a landing could be made.

Gradually the fact that I would not be in the Ilaga for Christmas became evident to Don, and with that realization came a deep feeling of loneliness and despair. *No one cares,* he thought. *They have all forgotten me.* But God had not forgotten him. He wrote in his diary, "The Lord spoke to me this morning from Mark 10:45. I have come to the Ilaga as

He did, 'not to be ministered unto, but to minister.'"

Don turned his attention away from himself and toward the Damal people—a people who so needed to be changed by the love of God. One of the young men at Kunga had just completed marriage payments on the girl he had chosen to be his bride. Her family was about to force her to go to him even though she could not accept the thought of marriage to him or any other man because she was so young. She chose the only way out that she knew—she committed suicide by jumping into the Ilaga River.

In the months Don had been in the Ilaga he had seen a hundred women and girls with leaf bandages on their hands where fingers had recently been chopped off in mourning. One day he met a forty-year-old woman who had all ten of her fingers intact. It was so unusual to see a woman of that age with all of her fingers that the plight of the Ilaga women struck him anew. *Must these women always live with maimed hands and hearts?*

The Damals were a friendly, open people, but living in their heathen ways without Christ they had no hope. With the goal of bringing them hope through Christ, Don threw himself anew into winning their friendship and learning their language.

17

Together in the Ilaga

Christmas was fast approaching at Enarotali, and I also had to face the reality that Don and I would not be together. A week before Christmas I realized that for the sake of Kathy and Joyce I must celebrate as usual. We began by making spritz butter cookies with a Swedish cookie press, and then we made gingerbread men. Kathy was delighted with her part in decorating the gingerbread men, and thus we began a family tradition of making cookie men every Christmas.

For Christmas dinner the table was set for fourteen and decorated with candles, evergreen boughs, and placecards. Our menu included Jello salad, candied yams, and in place of turkey we had two rabbits roasted whole with dressing. Rabbit was the only fresh meat we missionaries had, and compared to the canned meat we had every day, rabbit was a treat.

I knew that Christmas Day for Don was anything but traditional. There were no Christmas services or singing with the tribal people as we had at Enarotali. He did not even have a Christmas card. The girls and I had a special time scheduled to talk to Don but because of radio trouble the Ilaga never came on. The radio was transmitting again the next day, however, and we got our chance to talk then.

As the months of our separation dragged on, I felt increasing depression. But then the Lord gave me a renewed calling to take the gospel to the Damal tribe and the realization that this trial was part of that calling. In the years since we had been out of Bible School we had not yet seen anything noteworthy accomplished for the Lord—only one life touched here and there. The way had not been easy or especially rewarding. It seemed that the Lord's overall purpose for us was one of being faithful in a hard place without seeing much fruit.

Not until I began to write this book did I see one of God's purposes in the months of separation that we endured. Don had almost two months of waiting after the strip was finished, and much of that time he spent living very close to the Damals. He was learning their language and winning their friendship in a way that would not have been possible had the girls and I been with him in the Ilaga. In every trial that comes our way God has a purpose, but too often we are so overwhelmed by the problem that we cannot see His purpose. Certainly that was the case for Don and me.

Near the end of January, pilot Ed Ulrich and our field leader, Ken Troutman, flew to Homeyo to begin their overland trek to the Ilaga. The Homeyo airstrip had been repaired, and the plane was now able to land there. Ed gave up his vacation in order to make a ground inspection to open the Ilaga strip. No government inspector was willing to attempt that long hike, and it was no easy thing for Ed, a heavy man, whose usual job was sitting in a cockpit *flying* over the New Guinea mountains—not *hiking* over them.

Ken Troutman was experienced in hiking the mountain trails, and he knew how to work with native carriers on a trip of that kind. In 1952 Ken had been with the exploration party that first discovered the Ilaga Valley. Knowing the trail did not make the work of hiking any easier, but Ken gladly did all he could to help reach the Danis and Damals. Opening the Ilaga was accomplished not by Don and Gordon alone, but by a team of missionaries, both pilots and tribal missionaries, each doing his part in backing the advance.

After thirteen days of strenuous hiking the party arrived in the Ilaga. Of course the airstrip was the first place they went. Ed listed several changes that he wanted made before the first landing, and he told us on the radio that the work would take two weeks. Ed must have underestimated the enthusiasm with which Don and Gordon would tackle the job, because the plane was able to land in just five days.

Ken returned to Enarotali with letters for me and also some impressions of Don and his life-style in the Ilaga. For almost seven months now my only contact with Don was on the shortwave transceiver. Don was living quite like a Damal—more so than would have fitted Ken's conservative Pennsylvania background. He had grown a full beard in the Damal pattern, and his hair had grown quite long. Ed Ulrich gave him a haircut, but the beard was to wait until just before I flew to the Ilaga. Don had no furniture except a box for a chair. That was too much for Ken, who was the son of a cabinetmaker, so he set to work and built Don a bench.

Don's letter to me gave another insight into his identification with the Damals. After writing of his personal excitement and anticipation of my joining him in the Ilaga he wrote at length of his involvement in arranging for a pig to be killed to celebrate my arrival. Since every important social occasion must include the serving of pork, any Damal man who was a leader spent many hours of his time haggling over pigs. In true Damal style Don had become deeply involved in bargaining for one pig, only to have the deal fall through and have to bargain for another. He ended up paying a knife, an ax, and some shells to a woman and two men for half of a hog—and Don enjoyed every minute of the dickering, too!

After Ed Ulrich arrived in Sentani he went to the government office of civil aviation and gave his report of the strip. The Cessna 180, whose payload at sealevel was 680 pounds, had taken off from the Ilaga with 465 pounds using only eight hundred feet of strip. That performance was much better than anticipated, but still the inspectors wanted to check the soil before it received government approval.

After the inspectors flew to the Ilaga we waited on pins and needles for their verdict. Three days later it came: permission was granted for our two families to fly to the

Ilaga, and then the strip must be closed for six weeks to remove a hump that covered an old stream bed. After seven months of separation I was going to join my husband. God had called us to the Damal tribe shortly after we arrived in New Guinea more than three years earlier. February 24, 1957, was to be the big day for me.

I began to pack in earnest. The plane would fly 1600 pounds of household goods and food for us before the strip was closed for repairs. In our family, packing had always been Don's specialty, but now it was up to me. Albert, a young Ekari who worked in my kitchen, became my right hand man to help with the heavy work. Everything we owned had to be packed, tied up, and marked with a tag giving the weight and flight priority.

I was up at 4:30 on moving day, too excited to sleep anymore. I made sandwiches for our lunch in the Ilaga, for Don had written that things might be "a bit hectic" when I first arrived. We were all down at the dock by seven o'clock and anxious to be off, but someone had forgotten the key to the boathouse so we waited half an hour for it to be found. Our two-hour boat ride took us to the Obano shore—the first time I had been back to Obano since the day before the massacre. Two little planes landed on the airstrip just as we docked. With a mile of muddy trail ahead of us and the Ilaga Valley beyond that, there was no time to reflect on the happenings of the past.

Today there were carriers enough for both Kathy and Joyce and the 300 pounds of essentials we were allowed above our body weights. Besides bedding, warm clothing, dishes, pans, and a kerosene pressure lamp, I had five large rabbits and six small ones plus celery, onion, strawberry, and rhubarb plants. I may have been a city girl, but I married a farmer. To begin with we would sleep on grass for a mattress and sit on a box for a chair, but before long we would have good food to eat.

Peggy Larson and her family flew with pilot Bill Paul in the new Alliance plane—the third Cessna to arrive in less than a year. Paul Pontier was my pilot in the MAF plane. The forty-five-minute flight took us over the very route that Don had walked. We flew at 12,000 feet, not too far above the high barren plateau, but clouds blocked most of the view. At last we broke through the cloud buildups that ringed a valley dotted with gardens, and Paul Pontier said, "This is the Ilaga. You're here!"

The plane touched down, and I climbed out to be greeted by one very excited husband and hundreds of black people pressing in on every side—more tribesmen than I had ever seen at any one time. Everyone was talking and shouting and trying to touch Kathy and Joyce, but the girls did not seem to mind.

When I stepped out of the plane the Damals saw that I was tall—taller than any of their men. I was thin like their men without the large, protruding stomach of a Damal woman, and I had long hair like some men—not the very short, almost shaven, hair of a woman.

Some of the Damal men greeted me, "Nedek amolo," which means, "Greetings, my father." All I could understand was "amolo,"—"I greet you with love," so I returned the greeting and shook their hands in the proper fashion of snapping fingers twice and then clasping hands. Don spoke to the men, and again I did not understand what was said.

"This is my wife. She is a woman. Say to her, 'Greetings, my mother.'" The Damals nodded and said to me, "Greetings, my mother." Still without understanding, I enthusiastically responded, "Amolo." The Damals began to use feminine terms in referring to me after Don corrected them, but it took time for them to fully realize we were not supernatural beings. I was a real woman who gave birth to children and would someday die just as they did.

There was much the Damals did not understand about the white man and his airplane. When they had observed that large birdlike object swooping down near the ground and spewing out all manner of marvelous goods, they did not understand that men were inside the plane. Don had told the Damals that the *padagalo* would one day sit down on the ground they were leveling. They understood his words but not the concept. Instead they had the idea that some sort of a long snake-monster would come down upon the ground they were leveling. Why else, they reasoned, would the *tuans* insist that the prepared ground be so long? Word had been passed around that all the brave men should run out and grab the snake the day I landed in the Ilaga. Fortunately there were no *brave* men that day.

The hike across the Ilaga Valley involved lots of mud holes to wade through, fences to climb over, and the main Ilaga River to cross on a single log for a bridge. Several hundred excited people walked with us, chanting and talking all the way. Then we climbed the last steep hill, and there was our honeymoon cabin. The view of the Ilaga Valley with its neat gardens and villages ringed by the mountains was just as breathtaking as Don had described it.

The bark cabin was fifteen by eighteen feet with two rooms downstairs and two sleeping rooms in the loft. Don had put translucent plastic in the windows because, of course, glass could not be dropped. The house was clean but completely empty—not a shelf, not a sink, not a piece of furniture—except for the bench Ken Troutman had just built. In back there was a separate little shed for cooking over an open fire. Our water was carried from the Kunga River, and all of our drinking water had to be boiled for twenty minutes in order to avoid infectious hepatitis and dysentery.

The people were most friendly and would have crowded into our house every daylight hour if we had not limited them. Outside, their happy, excited voices created a constant din. After dark when everyone had gone home it became quiet enough so that I heard the roar of the river for the first time—a new sound to me, a sound that was part of my new Damal home.

Kathy and Joyce were a special attraction, and when people who had not yet seen them came, they begged to have the girls come outside so they could view these "strange beings." Actually the girls felt quite at ease with all the new black faces crowding around them. Kathy entertained them by singing her Sunday school songs. Whenever the girls took their dolls outside there was a near riot, for the people could scarcely comprehend that the dolls were not living beings. Joyce was soon sitting on someone's shoulders being carried around, and Kathy followed along behind. Before a week was past Kathy had a special friend— one of the chief's sons her own age—and she began to pick up Damal words and phrases.

The week that I arrived there was unusually good flying weather and the planes continued to make two flights apiece each day. By the end of the week we had almost all of our household goods, not just the 1600 pounds we had counted on. Every morning Don hiked an hour over to the airstrip, met the planes, and escorted the things back across the valley. With Don's encouragement the Damals built a new bridge over the Ilaga River—one with eighteen-inch wide planking instead of the usual four-inch wide footing of a native bridge. By the time our small kerosine refrigerator was flown in, the bridge was ready, and the men carried it all the way with no mishaps.

Every day our little bark house was stacked higher with boxes and drums and cartons until we only had a narrow path left in the living-dining room. But then we began to make progress in turning our cabin into a home. Don set up our little wood range, which made cooking so much easier. The warmth from the fire was good, too, for some nights the temperature dropped into the forties. Don built some rough shelves in the pantry, and I stocked it with the abundant supply of food we now had. Next he nailed packing boxes to the pole framework of the kitchen, and I had kitchen cupboards. I added light green paint, and my kitchen began to look rather cheerful. With pictures on the walls and curtains at the windows the rough bark house had become our home.

On my first Sunday in the Ilaga I could hardly believe what I saw. Over 500 people gathered in the Kunga village yard for church. That included all the Damals living nearby, some Damals from an hour's walk away, and some of the Danis who were close neighbors. We had lived and worked in Ekari country but had never seen interest like this. Here there were people of all ages and fully as many men as women. They had set aside gardening and their daily activities to gather for church.

Everyone took part in the singing, for the music was native to the people. There was only the one song, and two young men sang the words from memory. They sang it twice, once at the beginning and again at the end of the service. Don stood and addressed the group, giving them a Bible story with the application that this message from the Bible was life-changing and that it was for them. Sam and Don had worked through the story on Saturday to make sure that Sam understood the meaning. Sam remained seated as he interpreted from Indonesian to Damal, because their culture did not permit a teenage boy to stand and address all those mature men. As a result not all of the men heard clearly, and very few of the women could hear at all, for they were seated on the outside edge of the group.

Don and I talked at length about that. We had hundreds of people who wanted to hear the message, but they could not hear the words being spoken. I encouraged Don to see if he could not speak to the crowd directly in Damal. He was accepted by them on the level of a chief, and he had a strong voice that would carry well to the entire crowd. I felt he could do it.

Three weeks later Don preached his first sermon in Damal. He continued to work with Sam ahead of time in preparing, but now he wrote out the text as Sam translated it for him. That first Sunday the sermon was short and rather halting in delivery, but everyone could hear. Several times he had to stop and ask Sam for a word, and at other points men corrected words in a sentence which he then repeated in the correct form, but all that was good. The men had to be following what he was saying or they could not have corrected him. Even with their help I am sure that many sentences had grammatical errors—a verb tense was wrong or perhaps a subject indicator was left out—yet they were hearing the basic story of a loving God who sent His Son to give eternal life to every Damal who would forsake his spirit appeasement and follow Jesus.

Each week that followed Don became more fluent in preaching and less dependent on his written notes. Being pressed into preaching before he was fully ready was another one of God's preparations for an event that was coming just two months in the future.

Gradually life in our home became more settled. Before the strip was closed for repair, the plane brought us enough sheets of aluminum roofing to cover one half of our little house. Don set up two fifty-five-gallon drums to catch the rain water from the eaves trough, and we had cold running water piped into our kitchen. What a luxury after using the murky water from a little stream and having to boil all of it for drinking!

Our cabin was built on a steep hillside, and the ground around it was constantly churned into mud by the hundreds of people coming and going. Even venturing up the slippery hill to the outside toilet was a dangerous journey until we got the Damals to build a path and stairs.

Another project undertaken was leveling an area below our house where we could play croquet and badminton. The process was like building a mini airstrip with scores of men, women, and children digging up the high spots to fill in the low areas. Kathy joined in the work with the other children, carrying clods of wet dirt, and she earned blue beads just as the Damals did. We did use the court at times for family games but the chief purpose turned out to be a parade ground for the crowds of people who came to sing and march on Sundays before and after church.

Although Joyce was approaching her second birthday she

did not talk. The many languages she heard confused her. Here in the Ilaga she heard five different languages spoken every day: Damal and Dani from the people, English from us, Ekari from Andy, and Indonesian from Sam. Andy and Sam were the only two boys in the valley with whom I could communicate, and that in two different languages. They had agreed to help me in the kitchen and with scrubbing the clothes. At four-and-a-half Kathy was ready to tackle a new language, for she already spoke English and Indonesian.

Both the girls wore Damal string skirts over their dresses and enjoyed going to the nearby gardens with their friends. Kathy prized the potato digging stick that her girl friends had given her so she could join them in their garden work. Their dolls soon lived in a net-bag like all Damal babies and were carried everywhere. Kathy was delighted in becoming a real Damal when she took the beads she had earned doing various jobs and purchased woven arm bands. On occasion both girls came home with faces striped with red and black greasepaint.

A baked sweet potato and native spinach became the best of foods to our girls, and even the mention of pork made their eyes light up. Damal value systems and culture became more and more a part of them. Caring about people and always sharing whatever they had were two positive traits learned from their Damal friends. Today in adult life these Damal characteristics are still a part of Kathy and Joyce.

Although our girls spent many of the daylight hours with the Damals, there were still times we were with them. Every morning for twenty minutes I brushed and braided Kathy's long blond hair into French braids, and as I braided I read to her. In the evening after a bath that made them clean at least through the night hours, it was again time for stories and prayers. But Kathy's favorite hour of the week was early Sunday morning when I had Sunday school just for her. I used a Sunday school quarterly written for beginners, and she learned every Bible story that I taught her.

Kathy was a little missionary in her own right. She understood our motive in coming to the Damals and spoke of her faith to the children. Before the Damals could receive our message about Christ they had to first accept us as flesh-and-blood human beings. Our religion could not be for them unless we were real people like they were. Their idea that we were *hai* people, supernatural beings who did not give birth to children and die like humans, had to be dispelled. Kathy and Joyce bridged the gap from the twentieth century quite naturally, and that did more to convince the Damals that we were real people than did all of our words. The girls were accepted by the Damals as one of them, in a way that we as adults never could be.

The final flight before closing the strip for alterations brought in three wheelbarrows to help in the strip work. They were the ultimate in modern equipment in contrast to nothing but gunny sacks and bare hands to carry the dirt for the original construction. Heavy rains had created a muddy spot on the strip, and due to a mix-up in reporting strip conditions the pilot was not informed about that soft spot. In taxiing up the strip the plane bogged down in the mud, and the pilot gunned the engine to get through. Instead of the wheels moving, the plane nosed forward, and the propeller hit the ground and was bent.

Ten days later the MAF Cessna dropped a new propeller by parachute. The pilot repaired the plane and took off for Sentani, closing our strip for six to eight weeks, or so we thought. It was three full months before the plane landed again.

18

The Angels Sing

Bridging the cultural gap between the twentieth century and the Damal culture was important, but even more important than that was to teach the Damals the message of the Bible in their own tongue, for "how shall they believe in him of whom they have not heard?" (Romans 10:14). Sam, the fifteen-year-old son of Chief Den, was our God-given link to the Damal language.

Sam was in our home much of the time, teaching us language and helping out in the kitchen. He was like a big brother to our girls, and when he expressed a desire to take a Bible name in place of his five-syllable Damal name of Nogombunime, Kathy said, "Let's name him Samuel," for she had been studying about Samuel in her Sunday school lessons. Samuel it was, and then later his name was shortened to Sam.

Language learning for me had to follow a much different pattern than it did for Don. Gordon commented about Don, "He learns a language like a child." I did not have that gift. I longed for a dictionary and grammar divided into lessons like those I had used in studying the Ekari language. Lacking those, I set out to write my own, using Sam to translate basic words from Indonesian. Of course Don was able to give me a lot of help, too. Although not a single word from the Ekari language could be understood by the Damals, yet the order of words in a sentence, types of verb conjugations, and most important of all, basic thought patterns were similar.

My first lesson began with greetings and commonly used sentences and then went on to a few nouns and pronouns.

Sam was an excellent language informant for me at that stage of learning, because he was very intelligent and bent his every effort to help me. He repeated slowly, emphasizing the syllables I had missed. He patiently conjugated verbs, and as I wrote them down I found that Damal verbs were much more regular in pattern than English verbs.

Each day I devoted several hours to language study, and gradually over the weeks and months I could discern progress. In my diary I noted that I had conjugated the verb "to be" and learned how to use negatives with verbs; I recorded the Damal equivalents of the words found on the first ten pages of the Ekari dictionary. Even abstract words like "deceive" were turning up, and after three months I had written six lessons. To be sure, there were many unanswered questions like how to spell verb roots that seemed to change with different conjugations. Was I correct in thinking that a number of one-syllable words appeared to be identical but had diverse meanings? Those questions would have to wait for a trained linguist.

Each week Don worked with Sam in preparing his sermon, and he was making good progress in public speaking and expressing spiritual concepts; but Don was not the only person learning from those sessions. Sam was learning the gospel message more clearly than any other Damal. On March 28 during a sermon preparation time Don asked Sam if he was ready to make his personal decision to follow Christ, and they prayed together. That was a red letter day for us in seeing the first Damal come to Christ.

In doing research to write this book I asked Sam a number of questions concerning his decision to follow Christ. Later Sam was to be one of the first graduates of the Dani Bible School, for he was equally at home in either the Dani or Damal languages, and today he is pastor of a Dani congregation at the large government center of Wamena in the Baliem Valley. We recorded his conversion in Western fashion, connecting it with a specific date and a prayer of decision. Sam, like most Damals, had little interest in pinpointing the time of a formal decision. In fact, in telling me his story he did not even mention the occasion we had recorded.

I had come back to my father's village after two years of schooling near the Lakes. When Gibbons and Larson moved into our valley, I liked both of them so it was easy for me to listen to them. I was amazed at their teaching, but I believed it. Each time I learned a new story I told my father and the other men of my village.

Then one day Nigil came to Gibbons asking him to come and pray for his wife who was in labor and could not deliver her baby. He feared she might die. [That was shortly after the decision recorded above.] Gibbons asked me to go with him, and he prayed in Indonesian for the woman, and then he said to me, 'Now you pray in Damal.' I was reluctant, but I had no choice, so I prayed a short prayer, and, lo and behold, the woman delivered her baby. I thought, God really heard my prayer, so I honestly believed in God right then.

After this I told everyone that God is real. At first the Damals did not believe. They thought that Gibbons and Larson were supernatural beings from above, and that belief was only magnified when their goods came from the sky. But I assured them that they were just men like Damals, for I had been to the Lakes and seen other *tuans*. Because someone from their own tribe had seen the outside world it was easier for the Damals to believe without misconceptions. In time my father believed because I taught him, and since he was an important chief the other Damals listened to him.

One Sunday Gibbons preached on sin and the punishment of hell for those who do not confess their sins. [According to my diary that was in mid-May.] I remembered the pig I had stolen and eaten some time earlier, and I came and confessed this to Gibbons. He told me the story of Zacchaeus and how after he believed he repaid what he had stolen. He suggested that the ax I had earned that month for teaching language would be a proper payment to the man. I went to the man and confessed what I had done, and when I gave him the ax in payment, he was very amazed. He was so taken aback by my action that he said, "This gospel must really be true, for no one before has ever made payment for a stolen pig unless he was caught stealing."

One Saturday afternoon the cry of war came from across the river, and in minutes the hooting and calling of war rang from every direction—passing from one village to the next until the entire valley was calling out the news. Don was home that afternoon. Three days a week he spent supervising work on the airstrip, but today was Gordon's day to oversee the strip work. Don understood what they were saying and then said to me, "It's probably just another false alarm. Since I've been in the valley there must have been a dozen war alarms and not one of them has had any truth in it."

But, by late afternoon we realized it was the real thing as people were returning from the battle area. Then a note came from Gordon saying he had treated two men with arrow wounds and seen several dead on the trail between his house and the airstrip. Looking across the valley we could make out black dots moving back and forth near the airstrip, their traditional battlefield.

A war party had come from the Beoga and Sinak planning to spend the night hidden at the forest edge and in the morning attack their enemy, the Taganit group, who lived across the valley near Kunga. The workers had just left the airstrip for the day and were all at the Larsons' house being paid when one man discovered the presence of the invaders and called out the alarm of war. Among the strip workers were a number of Taganit men, and fighting broke out on the spot immediately. Other Dani clans living near the airstrip joined with the Taganit group, and the Beoga and Sinak warriors were taken by surprise and completely overpowered.

Pursuit of the attackers continued the next day. Thirty of the Beoga-Sinak group were killed—seven of those right on the airstrip. Perhaps even more who were wounded died in the forest from exposure and neglect. To us the invaders were not enemies, they were the friendly Damals of the Beoga whom we wanted to reach with the gospel. My future friend Kok-Me was in the Beoga group, but he was one who managed to escape with his life. Certainly the renewed hostility would make entering the Beoga much more difficult.

Seventeen Ekaris from a Christian village on Lake Tigi walked into the Ilaga. Now that the missionary had moved into the Ilaga, trade routes were open to the Ekari. Those men came first as traders, but at the same time they had a clear Christian witness. On the way they had stopped off at Homeyo for three weeks and worked on the airstrip, and in the Ilaga they were ready to work just at a time when the Danis and Damals were afraid to venture up to the strip site for fear of another attack. They came from an area where the entire Giyai clan had burned their fetishes four years earlier, and as a group they were following the Lord enthusiastically.

Chief Widibi led the party. He had already had two wives when he first heard the gospel, and that disqualified him from becoming a recognized pastor or elder, but it did not stop him from being a very active witness. Don perceived that the testimony of this tribal chieftain would be very valuable in presenting the claims of Christ to the Damals. He arranged for Widibi to give his testimony on Sunday morning. Don interpreted for him from Ekari to Damal. His speech was excellent, and the people listened with rapt attention.

Seeing the response at Kunga, Don arranged for Widibi to speak in the Namagu area, the second large settlement of Damals and a group with clan ties separate from the Kunga people. From the very beginning Don recognized the distinction between the two groups with their separate chiefs, and he made an effort to cultivate their friendship even though the distance made visits more difficult. Chief Kip was a special target of Don's interest.

Saturday evening we took time for Kathy's Sunday school so that we could all hike the two hours on Sunday morning to the Namagu for church. That was the first time that the girls and I had walked to the eastern branch of the valley.

Kathy and Joyce rode on the shoulders of two Damals. The girls were in the lead, and when we entered a village their naturalness helped prepare the people for the shock of seeing a white woman, the girls' mother, if you please, walking into their village. Soon someone got brave enough to touch me, and others joined in poking and rubbing my skin. They were trying to determine if we were *real* people.

Word of our coming had been announced widely, and over six hundred gathered to hear Widibi speak. He talked of heaven and hell. "There are many *tuans* who will be in heaven," he said, "but only a few of us real people are ready for heaven. The *tuans* will be there singing their songs. Let us real people go and sing our kind of songs too." Everything that he had to say was on the same wave length as the thinking of the Damals. Here was a tribal chief, a black man wearing a gourd, telling them how he had put away the spirit appeasement of his ancestors and embraced the gospel.

The very next Sunday Kip walked all the way to Kunga to attend church. While the crowds were dancing and singing outside, Kip came to talk to Don. For the first time his conversation turned to spiritual things, and for an hour they talked. Kip said he was considering giving up spirit appeasement and wanted Don to come for regular services. Don replied, "I can't come to your village to have church on Sunday because so many gather here at Kunga, but I will come on Saturday and teach you." Over three hundred people gathered in the Namagu for church on the following Saturday, and each Saturday after that church was held for Kip's people.

Life was more than full for us those days. Don still spent three mornings a week working on the airstrip, for until the strip work was completed and the surface hard and dry there would be no plane landing. Every two or three weeks we received a drop of basic supplies and mail, but we had no way to contact the rest of the world other than short transmissions on our two-way radio.

Don had started putting up the pole framework of our permanent house. The Damals knew how to fell and carry in the poles, but beyond that the work was all Don's, for they knew nothing about using a saw and hammer. Language study occupied most of my hours. Sometimes Don joined me, and we worked together with Sam. In addition, Don had his weekly session with Sam to prepare a message for Sunday.

Woven in with all of that were frequent talks with individuals or groups of men. Sometimes the subject of the talks was the purchase of a piece of pork or bargaining for poles in exchange for an ax, but more and more the topic concerned spiritual questions. Some of the same men had asked questions earlier, but Don had not had the language ability to respond. Now, with their help in correcting a verb form or filling in a noun, he was able to communicate.

One day Den came to talk to Don about a matter that appeared to be very important to the chief. The two men went off into the seclusion of the tall grass to hold their conversation. Den explained that certain women had been known to eat the brains of a dead person. Would Don say something against that practice in order to help stop it? *A touch of cannibalism*, Don thought. Yes, he would be willing to lend his weight to the stamping out of the practice.

The following Sunday after the sermon he spoke against that deplorable practice of the women, and after his few brief remarks a number of the men made speeches on the subject. It was some months later that Don came to realize that he had correctly understood the nouns and verbs of Den's disclosure but lacking knowledge of Damal culture and thought patterns he had not really understood what Den was saying.

The Damal word *nat* means "brains," but it also means "spirit" or "mind." Den was actually saying that certain women were witches and in that practice of witchcraft they would eat the *spirit* of a man and thus cause his death. Don's response to his misunderstanding caused no problem, but it did illustrate the fact that the Damals' thought world is unlike our Western secularism. Their figurative speech and consciousness of the spirit world contrasts with our cold world of scientific reality. The Damals' thought patterns made it easier for them to accept the intangible truths of the gospel, and it was most important for the missionary to take advantage of that. At the same time he must recognize the pitfalls of error that might come through their way of thinking.

Not long after the Ekari chief had given his testimony, the Damal men began to come with questions like, "Would God be able to heal us if we no longer appeased the spirits when sickness comes?" Don assured them that if they put their trust in the Lord He certainly would take care of them. Already many Damals were coming to ask for prayer when they were sick. Some came to our house for prayer, and others, feeling too sick to walk, asked Don to come to their villages to pray for them. They saw plainly that God was answering prayer, whereas spirit appeasement had not helped them.

Sensing that the time was right, Don preached a sermon from Joshua's words, "Choose you this day whom ye will serve" (Joshua 24:15). He made very clear that if they chose to serve God they must destroy all their fetishes. The two did not mix.

Discussions followed about how they might destroy their fetishes. Someone suggested they gather them and have the airplane take them away. In their thinking the airplane was related to the supernatural. Don told them that was not a good method. He had made up his mind that he would not help them dispose of their fetishes. If their decision was real they must destroy them themselves. No end of problems could arise in the future if some of the people demanded that their fetishes be returned. Another suggestion was to throw them in the river. Someone vetoed that idea because, he said, "The Danis might retrieve some of the things downriver."

Don opened his English New Testament to Acts, chapter 19, and gave them a free translation of the story about the Ephesians who wanted to follow the Lord, but found they could not mix their old spirit ways with following Christ. They burned their magic books publicly, and the Word of God spread because of their testimony. Don did not need to say any more. The men decided that the method they would use should be public burning.

On a Saturday afternoon, after three weeks of discussions, Den and the other leading men from the Damal villages around Kunga came to see Don. For two hours they talked of burning their fetishes. The biggest fear remaining in their minds was the threat of war. If they burned their fetishes and then war came, they would have no defense, for the fetishes protected them and gave them victory in battle. They could not be replaced because many had been passed down through the generations. With the Taganit Danis as their close neighbors, war was always imminent. Just a month ago there had been another battle in this devastating war that showed no signs of ending.

Don answered their questions by telling them Old Testament stories of Gideon and others to whom God had given victory. God was able to do the same for the Damals if they trusted Him. They went home saying that tomorrow they would burn their fetishes.

We had no idea of what to expect and really knew very little about the Damal system of spirit appeasement or what their fetishes were. We were young missionaries without experience and had no one to advise us. No missionary in the mountains of Dutch New Guinea had ever been a part of a fetish burning. The earlier burning near Lake Tigi had not involved a missionary.

Our Bible school training had concentrated on the study of God's Word with little instruction in missionary methods. Don had the simple but strong conviction that the Bible offered guidance in every situation. The New Testament recorded that Paul had sought and found converts in newly contacted heathen areas, and we could expect our God to do the same today.

Sunday, May 26, 1957, was a beautiful sunny day. We went down the hill to the village to join the small group of Damals waiting there. I took our camera with us, but Don cautioned, "Don't stand up to take a picture. The Damals might think of the camera as something magic affecting the fetish burning. If you can get any shots from where you are seated on the ground, that's OK."

Soon a large group of men appeared, singing and dancing on a nearby hill south of us. Almost at once another group appeared on the hill to the west, and in a few minutes a third group of men came over the hill behind our house. They continued to chant for some time.

All of a sudden the group south of us charged into the village waving their spirit appeasement paraphernalia over their heads as they circle-danced in the center of the village yard. The other two groups charged down the hill, leaped over the fence, and joined the circle dance. Finally they all placed their sooty bundles in a pile and sat down. Men who were not part of the fetish burning group and all the women and children had slipped into the village unnoticed. Seven hundred were seated on the ground, the men with their fetishes in the center, women and children around the edges, and then still further out were a group of Danis who came to observe.

An ominous silence fell over the crowd as they waited for the service to begin. The women were especially tense, for never before had they been allowed to come near the fetishes that had just been carried into the village yard. The voices of the men rose in resonant response as a pair of Damal men led in singing the hymn-chant. During prayer every eye was closed, down to the smallest child. Don spoke to the people about the resurrection and the hope of heaven for believers.

Then came the invitation. Don challenged those who were committing themselves to follow Christ by destroying all of their fetishes to join him at the edge of the group. Before anyone else moved, Den stood up beside Don and in his deep voice and the eloquence of a chief he repeated the invitation in a negative way. "If you have a double mind about giving up your fetishes, then wait until a later time to make your decision." Almost as a unit, 130 men and teenage boys rose from among the men seated in the center and went to sit in a group by themselves. It was obvious that their decision had not been made during the service but during the days before as they had discussed and re-discussed the issue.

Den turned toward the women and challenged them with his same negative eloquence. "Do not come and join the men if you have any reservations about this decision." Ninety women rose to go and sit near the men.

When no one else came, Den turned and ran toward the men's house in the center of the village. Wong-Wong, his brother, and the other Kunga men raced after him. Inside the hut they tore down the rough board enclosure at the back where fetishes were kept. Out came the sacred objects— stone axes, knives, and shell-belts. The men gathered up those fetishes along with the wood that formed the fetish rack and ran with them out to the village yard.

Sam helped his father arrange the wood to build a fire. They took one of the sacred stone axes, never used before, and chopped the wood. After the fire had started to burn Den unrolled a four foot shell-belt and said, "This was given to my fathers in settlement of a war three generations ago, and we have used it as a fetish ever since. Now we are going to trust God to protect us. We are no longer going to use this charm. Nor will we attack anyone else. We are through with war."

The elders from the ten villages in the Kunga area proceeded to add the wood from their fetish racks to the blazing fire and then to open their bundles of fetishes and give testimony of what the objects represented, as they threw them into the fire. Most of the fetishes had been consecrated during a specific war and were irreplaceable, for they had been handed down from father to son. Each man was really burning his bridges behind him as he threw the fetish he owned into the fire.

One fetish they burned was quite different from the others. It was in a net bag and was known as "the mother of sweet potatoes." It was used to ward off famine and insure good crops. In that area also their decision was made; they would trust God for their food in the future.

When all the bundles had gone into the fire Don said, "If you have now burned all your fetishes we will pray." Immediately the women cried, "Wait, wait," and began to tear off some of their necklaces and bracelets and threw them into the fire. Men too tore off necklaces and added them to the blaze. Those charms had been consecrated to an evil spirit in a time of sickness, and their owners had depended on them to ward off that same spirit from bringing on another illness. To us those decorations of shells, pig tails, and other bric-a-brac appeared to be identical with the regular jewelry worn by every man, woman, and child. In substance they were, but their owners knew which ones had a spiritual significance.

At last no more fetishes were brought forward, and Don closed the service in prayer. His words in Damal were not eloquent, but the singing of the angels in heaven must have been magnificent! The chain of sin and darkness that bound the Damals for unmeasured time had been broken.

The first large rock had been thrown into the pool of heathen darkness, breaking the surface. From that were to come ever widening circles of fetish burnings, affecting all the tribes in the mountains. Kip and other leaders from the Namagu went home to discuss the burning of their fetishes. Danis went back to their people to recount the event in detail and predict that grave disaster would now come upon those who had defied the spirits of the ancestors. If that calamity spilled over upon the Danis they would make war with the Damals to set things in order again.

The fire of the fetishes blazed high, and the smoke rose as a testimony to all in the valley who saw it for they knew what it meant. As it began to die down Den gave a shout and led all his people in a victory dance. The men followed Den running in a circle, and then came all the women and children. Their pulsating shouts rang out over the valley. Their fetishes were gone. Now they trusted in the living God!

19
God Proves His Power

"After two sleeps I want all of you who burned your fetishes today to gather here in the village. Come early in the morning before you go to your gardens, and I will teach you the words of Jesus." Don made that announcement just before the crowd broke up after the fetish burning. All at once the reality of what had happened really struck him. All the ties to spirit appeasement were broken for five hundred Damals of the Kunga confederacy, yet they had very little knowledge of Bible truths. They must be taught right away.

At 8:30 Tuesday morning we went down to the village to begin our first inquirers' class. We were disappointed to find that only twenty people had gathered. After waiting a few minutes Don began with the twenty—at least they had come. Soon people began coming into the village yard. Ten minutes later we had a class of 200. They had gathered according to the Damal inner sense of time and had all come at once from the surrounding villages.

Our clock and schedule of time is linked with the position of the sun, whereas the Damals relate more to the temperature and weather. Without clothing to keep them warm they customarily stay close to their fires in the early morning hours. That was an adaptation on the part of the Damal to the environment in which he lived.

It did not take many inquirers' classes for us to realize that our teaching of Bible doctrines had to be presented in a very simple, systematic form if the Damals were to learn. Our church background had dictated that prayer was always spontaneous, never written, and that converts were baptized upon their confession of faith and not necessarily upon the completion of a catechism class. Putting that background aside, we wrote eighty-six questions and answers, which covered the basic teachings of the Bible. First the Damals would memorize the facts, then later they could express them spontaneously. Another advantage of the catechism soon became apparent. What we were teaching could be carefully checked to make sure we were not prompting an error due to a language misunderstanding.

The classes were actually our first rudimentary school. Our students were adults, many of them mature in years. Almost at once the leading men added a new dimension to the class. After the lesson was over and Don had closed in prayer, a man or sometimes two stood and repeated what he had learned, using the pattern of public speaking for a chief. Before long people were repeating the lessons during the evening hours while seated around the fire in their houses. What could have been better? That was not our planning; it was the direction of the Holy Spirit working through the medium of Damal culture.

Prayer for the sick had become a very important part of Don's daily activities even before the fetish burning. Back in December the teaching that God is powerful and does heal the sick through prayer—but only for those who do not seek spirit appeasement—began to reach the mind of the Damals. It was one or the other, not both. That separation of faith was quite understandable to the Damal, and it laid the foundation for their complete break with fetishes. In time of sickness people transferred their dependence upon spirit appeasement to dependence on God.

When Don had first trekked into the Ilaga, the government doctor at Enarotali had supplied him with injections of penicillin to treat yaws. He also gave him aspirin, bandages, and ointment for sores. Beyond dispensing those few medications, Don prayed for anyone who came asking for prayer. Often he was called to a village to pray when the person was too sick to walk to our house. In those days we

had neither the ability nor the time to diagnose the sick-
nesses of the many who came. A woman could not deliver
her baby; a man was miserable with a cold; another had
pneumonia. Whatever the sickness, those people who had
asked for prayer recovered.

The beautiful thing was that God revealed his omnipo-
tence to the Damals in ways they could understand. Two
days after the fetish burning, men called Don to come and
pray for Duk. He went and found that Duk had a bad cough,
a fever, and had been spitting blood. Several days later the
men returned to report that Duk was well and that he
improved greatly the very night on which Don had gone to
pray.

One of the first things asked of us in the inquirers' class
was, "Teach us to pray. We want to learn to pray." In their
old beliefs, spirit appeasement, charms, and taboos had
been an ever-present part of their lives. Prayer to God could
fill that vacuum. A short, memorized prayer of thanksgiving
for food was a place of beginning. From that they learned a
pattern for opening and closing prayer. Gradually the
Damals began to express their own thanks and requests in
prayer. Soon both men and women were praying in informal
village gatherings. Three months later Kama-Kama, a fifty-
year-old man, led in public prayer at a Sunday morning
service.

Inquirers' classes were held each Tuesday and Thursday
morning and on Sundays after church. The group numbered
between 200 and 250 on Sundays and about half that on
weekdays. Sunday had become a day set aside completely
for church. It is interesting to note how quickly and
completely the Damals accepted God's plan of giving Him
one day in seven when in their old culture they had no
special days. Crowds remained large at the church at Kunga,
and always they enthusiastically marched and sang in
Damal style before and after the service.

The music of the Damals fascinated me. Singing was a
part of almost everything they did—especially expressing

their joy in their newfound faith. In Ekari country I had
heard very little of their native singing, for all singing in
church used Western tunes. As I analyzed the chant tunes of
the Damals I learned that their music was built on a five-
tone scale rather than the seven tones of our major scale.
They did not use the two half steps, the fourth and seventh
notes of the scale. (Years later I learned that many tribal
people of Africa and other parts of the world also use the
five-tone scale.)

There were only two hymn-chants, and I thought we
needed more songs. The Ekaris sang Western tunes reason-
ably well until they came to a note not in the five-tone scale.
At that point each person made his own adaptation of that
note according to what he heard, and the result was
cacophony. I decided to find a tune that was built on the
five-tone scale. The hymn tune "Revive Us Again" offered
just that with the exception of one note. Changing that one
note I had a tune built on their five tones. Don wrote the
words to the chorus.

> I love Jesus, I really love Him;
> I love Jesus, He loves the Damal people.

Den was in our house soon after we wrote the song, and I
sang it for him. His eyes filled with tears, for the words were
real to him. Next I began teaching the new song at each
session of the inquirers' class. They were excited about it
and tried for some weeks to learn to sing it, but they just
could not. The entire form of the music was foreign to them.
Had we been working with children, they would have
learned, but these were mature adults. Their mode of life
and expression was already formed.

We simply dropped the project. It was not working, and
we felt there was nothing intrinsically "Christian" about
Western tunes. If Damals could praise the Lord better with
their native music, then why should we insist on their using
music that was foreign to them? At the time the decision
seemed to be of little import, but it was not so in the plan of
God. Today tens of thousands of Christians all over the

mountains of Irian Jaya use indigenous music in their worship—a situation rather unique in missions.

Four days after the fetish burning Chief Den came to Don with a question about war and its ramifications. The Kunga Damals had never wanted to join in the Taganit War in the first place, but because they lived as neighbors to the Danis, and because tribal custom demanded that the community act as a unit, they had been pulled into the fighting.

Now the Taganit Danis were getting ready to make indemnity payments to their allies, the Kunga Damals. Chief Den said he felt that they as Christians should not eat pork given in payment for men killed in war. It was the price of blood. He explained that the arrangements for those payments had begun a number of months earlier and that the Danis would probably pay forty pigs to them. Don, who did not yet understand the scope of indemnity payments, replied that as long as the Damals made no threats of war he saw nothing wrong in their receiving the pigs if the Danis wanted to pay them.

Den and the other men did not take Don's advice. God gave them the wisdom to see that if they received war payments they would have to make them as well, and the whole process would only lead to further fighting.

Before the week was over the local town criers announced the arrival of a party of Danis from the east. These were leaders from the group that the Taganit warriors had driven out of the Ilaga. They had come to negotiate peace and the return of their people to the valley. In God's perfect timing, as the Damals had burned their war fetishes those Danis were already on the trail from the Baliem to take the first step toward peace.

The Taganit warriors had had definite plans to go to the Beoga and return the recent attack, but that never happened. The battle on the airstrip was the last battle of the Taganit War.

When those events occurred I recorded them in my diary, but it has taken the passage of time to see, at least in part, the hand of God in all that took place. We did not realize the scope of the Taganit War nor that the peace being made by the Danis was a vital step in preparing for the coming fetish burnings of the Dani people living all the way from the Ilaga to the Baliem. Certainly another battle in the Beoga would have delayed our entrance there. Although the Damals and Danis had lived for centuries unknown to the rest of the world, God had not forgotten them in His perfect plan.

Time was at a premium for us. Every waking hour was filled with some project—supervising the airstrip work, putting up the frame of the permanent house, teaching inquirers' classes, preparing sermons for Saturdays and Sundays, preparing meals and scrubbing clothes, helping the sick, tending the vegetable garden, counseling the men who came for advice, and always striving to learn the Damal language. In all of that you might think that our girls were left out, but really they were a part of everything that we did. Their dolls and Damal playmates attended "inquirers' classes" that Kathy taught, a new word learned in Damal was exciting and had to be written down at once, and a treasured possession was their potato digging stick. Kathy faithfully weeded in our garden, helping to supply our family's food just as her Damal friends did in their gardens. It was as exciting as going to a circus when we packed a picnic lunch, found men to carry the girls on their shoulders, and all set off to attend a church service at a distant village.

I wrote about Joyce's second birthday in a letter to my family:

> We cut our afternoon language work short, and the girls got dressed up in their best clothes. Don put on a white shirt and tie, and I wore my new jumper, hose, and heels. For supper we had macaroni and cheese, the first tomato from our garden, and chocolate cake and ice cream. We ate by candle light and even had music. Our kitchen helper cranked the phonograph and changed the records. [They were 78 RPM in those days.] Afterwards Joyce opened her

presents—two little toys from missionary friends and a couple of things I found to wrap up. Kathy and Joyce thought it was really special.

One afternoon Kathy burst into the house followed by a crowd of friends. One of the Damal children blurted out, "Look at Kathy's hand." I turned to see a neatly made bandage of banana leaves with only her two fingers and thumb sticking out. "Kathy's fingers are cut off," they chorused.

Of course it was only a game, and her fingers were bent down under the bandage, but it looked real. I played their game with them and acted very shocked. When they went out again I stopped and reflected. Chopping off fingers in mourning had recently been part of life for those Damal girls; now it was a thing of the past. The Damals who burned their fetishes had needed no instruction from us. After the gospel came they simply stopped the practice.

Not all of their heathen customs fell away so easily. Shortly after the fetish burning, a woman who was accused of being a witch and of eating the spirit of her neighbor was executed. Another time a bereaved father came begging us to have our "talking box" (the radio) tell him who had eaten the spirit of his baby. We could find no evidence of any woman practicing witchcraft. Rather it seemed that the men in their frustration of facing death were seeking a scapegoat. For us to deny the existence of witches did not solve the problem, for the Damals would feel we just did not understand. So we prayed with them and for them. We lived with them, taught them, and counseled them.

Superstition as to the cause of death did not leave the Damals overnight. Some remains to this day. Although the root of superstition has not been completely eradicated, God has led most of the believers to simply trust Him in times of sickness and death.

God must have known that those new Christians could not bear too heavy a test of their faith, for it was over two years before the first adult from the group who had burned its fetishes died. That was a direct miracle from God in answer to the faith of a people coming to Him from animism—and their unbelieving neighbors watched and wondered.

A third area in which the Damals had trusted God when they burned their fetishes was for their food supply. With peace coming to the valley everyone applied themselves to garden work, God blessed their efforts, and there was an abundance of food.

A special garden wonder came to the Damals in the form of a squash. The Ilaga people had a small, pale variety of squash growing in their gardens when we entered the valley, but it was rather tasteless. Don enjoyed experimenting with new varieties of seeds to see which might adapt better to the climate, and among those was a pumpkin type of squash. He planted some in our garden by the Kunga village. The squash took root well, and then began to grow. Everyone that came to Kunga—and that included hundreds of people from all over the Ilaga—always inspected our garden to see what new things were growing.

The squash were bright orange, and they grew so fast the people could almost see them grow. Soon seven of the squash weighed forty pounds apiece and would have won a blue ribbon in any county fair. We served them in a pit-cooked feast, and everyone gave God the glory for this small miracle and also thanksgiving for His blessing on all of their gardens.

According to Damal superstition certain evil spirits lived in a grove of trees clustered in a flat area near the Ilaga River. No one dared to enter the area lest they provoke the wrath of the spirits. After the fetish burning men fearlessly went into that grove, cut the trees for firewood, and planted gardens in the fertile soil. God honored their courage in breaking Satan's taboo. The potatoes grown there were huge, but not as exciting as the squash and cucumbers. The squash grew to an unheard of size, and the Damals said, "So many cucumbers set on the vines that they had to grow one on top of the other. There wasn't room on the ground for all of them."

When the airstrip was reopened after three months we were able to send out reports to our colleagues and friends of God's amazing work among the Damals. We learned that the Alliance was phasing out its flying program and turning it all over to Mission Aviation Fellowship.

Language learning was still our most pressing occupation. The plane brought us a tape recorder, and I taped the lessons I had been writing. That made it easier to drill by mimicking the sounds and intonation. At that point I began visiting the women in the village, trying to practice what I had written on paper.

The women were delighted with the special attention that gave them. One afternoon as we were chatting they decided that I should have a native skirt of the style worn by married women. I could wear it over my own dress on Sundays for church, they told me.

Don was commissioned to buy the yards and yards of braided string that were needed. The people had taken plain bark thread and wrapped it with the colorful yellows and browns of grass from the high plateau. The skirt had to be created on me; it had to fit just right in order to stay on my hips, and there were no zippers or elastic inserts to help. The women began winding the string around and around my hips. For three hours they worked, adjusting and wrapping until each string hung just a little lower than the round before. Finally it was finished, and they were most delighted with their creation!

When I came to Kunga the yard around the bark cabin was nothing but a chaos of mud and rocks. Grass and weeds had long since disappeared under hundreds of trampling feet. I soon realized that a lawn was out of the question, so I settled for flower beds close to the house. A low fence around the flowers also served to keep the people back a little way from the windows and made their curious staring less obvious to us from the inside.

When I flew from Enarotali I brought flower cuttings with me. Those I planted in the vegetable garden, waiting for a time when essentials were less pressing. No one seemed to object to my flower beds until I sent my Ekari helper to the jungle to get some colorful native plants. Inadvertently he brought back a plant that was used in spirit appeasement by the Damals. The leading men came to Don asking, "Are these plants part of your religion? We see you have planted leaves we formerly used in spirit appeasement." For a while it looked as though all the flowers would have to go, in order not to offend some weaker brother, but in the end the Damals understood our motives and only the one plant was pulled out.

Always we needed to see each situation through their eyes. Although we wanted to stand firm in every teaching of the Bible, we did not want to incorporate our Western culture into their faith. In those first years of work in the Damal tribe none of us missionaries understood very much of the underlying ideas or evils of the native culture. It was the Damals themselves, guided by the Spirit of God, who brought forward and dealt with them item by item.

When Don had first observed the courtship sing he saw nothing wrong with it. The young people were fully chaperoned by their elders. *Every society needs a way for young people to meet and court,* he thought. So when the new believers first raised the question about its legitimacy for Christians, he believed they were being too strict. The men were past their own courting days. But the leaders persisted in their conviction. They said to Don, "You don't know what sin is ignited under the emotional stimulus of a courtship sing. It may or may not be consummated the next day, but the very thought is sin."

The young church did ban the courtship sing. In its place the youth saw each other on Sundays or at a feast.

For two months the unrepentant Namagu Damals watched their Christian Kunga cousins, and in every instance God provided completely for the needs of the Christians.

He brought the Taganit War to an end. When the Christians were sick, God made them well. They cut down the "devil" trees and God protected them. They planted taboo land and their gardens flourished. They had nothing to fear; their God could do anything.

Now the Namagu Damals were also ready to make the break. Kip led two hundred of his people as they threw their fetishes into the fire. To all who watched, God had proved Himself strong.

20
From Whence This Movement?

In his report to conference in July 1957 Don chronicled a year and a half of his missionary work in reaching the Damal people. He wrote of two exploratory trips and then the entrance into the Ilaga followed by the unbelievable response of the Damals. Without pausing, Don went on with population facts:

> Although twelve hundred Damals live in the Ilaga, they represent only ten percent of the total tribe. Perhaps four thousand live in the Beoga and six thousand south of the Puncak Jaya Range. The southern population center is the Jila Valley, just three days' walk from the Ilaga. Men have been coming over the mountains from the south since they have heard what is happening in the Ilaga. From their reports I have learned that the people in Jila are open to a missionary's coming, and most likely an airstrip site could be found. The Ilaga Damals agree they can take me to the Beoga Valley with no danger from the Taganit War. I could leave immediately for the Beoga if it were possible for someone to stay with Alice during my absence.

Further down in his report Don continued:

> Assuming the Beoga trip is to be in August, I would like to plan a trip to Jila in November. If the door to the Beoga should be closed during August, then I want to go to Jila at that time. . . . One missionary couple can handle the Damal work in the Ilaga once the airstrip and house construction are completed, but we need two more Damal missionary couples, one for the Beoga and another for Jila.

As I reread that old report, I wondered how Don thought it might have been accomplished, for Larsons were to leave for furlough that same month, and our furlough was due just four months later. But Don had the vision, and God had the resources to carry it out, although on a slightly different timetable than Don had outlined.

John and Helen Ellenberger arrived in the Ilaga in October to join us in the Damal work. They were newlyweds—married only five weeks before they set sail for New Guinea. John was born in Guinea, West Africa, to missionary parents who worked among tribal people with a background not too different from that of the Damals. John had completed six years of college work in theology, anthropology, and linguistics. His language work included two years at the Summer Institute of Linguistics, but his natural gifts in language learning even surpassed his training. He assimilated a language almost as easily as breathing and enjoyed every minute of the process.

Helen's parents were David and Muriel Ellison, lifetime missionaries to Cambodia. After graduating from Nyack Missionary Institute, Helen went on to earn her degree as a registered nurse. With their training and background as MKs (missionary kids), John and Helen were as well-seasoned in missionary life when they arrived in the Ilaga as most missionaries are after a full term of service.

The Ellenbergers' arrival in the Ilaga had none of the unending delays that had preceded our coming. The plan was for them to have a month of orientation at the Lakes before joining us. But when they arrived John was anxious to begin his work, and the pilot said, "We'd better fly them in now while the weather is dry. The strip may be closed again in a few weeks." At five o'clock one evening we heard on the radio, "The Ellenbergers are coming on the second flight tomorrow."

The first flight brought a load of hardboard for bedroom walls and a sheet of plywood for a tabletop. Our dining room table was only a folding table hardly big enough for our family of four, and now the Ellenbergers were to live with us. The bark cabin was already bulging at the seams, so we planned to ready one upstairs bedroom in the new house for them. The framework was up, the roof on, and in the one bedroom the flooring was laid, but the room had no walls. That afternoon Don and John nailed the hardboard onto the bedroom walls, we borrowed beds from the Larson's house, and John and Helen were at home with us.

The next day a *mo* feast was planned at a village an hour's walk from Kunga. John showed interest in attending, but Don was not free to accompany him. The solution—John and Helen set off by themselves to attend the feast. We found a Damal man to guide them there and home again. They carried a canteen of drinking water, and John had his note pad and pencil in hand, the badge of every true linguist. He was writing down the words and phrases he heard.

One day several men came to Don and asked him why he did not smoke. Did it have something to do with his religion? They knew that there were other nonmissionary *tuans* who did smoke. His answer was both yes and no. "Smoking or not smoking," he said, "is not mentioned in the Bible as part of what makes a man a Christian. This is why I haven't taught you about smoking before—because it is not in the same classification as fetishes, for example. But the Bible does give me a reason why I do not smoke. First Corinthians three tells us that the body of a Christian is the dwelling place of the Holy Spirit. Thus we should keep our bodies clean and in good shape."

At that point Don pointed to the black tar and soot covering the inside of the hut where they were sitting. "A man who smokes tobacco collects tar inside his lungs just like the roof of this house." The Damals nodded their heads in understanding.

Don went on. "Let me ask you a question. Is there any

difference in the way a nonsmoker climbs a mountain compared to a heavy smoker?"

They all had the same answer. "The heavy smoker has to rest frequently because he is out of breath. He coughs a lot, too."

"That is why I do not smoke," Don said. "I want to keep my body in the best health I can to serve God."

The teaching spread and before long a group of Christians burned their tobacco publicly. Although men, women, and children all smoked, the men had the hardest time breaking the habit, for they were usually heavier smokers.

Pneumonia was the number one killer in diseases among the Damals. They lived in a wet, cold climate without clothing to protect them or penicillin to combat the disease. When they stopped smoking there was a dramatic decrease in pneumonia cases. Perhaps ten years have been added to their life span. Today most cases of pneumonia in adults are among the few men who do smoke.

In less than a month after the Ellenbergers arrived in the Ilaga, Don was on the trail for the Beoga. The Damals felt sure it was safe to travel there, but when Don tried to sign up carriers no one wanted to go. Finally three Damal men and two women carried loads and set off with him into the unknown.

John Ellenberger and Sam joined the party for a half day just to see what the forest trail was like. John was enjoying the beauty of the forest and of course picking up lots of new words.

The path they took leading up the mountain to the Beoga was the same one used by some of the Beoga warriors as they fled after their defeat in the last battle of the Taganit War. It was overgrown now, from lack of use. On the way they passed nine skeletons. Those were evidently the remains of men who had died fleeing from that final battle, and no one had ever come back to properly cremate their remains. It is likely that Nanol and his brother Nil had fallen here. The party was shaken by what they saw, but they hurried on.

At dusk the next day they reached Wang-Be, the first village in the Beoga. The people wept with joy when they saw the Damal carriers, relatives they had not seen since before the war. The word soon rang out from village to village, "Our Ilaga cousins have brought a *tuan*. Come and see."

That night in the men's house, Kama-Kama, an older man who had carried from Kunga, told the story of the fetish burnings in the Ilaga. He gave his own testimony and continued with Bible stories. It all came from his heart, spontaneously. He had faced the possible dangers of going to the Beoga so he could share his newfound faith with his relatives, and they listened with open hearts. The first bridge of family ties had been crossed and the mighty movement toward God began. The next day everyone in the immediate area gathered for a service, and several chiefs from some distance were there too, taking in every word that Don and Kama-Kama spoke.

Back at Kunga things did not look so good, for Don did not respond on the radio when we called at the scheduled hour in the afternoon. On the fifth day when there was still no radio contact, plans were made for a Cessna to come and take John Ellenberger and two Kunga men up over the mountain to Beoga in hopes of locating Don from the air. That night after dark two carriers came in from Beoga with a note from Don. He had left one of the radio switches turned to the "on" position, and the battery was dead when he tried to broadcast. The plane search was canceled, but my anxiety for Don was not yet ended.

Three days later two Ekaris came with a detailed story of how Don had been shot. That story came from the Danis, so John and I went down to the Kunga village to check the Damal version. We concluded that it was only a rumor invented by the Danis, who were still very jittery about war reprisals.

From Wang-Be Don walked through Wung village, and then turned and went upriver. He was surprised to see how the population had been depleted by the war. The entire north side of the Beoga River, where the Ndugas had lived, was deserted. The people were also in much poorer health than in the Ilaga. All along the way Don gave penicillin injections for yaws. On one day alone he treated forty people for yaws, but he had nothing with him to help the many women who had huge goiters.

When Don arrived at the strip site he could hardly believe what he found. His little hut and the supplies inside had not been touched during the nineteen months since he left. They even brought him the cans of food that they had found in the forest some months after the airdrop. All they asked was that he give them the empty tins after he had eaten the food.

The airstrip site had grown up with six-foot-tall grass, but no one had replanted the area in gardens. The soil was gravel, well-drained with streams on both sides of the strip. There were no muddy spots—a very welcome contrast to the soft, wet ground they began with in the Ilaga.

Don surveyed the strip site again and then began working with the Damals in clearing and leveling the ground. Andy was left to supervise the work when Don returned to the Ilaga. He had taken that assignment as a ministry for the Lord and had pledged his loyalty to Don as a helper. Andy remained with Don when all the other Ekaris returned home; he learned to speak Damal and married a Damal woman. His talents were not great, but he used His gift of helps in building first the Ilaga airstrip and then others after that. His Christian testimony remained faithful. Truly, Andy left father and mother, brothers and sisters, for Jesus' sake and for the gospel.

The days and hours in the Ilaga were more than full with missionary activities for the four of us. As a rule we carried on our ministries individually because there was so much to be done. When there was strip work to be done or a plane to meet, either Don or John made the trip while the other worked on building the house, studying the language, or conducting midweek classes.

Inquirers' classes were held at four points during the week—two villages in the Namagu area and two near Kunga. Since the Larsons were on furlough we also had a burden to reach the Danis, who made up 75 percent of the Ilaga people. Half of the Damal men who burned their fetishes in the Namagu were married to Dani women, and those women joined their husbands in that decision. Only a few of the wives in the Kunga area were Danis, but a number of Damal women were married to Dani men and lived in our neighborhood. So we began two midweek classes in those Dani villages, using a chief who understood Damal to translate the lesson. Attendance averaged 120 each week. But there was not the responsiveness of entire groups that we had found among the Damals. Individuals were listening, though, and thinking about the claims of Christ.

Sundays were now the day set aside for church, and more and more people gathered at the one central service at Kunga. When the weather was good and there were no conflicting activities, the crowds reached 600 or more. Don was the preacher on Sunday morning until he began making trips to the Beoga. John, not wanting to turn the people away in Don's absence, read his first Damal sermon on the fourth Sunday after he arrived in the Ilaga.

John prepared his text in English, a simple Bible story with an application. Don translated it sentence by sentence into Indonesian, and Sam gave it back in Damal, speaking into the microphone of a tape recorder. From the tape John wrote out the text and with practice was able to be clearly understood by the Damals.

John, being the linguistic scientist that he is, saved the written texts in English and Damal of his first sermons. Some time later when he had become fluent in Damal he checked them for language accuracy and found they were correct. Although there were no Ekaris who were bilingual with Damal to serve as a language bridge for Don, God had prepared Sam in an unusual way in Indonesian, and through him the Damals heard the gospel clearly and accurately in their own tongue. That was another miracle in God's perfect timing.

When Helen arrived, Don was quick to turn over the medical work to her. With her easygoing temperament, she fitted beautifully into our team. No matter how dark the situation looked, Helen always pointed out something bright and positive that she could see. In the early months medical supplies were few, and most of her practice consisted of treating bad ax cuts, lancing boils, or giving injections for yaws. Helen always gave out medicine with the knowledge that it is the Lord who heals although He might use her training in the process. If a patient died, she did not blame herself, for after all, did not each one already belong to the Lord, and were they not all in His hands?

My activities included language study and being mother and homemaker in our now extended family of six. John, Don, and I had each taken midweek classes in the villages. I taught an inquirers' class a half hour's walk from our home. One Thursday it seemed I really was able to minister to the needs of a number of people. When I returned home I wrote a detailed account of the morning.

We were expecting a plane, and at 7:00 I turned on the radio and gave them a weather report—a dark, cloudy day. Other stations gave similar reports, and by 7:45 the pilot had canceled all flights for the day.

I sorted the laundry and left the boys to scrub the clothes by hand. Kathy and Joyce were already playing with their Damal friends when I put on my hiking boots and started up valley.

As soon as I reached the first house a village elder greeted me and said, "Come pray for my wife. I knew you would be coming, so I waited for you." He took me up to a house, and there was a sick Dani woman. They said she had been sick for three days with a bad cough, spitting blood and with pain in her chest. I prayed for her.

As I went on up the path I invited people to gather for the class. In the next village they told me there was a baby who had just died. Going in to see the mother, I found the house crowded with women who had come to comfort her. The baby was about fourteen months old—a very beautiful baby girl. It lay on a mat, and the mother sat in front of her, caressing the body and crying. She brushed the flies away with some leaves. I asked the mother if she would like me to pray, and immediately she said yes and stopped crying. At first I could not pray because I, too, was crying. I told the mother she could hope to see her baby again in heaven if she really loved Jesus, and that seemed to comfort her. I left with a heavy heart—weeping with those who weep.

At the next house a man asked me to pray for him, and I did; he seemed to have a cold. I also stopped in to visit the old blind man who always loves to have me come. Often they lead him down to the class. He is progressively showing more interest in the gospel.

Having gone back down to the main village yard I began to teach the lesson. The group was small, only forty-five, because the morning was so cold and damp. On a day like this it was unusual for even this many to leave the warmth of their fires. After class I tested four on their catechism questions, and they all passed.

I had time to reflect a bit as I slipped and slid through the mud on my way home. Was I the same Alice who in high school had been too shy to speak to anyone about Christ? The things I had done this morning, in the name of Jesus, were not within the scope of my natural talents. Yes, I *was* that same person, but God had called me to be a missionary. In each hour He gave me the necessary ability and courage to do His bidding.

After the Ellenbergers came we often discussed missionary strategy and laid plans to help build the infant church.

The only time we could find for those discussions was around the table and evenings after our girls were in bed. Each of us marveled that our approach to the work was so similar and that God had put us together as co-workers in the Damal tribe.

As others learned of this group response to the gospel, questions arose as to its genuineness and our handling of it. As a whole those questions had a positive effect, for they spurred us on to an examination of the work in order to find answers to them for ourselves.

When should the first converts be baptized? The traditional missionary approach was to wait for a year or two to test the sincerity of their decisions. That method was practiced in Africa where John grew up. We believed a more scriptural approach was to offer baptism as soon as the candidate offered a clear testimony in life and word as to his faith in Christ.

What about that group movement where the leading men made the decision to turn to Christ for all those under the umbrella of their leadership? We concluded that every decision in a Damal's life was a group decision, whether it was concerning a war, a feast, spirit appeasement, planting a garden, or sponsoring a marriage. The Damals burned their fetishes as a group, but their faith in Christ had to be an individual matter—rather like the child born into a Christian home who learns the teachings of the Bible through his parents' decision but still must come to a personal trust in Christ.

Could a man with more than one wife be baptized? What about the women involved in such a marriage? Chief Den and a number of other men who had led their people in following the Lord had plural wives. Traditional missions dictated that a man must divorce every wife except his first before he was baptized. We spent many hours considering that question—both from the teaching of the New Testament and the culture of the Damals. We concluded that the Bible teaches each man should have only one wife and that no man with two wives could take leadership in the church. However, divorce would be an even greater wrong for a converted polygamist than for him to remain in the married state he was in when he heard the gospel. We found no biblical grounds on which to deny him baptism. If a man were to divorce his plural wives, those women would be forced to live in unwed sin or become the second wives of unbelievers, for Damal culture provided no means of support for an unmarried woman.

As we looked at what was happening in the Ilaga we were continually drawn back to one basic fact: God's time clock had struck the hour. This was not man's doing. Although many different people had played an important part in what was taking place, God had drawn them all together in His time. It was His Spirit who was changing lives.

In November we asked the inquirers who wanted to follow the Lord in baptism to come and have their names written down. Each one who came was questioned briefly to see if he or she understood the basic teachings of the Bible. A month later, following a second trip to Beoga, Don and John met with a group of village elders to consider the testimony of each candidate. Every person approved had a positive testimony of his faith and was not violating God's commands concerning his relationship with his fellowmen. He had burned his fetishes and no longer ate pork sacrificed in spirit worship. A number were approved on every point except one, and those were told to wait until a later time for baptism.

The Damals were more cautious in approving candidates than we missionaries might have been, but basically that was healthy. Being a close-knit society, the Damals not only acted as a group, but the affairs of each person were community knowledge also, even in distant villages. A man from the Namagu, who later applied for baptism, had burned his fetishes and answered all the questions, but the examining elders turned him down. Several months before the fetish burning he had secretly taken two of his fetishes to a southern valley for safekeeping and had burned only the remaining fetish. He tried to hide his actions, but he was found out.

Fifty-one men and women were baptized on the first Sunday in January 1958. Among the group was Chief Den and his son, Sam; two Dani women married to Damals; Andy, the Ekari who had become a missionary helper; and Kama-Kama, the man who first shared his faith with the Beoga people. Most gave a word of testimony before they were buried in the waters of baptism. The joy on their faces confirmed to all that their lives had been changed. A crowd of seven hundred witnessed the service, and after it was over many came asking to have their names written on the candidate list for the next baptismal service.

This movement was of God, and no man could stop it— even the gates of hell could not prevail against it. He was building His church among the Damals.

21

Hai Comes to the Beoga

"The hearts of the Beoga people are wide open to receive the gospel. I want to go back on another trip. I promised them I'd come soon." Those were Don's first words when he returned from his trip to the Beoga.

My response was, "Then I want to go with you." We asked our field leader, Ken Troutman, for permission to make the trip, and he agreed provided we take a transceiver radio with us to keep in contact.

Don consulted the Damals and decided we would visit all the areas of the Beoga this time, for he had only traveled through half of the valley on his trip in November. All the Beoga people had been cut off from contact with the Ilaga since the Taganit War had begun. That included a large group of Damals living near the junction of the Beoga and Ilaga rivers. One way to get there was to follow the Ilaga River over the trail that Gordon Larson and Don had taken in 1954 when they were raided. The Damals advised against that, suggesting a shorter trail up and over the mountain.

Before we started out I asked Helen Ellenberger to teach me how to give injections of penicillin for treating yaws. Nursing was certainly not my interest. Even in a minor family accident it was Don who stopped the bleeding and bandaged the cut finger. But I knew that yaws was epidemic in the Beoga, and if others could learn to give shots, then I could, too.

First I learned to draw the proper number of "cc's" into the syringe, according to the estimated weight of the patient. The penicillin was in an oil base so that its potency would be released slowly over a period of days. The oil was difficult to draw into the syringe, but I mastered that part.

The injection was given in the buttocks. At least the area of injection offered no problem, since the Damals wore no obstructing clothing. I can still hear Helen's instructions to me, for I repeated them to myself each time I gave an injection. "Determine the upper, outer quadrant of the buttocks, and thrust the needle into the muscle with a quick jab—don't hesitate!" The Damals made excellent patients— only the babies cried or showed any discomfort. The others did not mind the pain of the needle compared to the life-saving potential of the penicillin.

We packed our supplies, cutting as many corners as possible. The tent and sleeping bags were packed, but we took no air mattresses. A pile of grass could be substituted for them. The cooking kit, canteens, and two changes of clothing went into the trail tins along with tins of corned beef, oatmeal, powdered milk, and margarine to supple-ment the native food we expected to get along the way. Altogether we had eight carrier loads of thirty-five pounds each, including the radio and battery.

We planned to leave the first of December, hoping to be home by Christmas. Join me on our trip through the pages of my diary.

December 2, 1957. It looked as though we were not going to leave as planned because most of the carriers backed out at the last minute. Don said, "Let's go as far as the airstrip and see if we can find more carriers." So we said good-bye to Kathy and Joyce and left them with the Ellenbergers. Parting was hard for me because I had never before left our girls overnight. By 10:00 we started up the mountain with an assortment of carriers; a man and his wife each carrying a load; Sam, who was pressed into going because no one else would go; and Pen-Me, the boy who first carried Don's canteen when he entered the Ilaga and more recently had worked in my kitchen washing dishes and peeling vegetables. After two hours Sam feared to go any farther, so Don took his load and we continued climbing. Of all the carriers only Pen-Me stayed with us for the entire trip; the others were afraid of war involvements and left us when we got to the first villages.

After two hours of delightful walking through the forest we came to a steep cliff area. Here we went up on a 60 to 65 degree grade, and at some places even an 85 degree grade. Don had to pull me up where the toeholds and hand-gripping roots were too far apart. I was thankful for my hobnailed boots and glad we were going up the cliff and not down. Rain began, turning to hail as we reached the 10,000-foot top.

The rain stopped, and we sloshed through a barren wonderland of peat and moss with stunted bushes and strange growths all colored in yellow and browns. At 3:00 we came to a campsite of eight large houses and decided to make camp for the night. The Beoga warriors had built these houses eight months earlier on their way to attack the Ilaga.

December 3. Today was the hardest day of the entire trip. I hiked 9½ hours. After two hours of walking on roots and logs we came to a stream that cut through steep mountains. For 3½ hours we were in and out of the water, climbing and sliding over boulders often taller than I was. Finally the trail left the stream, went up a cliff, and then up and down along the side of the mountain. I grasped for footing and clung to the roots and vines with my hands. Almost every step I took offered new danger of falling down the mountainside into the jungle below. There was no place to sit down and rest, much less any place to camp for the night. We had to go on. Late in the afternoon we reached the first village, where the people received us with open arms. I had blisters on my feet and was so exhausted I couldn't eat a thing that night, but I knew that would pass. I had reached the Beoga people, 1200 Damals living in this mountain pocket, and they had welcomed me—the first white woman they had ever seen.

December 4. We moved down into the center of the population on a path through gardens that were so steep I could hardly keep from falling even with my hobnailed boots, a walking stick, and the steadying hand of a Damal man. I wondered how Damals could plant gardens in a place like that. We must have dropped a thousand feet in an hour. Six hundred people were waiting for us in Oga village, and Don had the privilege of telling them the gospel story for the first time. They listened eagerly. We were showered with gifts of food—far more than we could use.

When I started giving injections for yaws I could hardly believe what I saw. Huge running ulcers ate away at their bodies. Some had fingers and toes missing. One woman's breast was almost gone, and the face of her nursing baby was covered with ulcers. Ten women and children were so near death that their relatives had to carry them to me. Many two-year-olds had four or five sores two inches across—eating away at their little bodies. One man's nose and lips were gone, and the ulcers eating at his eyes would soon have made him blind. That day I gave 120 injections of penicillin. What a joy to know that within ten days their bodies would all be cleared of infection.

Don preached to the crowd again in the afternoon. I have never seen such friendly, helpful people. They knew we came because we love them—and we do! They loved us and we loved them for Christ's sake. Don taught them our two hymn-chants. They sang all night—such rich, beautiful chants. I didn't sleep well, partly because of the singing and partly because I knew we would leave them in the morning. I longed to stay and tell them more of the gospel. They were all smiles and kindness to us! My heart goes out to them in love. Oh, that they might hear more and believe.

December 5. A group of 200 went with us to the top of the first mountain, marching and singing and saying, "We love you." It was so hard to leave them. All day we hiked up and down a mountain covered with jungle. At 3:30 we reached a small village. At first the people were afraid, for they had never seen white people before; but soon I was giving injections for yaws, Don was treating infected eyes, and then everyone sat down to listen to Don tell the story of Jesus.

Their fears were gone, and they listened with interest.

December 6. We traveled on—up and down over fallen trees, dense jungle, and landslides. Our carriers were all Beoga men now. The Ilaga people had left us, fearing revenge from the Taganit War. As the carriers walked along they sang, expressing their excitement and joy in our coming. In their song they gave Don and me new Damal names: *Damal-Neme* for Don, which means "Friend of the Damals," and *Damal-In* for me, which means "Damal woman." The Beoga people had adopted us, and from then on everyone called us by our Damal names.

> We love Damal-In; we love Damal-Neme,
> Let's all pray; let's go to school,
> No more war, no more serving Satan,
> We love all the Damal people.

In the afternoon we climbed a steep hill, found a few houses, and drained the last bottle of penicillin. Going on we came to a large village—Piloma. I was covered with mud, wet from the falling rain, and nursing blisters, but those were forgotten with the reception the people gave us—the first missionaries they had ever seen. I have never met more friendly and loving people, anywhere!

December 7. We declared the day to be "Sunday." It really wasn't, but who besides us would know the difference? It gave me a chance to rest my aching muscles and wash our clothes. Don preached three times to a crowd of two to three hundred.

Chief Kawa, a man with five wives, joined our party at Piloma. Don did not recognize his importance at the time. He along with a growing number of other men wanted to learn more. Since we would not stay longer in their village, they decided to travel with us.

(When Don asked about the trail upriver, the men never mentioned the dangerous trail that led to Wung village. Instead they directed us to cross the Beoga river at Piloma and hike upvalley on the north side. Don had never been over any of the trail we had taken from the Ilaga, so we simply followed their directions.)

December 8. At 6:30 I left Don to pack up camp, and I
started down the trail to the river. We decided that I had
more energy for hiking in the morning hours and maybe if I
started earlier I could get to camp before the afternoon rains
began.

I found the Beoga River to be a river indeed. It was more
than twice as large as the Ilaga River where we crossed. The
rattan bridge was 125 feet long and swung 40 feet above the
roaring water below. No one could help me cross this bridge;
I had to go it alone, for the footing was only four inches
wide. Heavy rattan vines served as handrails on each side,
and small vines were laced every foot or two to help keep
the walkway and handrails together. Even with the lacing
the handrails varied in height between my waist and my
shoulders. I concentrated on putting my feet in a firm
position, one in front of the other, and ignoring the water
that was below. Everyone was glad when I reached the other
side.

We came to a village midmorning where Don had
planned to camp for the night, but since it was still early we
held a service and continued upvalley. About noon we
crossed a huge landslide. It was still active, and I was glad to
be across it. [We were now walking in abandoned potato
gardens left by the Ndugas during the Taganit War. Kelandi
village had been here, too.] Don asked our guides how
much further to the bridge, and they said we were almost
there. I could see the Beoga River not far below us, and I
noticed three logs lashed together go bobbing down the
river. I wondered where they came from, for usually you do
not see anything in the river water.

In ten minutes we came to the Kelandi bridge site, but
there was no bridge there. The logs I had seen float down the
river were part of the temporary bridge the men were
building. I took one look at the men working on both sides
of the river and said to Don, "The bridge is gone. I *cannot*
cross the river here." When Don consulted the Damals, they

assured him that in a short time the men would have a bridge ready for crossing. He asked about another bridge upriver, and they said, "The Jugu bridge is a long way upriver, and the trail is very bad between here and the bridge."

Don turned to me and said, "We don't have any choice. We'll have to cross here." So I sat down on the ground and watched the men work. On the opposite side near the edge there was a dead tree lodged in the water. Men were building a pole walkway from the bank to the tree branches and another one from the tree to the side where I sat. As I watched my fears mounted. I could not swim, but I also knew that the best of swimmers would be lost if they fell in here where the water dashed over boulders in the river bed. I kept thinking, *If I'm going to get home to Kathy and Joyce in time for Christmas, I have to cross this river. There is no other way.*

Soon the men had the three poles across the river and they were out over the water lashing them together. They seemed no more afraid than if they were working over a mud hole. A strong, young man came over the bridge and offered to help me cross. [That was my first meeting with Kok-Me, but it was still to be many months before I learned to know him by name.]

I started out with the young man grasping my arm in front and another man holding my arm in back. The poles bent to within a foot of the water with our weight, and the black, boiling water rushing under my feet brought a feeling of dizziness. I prayed and tried to concentrate on finding my footing on the irregular logs. When we reached the branches of the tree in the river I wanted to hold onto a branch, but I could not free my arm from my helper's grasp. He was not about to let me fall in the river. Finally I told him what I wanted, and he allowed me to hold onto the branch for a minute before we continued on across.

A crowd of people gathered on the south side of the river and escorted us on to [Wolo's] village of Tingil. There Don preached to two hundred people, after which we joined them in a greens feast before setting up camp for the night.

[While preparing to write this book, Kok-Me and I were discussing my crossing the makeshift bridge, and I learned that there *had* been another bridge upriver less than an hour from where we crossed. The river cuts a narrow passage between two rock cliffs and a ten-foot log spans the crossing there. I have now crossed that bridge a number of times. The Damals did not tell us about the bridge then, for it crosses upriver from Tingil, and they figured we would have bypassed the greens feast they had prepared for us. How typically Damal to shade the truth for their own ends. Just think, had I known of that other bridge I would have missed my most unforgettable experience on the trail!]

December 9-11. We hiked upvalley to the airstrip site at Milavak and found three hundred people waiting there for Don to hold a service. The people showered us with gifts of food. They knew we could not possibly eat it all, but they were expressing their love to us through their gifts. A delegation came and presented me with three female pigs— very nice ones. They said, "These are for you, Damal-In, to start your pig herd. We want you to come and live here. We'll take care of the pigs for you until you come and take them yourself. When will you bring your two girls and come to live with us?" I was overwhelmed. These people had given us everything they had.

While Don worked on the airstrip, making payments for completed work, I went to the village to be with the women and gossip the gospel. Although my language was very faltering, they understood me because they *wanted* to understand with all their hearts. One night they all marched and sang on the airstrip until it started to rain at 3:00 A.M.

December 12-13. We packed up part of our gear and hiked to the top village in the valley. The people gathered, and we held two services. In the afternoon before a very nice greens feast held in our honor, the men gathered for discussions with Don. Here they really talked out the crucial issues facing them—witchcraft and its threat from the women, accepting the gospel as a new way of life, and building the airstrip.

December 14. Back at the airstrip we treated the day as Sunday and invited everyone to gather for a day of church. Five hundred people came for the three services. In one sermon Don wanted to challenge them as individuals to consider following Christ. Not expecting a response, he asked them, "Which way will you choose, Satan's way or the Lord's way?" In unison they said, "We want to follow the Lord." The crowds expressed their joy by marching and chanting between services. Three village headmen took Don off into the privacy of the tall grass to talk. For over an hour they discussed burning their fetishes, deciding that they would wait until Don's next visit—but that he should come back soon.

December 15. We packed up and said good-bye. It was hard to leave—many women came and lovingly told me good-bye. We reached Tingil before noon and had an afternoon service. That night in the men's house we talked to an old gray-haired man. [Years later we learned that he was Ambo, the boy who ran away to Hitadipa when the villagers were planning to offer him as a human sacrifice to the spirits.] "Will you come back before I die?" Ambo asked. "I want to learn this new talk, the gospel, and I want to go to heaven." The old man continued, "My father taught me about *hai*. Once there were people who knew the way to the place of *hai*. They went there, but left us behind—here on earth where men keep dying. In the future Damals will learn the way to *hai*. My father taught me this song." The old man sang softly,

> O we pe-ai, O we pe-e
> We long to be joined with *hai*
> Let's be united in hope
> We look for the covenant of our people
> Let's join in expectation
> E mo go-ni E mo go mi-e

December 16. Another "Sunday" with three services. We prayed for many sick people who came requesting prayer. The Tingil people served a greens and sweet potato feast, and we added salt. All day long people came asking us to teach them to pray, and we taught them a short prayer. [Wolo, Kok-Me, and Meyong were all there, but we did not yet know them by name.]

December 17. It was so hard to say good-bye to the inquirers. I feel many will really stand in the light they have. We left at 7:15 and had a service in the villages on the way to Wang-Be. I'm getting anxious to be home for Christmas.

December 18. After breakfast we packed and condensed our loads, planning to spend the night in a village near the trail to the Ilaga. Don held three services, and the people had a pit-cooked feast for everyone. In talking to a woman with a huge double goiter I said, "In heaven there are no goiters—yours will be gone." Later two men of her family brought the same woman to me and asked that I give her a shot for her goiter. I explained that I had no medicine to help her. Then she turned to the men and said, "In heaven my goiter will be gone."

Later, when the men were singing between services, a woman sitting next to me said, "We are so happy to hear the gospel—that is why the men are singing and dancing. I want to put away all my sin—lying, stealing, witchcraft, and adultery—and follow Jesus. I want to go to heaven. I'm excited with joy."

Many of the chiefs had followed us up the valley and down again. They made speeches after Don preached, exhorting the people to put away all fetish worship and follow the Lord. We came to know Chief Kawa as an unusual man. He was a war leader as well as a shrewd business man and had five wives to prove his financial prowess: three Damal women, one Dani, and one Dem. [Kawa is the only Damal we ever met who had more than three wives.] He asked Don to listen to his recitation of a sermon Don had preached at several different villages on our trip. He gave the sermon without error. Kawa had developed his memory in his business dealing and spirit appeasement rituals. Now he used his keen mind to grasp the gospel. After we left he traveled around repeating the sermons he had learned from Don and exhorting people to follow the Lord.

In the late afternoon we walked for an hour and a half to a village on the edge of Wang-Be. A large crowd of people went with us singing all the way. No rain fell until after dark.

December 19. We were up with the first ray of light, and at 6:30 I left Don to finish packing. We fought our way through heavy brush at first, but then we were in the forest and the trail under the trees was quite open. We climbed steadily, reaching 10,000 feet at 11:45. There were no trees at that elevation. We reached the 11,200 foot summit at 12:30, having climbed 5000 feet in six hours. I kept up with the carriers all day and sometimes got ahead of them. The other side was a gradual slope for an hour and then down through jungle for two more hours. Once when the clouds lifted we saw the dazzling snow on the mountain range south of the Ilaga. We made camp at 4:00 at 9,500 feet. It was really cold that night!

December 20. I was on the trail by 6:30. We passed through sections of woods and then sandy areas. We saw the plane go over midmorning. We cut a Christmas tree before leaving the forest. By 12:30 we reached the first population and crossed the Ilaga River and were home by 2:30. It was so good to see Kathy and Joyce, and were they ever excited to see us! Our two-and-a-half-year-old, Joyce, is talking more, but only in Damal.

At supper we heard an interesting story about Kathy and Joyce. Damal children enjoy catching mungs—a little green bug related distantly to a grasshopper. The mung is roasted a bit in the fire and then eaten. Only the children eat them— adults do not like their strong flavor. Kathy and Joyce ate

mungs with their Damal friends. Being an MK himself, John
Ellenberger enjoyed watching the ways in which our girls
were so like little Damal children.

John suggested, "Why don't you bring some mungs home,
and Aunt Helen will cook them for you with scrambled
eggs." The girls thought that was a great idea. Helen fried the
mungs and then scrambled them with the last eggs she had.
At the table Kathy looked at them and passed them to Joyce.
Joyce took one bite and said to Uncle John in her best
Damal, "I don't want them. You eat them." And so he did.

December 21. I baked three fruitcakes, and Kathy and
Joyce helped make gingerbread men. We all decorated the
tree in the evening.

December 22. Sunday. John preached in church today,
and Don gave a report of our trip. In the evening the six of us
sang Christmas carols.

December 23. Don spent the morning checking the work
on the airstrip. In the evening we all made Christmas candy
together—three kinds—and sang Christmas carols.

December 24. Five-year-old Kathy was working in her
room and would not let me come in unless she put her work
away first. She said she was making a Christmas present for
us. She came to lunch late, explaining that she just could
not stop in the middle of her work. She wrapped her gift
and put it under the tree—a very nice pot holder, woven on
a loom with colored loop string.

Everyone dressed in his best, and we had an early supper
by candlelight. After Don read the Christmas story from the
Bible, we began opening the gifts. I've never seen such a pile
of presents. Packages had come from the Grandmas and
Grandpa and two large boxes from the Bend, Oregon,
Alliance Church—fun gifts and clothing for each of us, too.
The gifts came in pairs for the girls, including two 18-inch
dolls with rooted hair.

December 25. Christmas dinner was roast rabbit with
dressing, candied sweet potatoes, and beans, carrots, and
tomatoes from our garden. Fruitcake was dessert. Our hearts

are overflowing with praise to God. Our family is together in the Ilaga this Christmas, and hundreds of Damals have decided to join us in following our Lord and Savior.

22

The Sweet Potato of Life

The next step to be taken with the growing body of believers was serving Communion to those who had been baptized. The question facing us was, What should we use for the elements of Communion? Should we provide bread and grape juice in some form, as some missionaries had done? The four of us discussed the matter and saw some problems in that. The Damals might well be thinking about this strange food of the foreigner rather than of the Body of Christ. Would they feel there was magical significance coming from the white man? Also, we could foresee hundreds of Damals taking Communion, and the missionaries' supplies might not always be available.

In Jesus' day bread was the staff of life, and wine was a common drink. The staff of life for the Damal was the sweet potato, and they had no drink but water. However, they did have a wild raspberry which could be substituted for the fruit of the vine. Thus we chose the sweet potato and raspberry juice to serve as the elements of Communion.

John Ellenberger was also thinking ahead to the translation of Scripture and the passage where Jesus said, "I am the bread of life." To translate this, "I am the foreigner's food of life," might suggest heresy; but to say, "I am the sweet potato of life," would speak to the hearts of the Damals through their own culture.

The Communion service was announced, and after Sunday morning church all the baptized believers crowded into Den's hut to partake of the Lord's Supper. The sweet potato was broken and passed around on a banana leaf, and the raspberry juice was served in a Damal drinking gourd from which each drank in turn. In that setting Communion was not a foreign ritual to those Damal Christians. It was the sacrament established by Jesus Himself.

Both sacraments, baptism and Communion, had a profound meaning for the Damals from the very beginning. True, they were not distracted with foreign elements in the service, but the reason for their understanding goes beyond that. Those sacraments are directly taught in the Bible, commanded by God for all Christians. The Holy Spirit enlightened the hearts of the primitive people, and they understood because they had a sincere desire to know the truth.

In other ways the Damals still did not understand us as foreigners. Don had two reasons in mind when he built our bark cabin with an upstairs. First it gave us twice as much floor space for the number of sheets of aluminum roofing, and second it gave us a place of privacy from the curious eyes and the feeling fingers that were always with us. No Damals, except my kitchen helper when he swept the bedroom floors, were allowed upstairs. The people could not understand our need for privacy. Nothing from birth to death was private in their villages. They reasoned that we must have some secret thing hidden up there.

A rumor got started that I had given birth to a baby and that it was hidden upstairs. Visitors had heard the crackling noise that the metal roof made as it expanded from the heat of the midday sun. That, they said, was the baby crying. It was obvious to them that I did not have the protruding stomach of a pregnant woman, but neither did I have the silhouette of a Damal with no waistline or distinct hips. Perhaps my clothing further confused them. At any rate, the rumor was that I had carried my pregnancy in back and had kept the birth of the baby a secret.

Those same Damals, who were confused about the ways of the *tuan*, were amazing us with their knowledge of God's Word. Many of the Christians, and especially the men, could retell quite accurately the Bible stories given with the

Sunday sermons. One man, in an examination for baptism, was asked the question, "When is Jesus coming?" He replied, "After all the people of the world hear the gospel—the Danis and the Ndugas, and the Dems and the Monis." Those, to him, were all the people of the world. The answer he gave, although correct, was not in the catechism answers, and none of us missionaries could remember even mentioning that aspect of truth. The man must have picked it up from a passing comment in a sermon.

More and more people came asking to be baptized. They had burned their fetishes and put away their old way of life, but some had not learned enough of the positive teachings of Christianity. We missionaries believed that lack fell back on us, and we went out even more diligently teaching in the villages. Each week John and Helen walked the two hours to the Namagu to teach, Don went an hour upvalley to a receptive Dani village, and I went to the villages a half hour's walk behind Kunga. In January and February we had two more baptismal services. When believers were ready to follow the Lord in baptism, we thought it was important not to keep them waiting.

In all of our work with the Damals, speaking their language accurately was critical to their understanding our message. One day John Ellenberger was going over the language material that I had written. There were lots of blank spots in my understanding, and one of those involved a number of short words that seemed to have two or even three completely different meanings. For example *kop* means "place" or "area," and *kop* also means "spear." John checked that out with an informant and came up with the pronouncement that Damal is a tonal language. *Kop* meaning *place* has low tone, and *kop* meaning *spear* has high tone. To the Damals they are two completely different words because of the tone given the word as it is spoken in the sentence.

In time John completed this analysis of the Damal tonal system, the only language in all of the mountain tribes that is tonal. It has three tones and a glide. The language is full of one syllable words, and 25 percent of those are minimal pairs—only the tone differentiates the meaning of the word. Besides the complications of tone, the verb system is very intricate. Several hundred forms can be built on each verb stem by adding prefixes, suffixes, and infixes, and each time the meaning is changed. For a Westerner that makes learning to speak Damal more difficult than learning any of the European languages.

One of John's first tasks was to devise a phonetic alphabet, one in which each sound was represented by one letter and each letter represented only one sound. For example, in Damal the letter *a* always represents the sound in our English word *father*, never the *a* found in *cat* or *day*. With an alphabet, John began work on his first primer to teach the Damals to read their own language. Leaves would *talk* for Damals just as they did for *tuans*.

Five weeks after our trip to the Beoga, Don was back on the same trail again. That was his last trip to the Beoga before our furlough, which began in April of 1958. The people gathered in Ogam, and for two days they listened as Don preached to them, explaining the way of following Jesus. They talked of burning their fetishes, but Don suggested they wait until the next missionary visit. In the meantime they should tie the fetishes up and only pray to the Lord.

At the next village Don found a group of Ndugas waiting for him. They were men from the Sinak Valley, who had come four days by trail to hear the new message. In the Taganit War they fought on the Mudip side and still could not visit the Ilaga. Everything that Don said was translated into Nduga, and there were also some men from still another untouched tribe—the Dems—who heard for the first time.

Don's next stop was Piloma, the home of Chief Kawa. Kawa was not there, for he had gone to Sinak to witness of his new faith. He wanted to share it with the Danis there who had been his allies in the Taganit War. The Piloma people told of how Kawa had put away all spirit worship and was praying before each meal. He had stopped smoking and chewing betel nut. Because of Kawa's testimony the Piloma people decided to burn their fetishes. Theirs was the first fetish burning in the Beoga, but more were soon to follow.

From Piloma, Don took the trail on the south side of the river up past Wung village to Wang-Be. John Ellenberger was at Wang-Be waiting for him. John had left the Ilaga a week after Don and had come over the trail directly to Wang-Be.

The Wang-Be people could hardly wait for Don to return so they could burn their fetishes and publicly declare their faith in Christ. The scene was repeated in each village center as Don and John moved up the valley. From Piloma upriver 80 percent of the people burned their fetishes. Those Damals had learned to pray on our last trip, and prayer had become a very important part of their lives. Their knowledge of the Bible was very limited, but I believe God honored their faith because they obeyed every bit of light as it came to them.

Back in the Ilaga, Helen and I were having some adventures of our own. The letter that I wrote to my parents on February 9, 1958, best tells the story.

> We expected to have a bad time with Danis stealing when both Don and John were out of the valley. A number of things were taken when John and Helen were here alone on our last trip, and the Danis have continued to become more bold. I've lost at least four knives off my table in the last two months. Those were wedding gifts from Uncle Karl and Aunt Bertha. This week I caught a Dani in the act and got the knife back. The Damals also returned another knife they retrieved, but the Dani had already sharpened the cutting edge to use it for cutting up a pig. [I still have that sharpened knife today, and when I put it on my table it brings back lots of memories.]
>
> On Thursday night there was a full moon. At midnight

Helen awoke to see a man standing beside her bed. She screamed and he ran—evidently he was after the mirror on the wall but didn't get anything. The Ekaris who live nearby came running, but the man was already gone. Before going back to bed she locked her door with the makeshift chain and padlock—she hadn't bothered earlier.

The next night a little noise awoke me at 3:00 A.M. I called the Ekaris, and we found a hole in the storage shed wall, where our thief had cut the vines that held the wall together. We don't know if he got anything or not, but all our tools, nails, and extra food were in the shed. In the morning Helen and I boarded up the windows in the third bedroom in the big house and fixed the lock so it would work. We moved all the food there. Then I asked a Damal boy to sleep in the storage shed. This morning at 1:00 A.M. the boy sounded the alarm of the thief's arrival. That Dani must have been surprised! He was gone by the time the Ekaris arrived.

We are most happy to have outwitted that thief last night— it must have been the same man every night. The boy will continue to sleep in the toolshed. Today after church there were speeches about it, and Den was very concerned. If I thought you would worry I wouldn't write this—so please don't. I just hope this thief lets me sleep all night tonight!

It was on that same Sunday that I was the "preacher" in church. Don and John were both in the Beoga, so either I spoke or there was no church. To illustrate my talk I made stick figure drawings.

The Damals were not able to look at a picture and understand it as we do. Pictures made no more sense to them than letters on a page. I knew if I used flannelgraph to illustrate my story they would never recognize the figures as men and women. The only picture a Damal ever drew was a stick figure drawing of a lizard, drawn with charcoal on the wall of his house. I do not know if my Damal congregation understood my drawings, but they certainly listened very quietly—all 450 of them.

The guardian angel of the Lord was with us another day, too. Kathy and Joyce had gone out to play after lunch. Later I wanted them to go with me to visit a village, so I started calling for them. When I got no answer I went down to Kunga village, but they were not there. Someone said they were at the Kunga River. I assumed they meant they were down in that direction, as the girls were strictly forbidden to go near the river. The Kunga River is a large mountain stream, too swift for me to wade in places. I continued on down the path, and there I found them both with their shoes off, wading on the edge of white water rapids. Worst of all, they were alone, without the usual helping hands of Damal friends. Kathy's first words were, "How did you know I was here?" I knew in my heart that God had sent me. After I recovered from my fright I spanked them both—the only real spanking I ever gave Kathy. She remembers it to this day, and has never disobeyed like that again.

With our plans progressing to leave on furlough, we were under pressure to finish the work on the permanent house—at least to the point that the Ellenbergers could set up housekeeping. We were expecting an Ekari who had served as a carpenter's helper to be flown into the Ilaga, but just as the men left for the Beoga word came that he would not be coming. It was obvious that if the two men stopped their missionary work to build the house, Damals needing spiritual help would be turned away. Helen and I had a plan. We would put the boards on the downstairs walls ourselves, using two Ekaris to do the heavy work.

The boards that we had to work with were sawed by hand. They were neither straight nor smooth, and the width and thickness varied with each board. Our aim was to nail the boards on securely to keep out any night visitors and at the same time to leave no cracks for peepholes. Helen and I took turns working with the two Ekaris. We planned which board would go on next, measured it, squared the end, and then checked to see that it was level. Our helpers did the actual sawing and hammering. When our husbands returned from the Beoga we had put on the downstairs walls all around the house.

Five men came from the Beoga to attend our Witness School. We were delighted with that prospect, because later they could return and teach their people what they had learned. But on Sunday the church service was disrupted when nearly three hundred Taganit warriors burst into the village yard, all painted with red and black pig grease and brandishing spears, bows, and arrows. One Dani after another made a speech, running back and forth and punctuating his remarks with shouts of anger and threats to throw his spear. The Damals were not armed, so they had no defense except prayer—and pray they did. Finally the warriors left, saying, "We will let you Beoga people go, but see to it that no more of your people come here, and no Ilaga Damals are to go to the Beoga." After that episode the five students were afraid to remain any longer and returned home.

The three-week Witness School began with lots of enthusiasm—the very first school for the Damals. Everyone was invited to attend, and three hundred turned out on the first day. We missionaries were as excited as the Damals and had been preparing our lessons for some weeks. The subjects taught were life of Christ, instruction in prayer, church organization, and a class in singing Christian songs to native chant-tunes. John Ellenberger had his first primer ready to teach reading. The Damals thought they would learn this new art of reading in five easy lessons. Although we spent a lot of time each day on reading, it did not work that way, and some even stopped coming to school in their disappointment.

Witness School was going on in the mornings, and doors, windows, and a kitchen counter were going into the house in the afternoons, and we were packing to leave on furlough. Don and John were also meeting with village elders to examine the life and testimony of baptismal candidates. On Saturday the four of us each went in different directions to check on the Bible knowledge of the men and women who had been approved.

Our last Sunday in the Ilaga before furlough was a wonderful day. Six hundred gathered in the Kunga village yard for church, and then, with marching and singing, everyone moved to the baptismal site. Forty-four men and women followed their Lord in the waters of baptism. Again we went back to the village, this time for a communion service. With the newly baptized there were too many for Den's house alone, so a second men's house was also filled with believers. A spirit of love for the Lord was in our midst as we partook of the sweet potato and raspberry juice—in remembrance of our Lord until He comes.

Can this really be true? we asked. Eighteen months earlier Don had finally reached the Ilaga, and already we were sharing the Lord's Supper with 130 baptized Damals. Yes, it was real. God's Spirit witnessed with our spirits that we were all one in Christ.

Early the next morning we hiked once more across the valley to the airstrip. A large crowd of Damals were there to see us off. They showered us with presents of beads and shells and woven belts—gifts from their very hearts. We said good-bye, promising to come back. When we came we would go to the Beoga and teach the people who had so recently won our hearts. As we left the Ilaga we thought it would be for just a year, but God had a different timetable in mind. The Cessna came and took us aboard to fly east to the Baliem Valley. In every direction we saw sources of valleys filled with still thousands of tribal people who knew nothing of Christ the Savior.

PART 3

23
Two Thousand Amens

The single engine Cessna took off from an airfield nestled in the jungle at the coastal settlement of Nabire and flew out over the ocean to gain altitude. Then pilot George Boggs turned the plane back over the jungle and headed toward Enarotali and the Lakes en route to the Ilaga.

Twenty months had passed since our family left for furlough. On our trip to the States Don did not feel well, and when he went in for a medical examination the doctor discovered he had a new case of infectious hepatitis. Every two months I drove Don to the doctor for tests, but there was very little change. His orders were for complete bed rest, and for some time Don was so exhausted he could do nothing else. Although our doctor was a competent physician he had little sympathy for our missionary work. On one visit he used some rather strong language and then said, "Mrs. Gibbons, your husband has permanent liver damage. If you don't want to become a young widow, you'd better forget about going back to New Guinea."

The Damals had been counting the new moons until our planned return, and then John Ellenberger gave them the news that Don had a "liver sickness," and that he could not come back unless God healed him. They understood something of infectious hepatitis, for occasionally their people had the disease. Even Kok-Me had had hepatitis as a child. However, it is rarely a serious disease to the native people, for it is endemic and their bodies have a built-in resistance. When the American doctor said, "Don has permanent liver damage—forget about returning to New Guinea," it spurred the Damals to prayer.

The Beoga people had learned to pray in simple faith, and now they asked God for a miracle. They kept on praying, for they were desperate. There was no other missionary to come and teach them. They prayed when they gave thanks for their potatoes, in their huts at night, and in public meetings. "Lord, heal Damal-Neme's liver sickness." "Our God, give him a mind to come back to us." "Lord, Damal-Neme is sleeping now because it's dark there while it's light here. Visit him with a dream and make him sick and tired of America."

After sixteen months the doctor wrote a letter to our Alliance mission headquarters reporting that the liver function tests had improved although they were not fully normal. "Don's health," he wrote, "is as good as it will ever be." In spite of what the doctor wrote, God answered the prayers of the Damals with a miracle. To this day Don continues to hike over these rugged mountains—not just on the easy days when I am along—but ten-hour days of strenuous hiking. Could a man with liver damage ever do that?

At last we were on our way back to the Ilaga. In the plane with us were Joyce and her eleven-month-old baby sister, Lori. Kathy had already flown to Sentani to enter the second grade in the new boarding school for missionaries' children. Below us we saw the Lakes and then picked out the Homeyo airstrip and the aluminum roofs of the missionary houses beside it. We flew on over the Dugindoga Valley with its river winding through the mountains all covered with a patchwork of light green gardens and darker forest. Most of the Dugindoga people were Monis, but there were also Danis, Ndugas, and Damals—all without anyone to teach them the words of Jesus.

We flew over a 9,000-foot pass, and for the first time I saw the Beoga Valley from the air. George Boggs had chosen to fly that longer route to the Ilaga so he could show us the progress being made on building the Beoga strip. George had played a major part in the decision to OK the Beoga site for MAF Cessna operations. After the Alliance aviation section rejected the Beoga site, MAF agreed it was workable, only to reverse their decision for the same reason the Alliance pilot had given—the approach to the strip was too crowded with towering mountains to provide adequate room to maneuver. George Boggs had been a US Navy pilot in the Second World War. If he could land an airplane on an aircraft carrier, then he could land one on the Beoga strip, and once again approval was given to construct the airstrip.

On we flew down the Beoga River, past Tingil, where the people were no longer afraid of the *padagalo;* over Piloma and a mountain that did not seem nearly as rugged from the air as it had from the ground; past Ogam and the spot where the Danis raided Don and Gordon; and then, following the Ilaga River around the bend, we flew into the open expanse of the Ilaga Valley.

The plane touched down and taxied to the top of the airstrip, and we were immediately engulfed by a mass of shouting, smiling nationals—perhaps two thousand of them. Here we were on the traditional battleground of the Ilaga Valley—the very site of the last battle of the Taganit War, where thirty had been killed. Now we were pressed by happy, excited men, women, and children with no fear of a surprise attack, and there was not a single bow and arrow or spear to be seen. The Danis and Damals were all mixed up in one big, happy crowd. Many things had transpired during the twenty months of our absence.

Soon after we left, villages from the Namagu held a fetish burning. That completed the destruction of all the spirit appeasement paraphernalia of the Ilaga Damals. Because of the free intermarriage between the tribes many of the people were, as the Damals express it, "Damal on one side of their face and Dani on the other side." All of the Namagu people spoke both languages, and their turning to Christ had a strong effect on their Dani neighbors.

Several men took part in the fetish burning, who had taken part in an earlier one. They had held back one or two of their fetishes in an effort to embrace the new without a complete break with the old. One chief had kept the fetish that was supposed to make his gardens prosper. When he finally burned that fetish his entire village began to seek the Lord with their whole hearts.

The lives of the twelve hundred Damals had been swept clean from their ancestoral practice of evil spirit appeasement. They had turned as a unit from their former religion of animism to Christ without breaking away from the social structure of their tribe. The first part of the Great Commission as Jesus gave it in Matthew 28:19 had been realized in their lives: "Go ye therefore and [make disciples] of all nations."

The second step was an individual one when each man, woman, and child believed in Christ as his personal Savior. For some that may have taken place on the day they burned their fetishes, but for most it came when they more fully understood the teaching of the Bible. Jesus' words to baptize "them in the name of the Father, and of the Son, and of the Holy [Spirit]" were followed as individual Damals knew they had been born again.

The first two steps alone were not enough. The third part of Jesus' command says, "Teaching them to observe all things whatsoever I have commanded you." That was the challenge that faced John and Helen Ellenberger and Mary Owen, who had joined the ranks of the missionaries to the Damals. Their answer to the need of teaching the believers was to establish an adult Leadership Training School.

The students were to be ten men and their wives, chosen by the Damal Christians from five geographic areas of the Ilaga. Entrance requirements were that each man have only one wife, that his testimony in his village be clear, and that he have a strong desire to learn and teach his own people. Not all of those chosen would have been the missionaries' first choices, but here, as in each decision, the Damal Christians were allowed to decide unless direct scriptural teaching would be violated.

Classes were held five mornings a week in the newly constructed church building. Studies included stories from the Old Testament and from the life of Christ. One story a week from each was enough, and with repetition by the missionary and recitation, the students really mastered the lessons they studied. Reading, chapel with singing, prayer, and memorization of verses were also part of the daily schedule.

The most important feature was the class in which John Ellenberger gave the men a sermon complete with application and memory verse to memorize. Every other weekend the ten men fanned out across the valley to hold a Sunday service in all five of the Damal areas. John wrote, "It is unsurpassable joy to sit in silence in a service completely conducted by one of these men." The students not only multiplied the voice of the gospel, but they also expressed it in native idiom more clearly than any foreigner could ever do. The stories were presented in the Damal way of thinking, which made the gospel click in the hearts and minds of their listeners.

Another very Damal way of teaching the gospel sprang up in the Christian villages. Following the pattern of the courtship sing they initiated "talk-the-gospel" evenings. Everyone gathered in the men's house after dark. Anyone who knew a memory verse recited it, phrase by phrase, and all the others repeated the phrases in unison after the leader. Men, women, or young people could lead in the recitation, and the verses were interspersed with singing of hymn-chants and telling Bible stories given in the same format of sentence-by-sentence repetition. The catechism was also reviewed, and anyone who did not know any item on the program was taught through repetition until he had memorized it. Like the courtship sings, the talk-the-gospel evenings sometimes lasted until the birds began to sing in the morning.

Approved candidates for baptism increased in number with the Leadership Training School men teaching the inquirers. By the time we returned to the Ilaga, 510 Damals had followed their Lord in baptism.

War, for the Damal Christians, was a major part of the old way of life. They believed that the existence of bows and arrows was a direct temptation to war. For a number of months they kept their bows and arrows tied up in Chief Den's house while they discussed the possibility of burning them. John Ellenberger cautioned them against doing so because they might need to defend themselves if they were attacked. Finally, on a Saturday after listening to John's advice once again, Den put his arm around John's shoulder and said, "Now, Ellenberger, tomorrow you are not to say a word while we burn these bows and arrows."

Young boys gathered on Saturday from all over the valley and danced in the evening. Sunday morning there was dancing again before church. When everyone had gathered, the boys sat in a central group while Den and other men made speeches saying, "These boys represent the coming generation. They will grow up in a peaceful valley where there will be no killing, revenge, and war payment."

Men broke the bows and arrows and set them ablaze. As the weapons crumbled into ashes a Damal chief prayed, "God, we earmark these boys as your children. This generation is branded for you." That is why there were no bows and arrows on the airstrip when we returned, but there was to be still more to the story.

The Damal Christians did not become "saints" overnight. In fact, they are still like Christians anywhere in the world and have their ups and downs. In those first months a wide chasm of resentment and even hatred lay between the Damals and their Dani neighbors—especially against

Taganit's group. Through the years the Danis had pushed many Damals out of their homeland, and the fighting and war they had brought were not easily forgotten. Damal men frequently expressed their hatred of them. "I detest those Danis," they said. "They are like animals and will never believe. Let them go to hell."

Then a change began to take place. Damal men prayed in public for their Dani neighbors. They listed villages and chiefs by name in prayer. Their comments changed to, "The Danis will soon believe." Danis were invited to the Damal Sunday services, and before long two hundred were attending regularly. A capable man was assigned to translate everything into Dani and add words of special exhortation after the sermon.

The Danis began to burn their fetishes in December 1958 just two months after Gordon and Peggy Larson arrived back from furlough. The first group to respond was located just below Kunga village, and they were led in their break with fetishes by the father of Den's third wife. Den not only led the Damal tribe, but his influence through marriage ties also encouraged the first Dani chief to follow Christ.

Dani fetish burnings erupted all over the valley like popping corn, so that when we arrived a year later, twenty-two village areas had burned them, representing 3,500 Danis from almost every part of the valley. Everything the Danis did was done with more flashy enthusiasm than was shown by their Damal neighbors. They had a more complex system of spirit appeasement, and their fetish burnings were larger, accompanied with more dancing, singing, and rejoicing as they did away with their ancestral objects.

The break with sin was almost unbelievable; it could be only the working of the Holy Spirit in their lives. In a tribe noted for thievery and raids, stealing was abolished. Smoking ceased among the believers. Their zeal for righteousness may have sprung from fear of punishment, but it was real nevertheless. The Danis carried their witness for Christ everywhere they went, just as the Damals had done. A training school for twenty men and their wives began, and they in turn instructed others. Desire to learn of their new faith knew no bounds. Within a year, 502 Danis were baptized.

To be sure, there were some misconceptions among the Danis—that is inevitable with a primitive people whether the converts come by ones and twos, rejecting their society in their conversion, or whether like the Danis they turn to Christ as a unit. In that open-faced society there were no secrets, and the misunderstandings were repeated publicly, so specific teaching soon corrected them.

Some thought they must not touch the water drained from the baptismal pool because sins were in the water and they could become contaminated. One man concluded that since his wife was baptized before he was, he could not sleep with her until he had been baptized. Because their old spirit worship contained so many taboos, several men decided it was forbidden to eat anything for a full day after being baptized. Direct teaching was given from the Word of God, and those false concepts disappeared as quickly as they had sprung up.

The Dani church had been born, not by tens or hundreds, but by thousands, and their faith was soon to spread to tens of thousands. They were newborn babes in Christ. Just like new converts anywhere in the world they had a lot of growing and learning to do before they became mature Christians, but their conversion was genuine.

Those were the happy shouting people who greeted us as we stepped out of the plane. Seeing Don again was tangible evidence to the Damal people that God does answer their prayers. They had prayed fervently and without ceasing that God would bring Damal-Neme back to them, and He had!

The airstrip turned into an open-air cathedral as the crowd sat down around the airplane. Chief Den stood and welcomed us back, and then he prayed, thanking God for our return. Den's "amen" was repeated by every person there. Then another chief and another prayed, each followed by that resounding two-thousand voice "amen."

24

Village Prayer Leaders

John Ellenberger went back to the Beoga on another evangelistic trip two months after we left on furlough. As he traveled up the valley, several more village areas burned their fetishes. At one place near Piloma the people had already gathered their charms and were waiting to burn them when he arrived. During their joyful dancing immediately following the burning of their fetishes, they stopped abruptly several times to remind one another of what they had just done. "We need no longer fear the evil spirits"—a fear that hung over every hour of their lives. "Now we are to live according to Christ's commands."

John found that those who had burned their fetishes very rapidly learned to pray. Prayer and dependence upon God for all their needs was a complete turnabout from their former practice of animism.

The people at Kelma showed John the grave of a man who had died since his last visit. No spirit appeasement was made during his illness, and no woman had been killed as a witch. What a victory this was! It had been just a year earlier in that same village that the old mother and sister had been executed after Chief Nanol was killed in the final battle of the Taganit War.

John Ellenberger wrote of his May trip: "The Beoga Damals are sincere and most ardent in their desire to follow God. But having burned their fetishes without much knowledge of the way of the Lord, and being left without further training in that way, they are making little progress and are easy prey to temptation. We who have the written Word of God have little idea of what it means for them to walk in a new way with no man to instruct them."

John surveyed the challenge before him. What tools did he have with which to work? A few memory verses had been translated from the Bible, but no Damal could read. No Damal witnesses were trained, and for that matter, travel between the Ilaga and Beoga was still very limited due to the recent war. He had hoped to make trips himself, but as it turned out he was only able to make two more visits to the Beoga in the next year and a half. Prayer was the only tool available to augment the working of the Spirit of God— prayer offered by the churches in the homeland on behalf of those babes in Christ, and prayer offered by the Damals themselves.

John wrote:

The primary teaching emphasis to both believers and unbelievers on this trip was *prayer.* For those undecided for the Lord, the effectiveness of prayer over and against spirit appeasement tended toward convincing them. God is answering the prayers of the Damals who call on Him in faith, but spirit appeasement brings no results. To those who are already believers, it encourages them to know of the powerful tool in their hands.

We missionaries sometimes refer to the Damals performing "spirit worship." On the contrary, those infants in Christ had no concept of worship in their old religion. The supernatural to them was either evil or unknown in nature, and any contact with the spirits was an effort to appease them in order to attain certain ends like termination of illness, protection in war, or certainty of success in hunting. From the appeasement of evil beings to the fellowship and worship of a single, loving, holy Being is a long step—one that every new tribal Christian is called to make. An understanding and use of that relationship must be culti- vated in the believer by carefully leading him into it. As Christ taught His disciples "how to pray," so we must help them by giving them opportunity and practice in prayer, and often a "format," at first, of what to say.

I encouraged them to pray by themselves when they awoke in the morning, to pray together as a village before scattering for the day's work, and to pray in their houses before going to sleep. In each village their desire to learn to pray was encouraging. Often at night the women would sit around the fire, practicing what they were to pray before going to sleep. In several places there were those who wanted a private session in learning how to pray—either because they had missed the main service or had forgotten what was taught.

In the villages that I believed were ready for it I instructed believers in meeting together every Sunday for worship. I gave them a piece of string with seven knots tied in it—quite like the string calendars the Damals used before we came. Each morning they were to untie one knot. When the final knot was untied it was Sunday morning—the day set aside for worship and rest from work.

In addition, I taught them the Ten Commandments, explaining and amplifying to include related areas of their Christian life. For example, "Thou shalt not commit adultery" was expanded to include the New Testament prohibition against fornication and the New Testament discouragement of polygamy. In pregospel culture, prohibitions were strong against adultery and incest, but fornication, trial marriage and taking plural wives were part of the way of life. In those areas the New Testament standards had to be taught.

It was February 1959 before John got back to the Beoga, and that time his party included his wife, Helen, their three-month-old baby daughter, and Mary Owen. The few remaining villages who had not burned their fetishes on the two earlier trips brought them at that time and destroyed them. One of the last fetishes burned was an arrow shot by Taganit himself in the war, and with its burning the chief said, "Our hate and desire for revenge against the Ilaga Danis is now gone."

John wrote of that trip:

The Beoga people have now made a clean sweep in burning all of their fetishes. Some have been living for twelve months without them, but what of the positive teaching of the Bible? Don Gibbons is sick with hepatitis and has not returned as planned to teach the Beoga people.

Although it is wonderful to see the Beoga people turning to the Lord as a unit, yet it is an exceedingly dangerous thing to have so many who have so little knowledge of the Way of the Lord. At the same time we cannot possibly forbid them to come. Rather we must somehow accept the challenge to teach those whom we have led to the foot of the cross. Otherwise, these many who have come sincerely to the Lord may develop into groups of quasi-Christians with only a veneer of the gospel.

Although John had heard good reports from travelers, it was encouraging to see that the Beoga Christians were gathering faithfully each Sunday to worship the Lord. In each church center a leader had sprung up who was taking the initiative to lead the Sunday service. John referred to those men as "village prayer leaders." Some of the men did little more than lead in public prayer. Others took every opportunity they had to memorize Scripture verses and stories from the missionaries' teaching. A witness school conducted on this trip provided new material for the groups of people who gathered on Sundays, and men like Palek from Tingil memorized the details with amazing accuracy. Later Palek with other prayer leaders visited the Ilaga, where they learned more, thus adding new Bible stories and verses to their repertoire.

Jak-Niti was another one of the village prayer leaders. He was among those who had welcomed Don and me when we walked to Ogam. His firstborn son had been a toddler at that time. The baby had had several large ulcers from yaws, and I gave him an injection of penicillin. Within a week the sores were gone. Jak-Niti had also heard for the very first time the story of Jesus, and it made a deep impression on him when he saw his baby's life had been saved.

Two months later when Don returned to Ogam, Jak-Niti joined the party as they traveled through the Beoga. He listened and learned as Don preached, and he asked more questions as they traveled. One day, walking along the trail, Don gave the creation story by counting off the seven days on his fingers, and Jak-Niti memorized the entire account.

In May after Ogam village had burned their fetishes Jak-Niti assumed the leadership of the Christians who gathered on Sunday to pray. Later he walked to the Ilaga to visit John Ellenberger and learn more. He gradually added Bible stories and verses to those he had memorized and recited them on Sundays. Because he had become a village prayer leader, his fellow Christians often called on him to pray for the sick. One day he was called to pray for a woman who had given birth to a baby several days earlier. Evidently an infection had set in, for she was burning with fever. He prayed for her in Jesus' name, and the next day she was well. "God did hear my prayers and healed many people," Jak-Niti told me.

Several years later Jak-Niti realized a new calling from God through a vision. He had joined an evangelistic party taking the gospel to Danis and Ndugas who had not yet made peace with his clan. The second night out from Beoga he had a dream. He heard a voice saying, "The Lord is with you as you go. You will not die." Then he saw a Man, a Man with long, straight hair quite unlike the shorter, kinky hair of a Damal. He came up to Jak-Niti and put His arms around him. Jak-Niti responded, "I pray to You and I follow Your teachings." The Man spoke once more. "I hear you when you pray, and I am with you."

Then the scene changed, and Jak-Niti saw a garden with *mo* planted on the side of a hill. The leaves were large and healthy—a beautiful garden to behold. Running through the garden was a wide stream of water flowing gently over the *mo* plants. Jak-Niti knew that *mo* can be grown without the stream to irrigate the plants, but that the tubers grown will be small and blighted. If the farmer wants to grow a first-rate crop he finds a source of water above the garden, ditches the water to the plot, and allows it to trickle down over the entire area. In his dream the *mo* represented people who had burned their fetishes, and the water was the Holy Spirit and the Word of God. That was Jak-Niti's call from the Lord to be a pastor.

He made plans to enter the Damal language Bible school. To enter school, a student must first be able to read, and Jak-Niti did learn, although it was not an easy task for a man of his age. In time he graduated with a four-year diploma and was later ordained. Through the years Jak-Niti had been faithful to his calling, in season and out of season, always guiding the water of the Holy Spirit and the Word of God over the members of his congregation.

As the feeling of hostility between the Ilaga and the Beoga lessened, Kok-Me decided to make a trip to the Ilaga. That trip included a visit to the Ellenbergers. John took him on a personally conducted tour of their house. They went upstairs and looked into each of the four rooms. "This is where my baby daughter sleeps," John told him, "and my wife and I sleep in this room."

The Damals were never allowed in the upstairs of our bark cabin. As a result they imagined that it contained some mysterious secret that led to the story of our keeping a newborn baby in our bedroom. The story grew even larger after we left on furlough. John was constantly on the lookout for false ideas that are inevitable when working with a people emerging from a Stone Age culture. Thus he made a point of taking every visitor who came from a distance on a guided tour of his house.

Coming downstairs John seated Kok-Me on a chair in the living room and said to him, "Now you've seen everything in our house. The things that we have in our house are just earthly things, and they are of little value. What's really important is the gospel—that Jesus died on the cross for the sins of all men, that He rose again in three days and has now gone back to heaven. Every man must come to Jesus himself and repent of his sins or he will be doomed to hell."

Kok-Me returned home to the Beoga with a new view of the *tuan* and how he lived, but even more important he understood more clearly the message the *tuan* had brought.

During interviews with Kok-Me in preparation for writing this book I asked him on several occasions about his experience of salvation. Each time he gave clear testimony of understanding the scriptural teachings of repentance from sin and receiving Christ by faith, but he did not point back to a time when he had accepted Christ. It was a growing experience as more light penetrated his understanding.

That to me was a satisfactory answer and one given by most of the Damal Christians. In their society they had no reason to measure events in time and thus had not developed a counting system beyond a few basic numbers. Birth, marriage, and death were important to the Damal, but the occasions were not related to time.

One day Kok-Me offered the story of his visit to see John Ellenberger, and he added, "I think this is the time when I first understood enough and made my decision to follow Christ." Kok-Me came up with that response because I, as a Westerner, had been looking for a point of decision.

The Beoga people were like dry sponges, soaking up every bit of teaching they could acquire. God was answering their prayers for more light. The ministry of the village prayer leaders blossomed after the Ellenbergers' second trip. More Beoga people visited the Ilaga with the specific purpose of memorizing new Bible verses and stories to take back to their villages. They also brought reports to John that the Beoga people were of a single mind to follow the Lord, no women had been killed as witches, the Wang-Be church was giving offerings on Sunday, a group near Ogam had built a church in which to worship, and the Christians in the upper Beoga, who had known the Lord for a longer time, were requesting to be baptized.

In October John Ellenberger once again set out on the trail, adding shoe leather to his prayers for the Beoga people. Traveling with John was Tita, the man who had watched Don read his Bible and asked about it. At that time Tita was one of the ten men attending the Leadership Training School in the Ilaga. Tita was a leader in whatever he did. That had been true in the Taganit War. He now came to the Beoga as a preacher of the gospel to people who had recently been his hated enemies. With Tita and John were forty-five other Ilaga people, the first major party to visit the Beoga since the war. Their testimony as they left their home was, "If they kill us, it's all right. If we live, it's all right. The important thing is the spread of the gospel."

That party, without bows and arrows, arrived in Wang-Be with some fear, but they were greeted with outstretched arms and tears of joy by relatives they had not seen for a long time. When they entered the first village, a feast had been cooked and was ready to be taken out of the pits. The gospel message as it had been received by the people who had fought on both sides of the Taganit War had knit them together in Christian love.

A week later as the party was preparing to travel downriver to Piloma they heard that Chief Komang was planning to shoot Tita in revenge for the death of his brother, who had been killed in the Tovegi battle. Tita took his fears to the Lord in prayer. "Oh Lord, you know that I'm like a woman without a bow and arrow, and I can't defend myself. We have to go through Komang's village to continue on our way preaching. Now, take the desire to fight out of Komang's heart. Lord, make him sick, so sick he won't feel like fighting. But don't let him die."

When the group arrived at Piloma, Komang was there, sick with malaria and very unthreatening. John Ellenberger wrote, "I was amused to hear one Ilaga man telling him, 'Oh, it's too bad you're sick. We have all been praying for you.'" John gave him malaria medicine, and the group went on their way.

The sequel to that story does not belong here chronologically, but I would like to relate it here. In all the years I have lived in the Beoga I never heard Komang's story until I began research for this book. He is just one of hundreds who could tell a similar story.

Komang's recovery was dramatic. He and the other villagers gave God the credit for delivering him from death.

From that time the desire for revenge began to leave his heart, and he sought the Lord in a positive way. A year later he was baptized. Because he had two wives he was not qualified to take any leadership in the church, but he still remained a leader in the community. Later, when an epidemic of Asian flu swept through the valley, his second wife died. That freed Komang from a marriage contract he had made before hearing the gospel, and when his church was organized he was elected to serve as an elder. He never learned to read, and now he is too old to learn, but through the years he has served faithfully as an elder and Christian leader in his home village. When pastors and elders come for meetings at Milavak, Komang is with them. And there are hundreds of others in the Beoga today like Komang— living in their isolated villages, tilling sweet potatoes as their fathers did in time past, but freed from war and killing.

Our family arrived back in the Ilaga on the first of December, and the logical move seemed to be for us to pack our things and move to the Beoga by trail, but that was not possible. Kathy would be coming home at Christmas for a three-week vacation, and she could not come to Beoga by trail for such a short time. We felt the Lord wanted her time with us to take priority over our missionary work. Through the years we have always followed that principle, and our missionary work has never suffered.

The solution for the hundreds of Christians waiting in the Beoga was for Don and John to temporarily switch places. John left for the Beoga by trail in mid-December and stayed on until we arrived five weeks later. During those weeks the people under John's supervision made real progress on the strip at Milavak and it looked for a time as though we might fly to the Beoga instead of hiking. I never really *believed* it would happen that way, though, and I was right.

In those weeks John also picked out a site for our mission house, started clearing the ground, built a native-style house to serve as kitchen-dining room, and put up the framework and an aluminum roof on a ten by twenty-foot building, which was to be our first sleeping quarters. The Beoga Christians could wait no longer, and on three consecutive Sundays John baptized 196 men and women from the three church areas of the upper Beoga.

In the Ilaga the mission executive committee met, and one of their decisions made it possible for the Damal church to take another step toward growth independent of the missionary. The committee decided that permission could be given to the pastor and elders to serve Communion in an organized church. Up to that time only an ordained man was allowed to serve Communion, and of course that meant that the missionary was the only person qualified—an impossible situation in the Beoga.

Taking up John's tasks in the Ilaga, Don worked on a building project and putting a large water tank together. In ministry to the Damals he held a baptismal service for a large group in the Namagu, including Kip, the chief whom he worked so hard to win, and he organized the church at Kunga with a commissioning service for the pastor and elders. That made Kunga the first church in the Damal tribe to be organized as a self-governing body.

The exchange of ministry between John and Don, with each man making active advances in the work of the other, was a beautiful thing to behold. It is rare for two missionaries to have such oneness in methods and approach to the people so that each can act in place of the other. That unity between the two men was another piece in God's master plan to reach the Damal people with the gospel.

25

"We Have Come to Stay"

The final countdown until our departure for Beoga was in progress. For days we had been sorting and packing for an hour or two each afternoon. Already we had sent basic household items over the trail—cots, dishes, a wood stove, a folding table and chairs, a kerosine lamp, tools, and a typewriter. Each load could weigh no more than thirty-five pounds, and had to be packed for a rough trip in the rain. It was my job to sort and plan what we would need, and then Don took over preparing the loads for the carriers. Other things we packed, weighed, and marked to come in by plane when the Beoga strip would be opened.

On Monday we did our final packing. I baked bread and made lunches to eat on the trail. Canteens were filled with drinking water. Any water added on the way had to be boiled twenty minutes before we could drink it. Lori's bottles were ready to accompany her, and more powdered milk was in a can with a measuring spoon inside. Packing diapers and rain clothes, salt, matches, and sweaters—that and a hundred other tasks filled my day. I knew that once I started on the trail I would have no energy for anything more than setting one foot in front of the other, so what I organized now would make a more pleasant trip for all of us.

In a candid description of heaven the Damals include, "And there will be no flies or mud in heaven." My description includes, "And there will be no packing in heaven, for we will be there forever." In my missionary career I wonder how many days and months I have spent planning and packing everything from thumbtacks to a four-years supply of shoes for a family of six. For a trip it included everything from the food we would need (and no extra, because our weight is always limited whether we walk or fly) to the stamps and glue for a letter to send to my girls away at school. And the axiom stands: whatever you forget, you get along without.

Tuesday morning the whole family was up at 5:30. We said good-bye to Kathy, and she walked across the valley to the airstrip to return to school. Our thirty loads were on the backs of carriers, and we were on the trail to the Beoga by 7:30. Perhaps I should add that two of the loads were Joyce and Lori.

Don had chosen a husky Damal man with a pleasant personality to carry our four-and-a-half year old daughter, Joyce. Even though his load was overweight he was happy to carry Joyce because she was once again chattering Damal and provided good company. The morning we left he asked for a large net bag, and it proved to be a good thing that we had it along. At one point as we were toiling up the mountain in the rain a carrier passed us, bent down under a rain cape. I said to Don, "What is that man carrying? I saw some cloth in his net bag." From inside the bag came the reply, "It's me, Mommy." Joyce's legs were tired from riding all morning astride her carrier's shoulders, and when the rain came she was content to be put inside a net bag and be carried like a Damal child.

Lori's carrier was a woman. Although I had never turned the care of my girls over to a Damal, for this trip I knew it would be different, and I wanted a woman with the instincts of a mother to carry my baby. There would be times when I would be separated from Lori on the trail, and she would know how to respond to Lori's needs. During our weeks in the Ilaga I had introduced Lori to riding on the shoulders of a Damal and sleeping in a net bag. Now she took traveling in stride as if that had always been her life.

In the Ilaga I also had gone in training—taking one- and two-hour hikes to get in practice for the trail. In spite of that

I was exhausted by noon. I felt that I could not go on, but I had to. When crossing a mountain, camp can only be made in certain places, and the campsite ahead of us was closer than any behind us. I hiked for fifteen minutes and then lay down flat on the ground, panting, for five minutes. As the Damals passed by, seeing me lying on the ground, they were shocked and expressed their pity and love. They had never seen anything like this before. "What is wrong with Damal-In?" they aked.

I wondered that myself. An hour later I lost my lunch—*Exhaustion*, I thought. It began to rain, but I kept pushing on—lying on the ground and then getting up to hike again. At three o'clock we reached the campsite, and I slumped in a heap on the ground while the rain dripped off the end of my nose. Don would have to take care of everything else.

Some weeks later I realized what my problem had been— I was pregnant. At that point I was really glad I had not known in the Ilaga, because our mission leader would never have allowed me to hike to the Beoga. Sheer determination that I would not be left behind again while Don pioneered a new mission station caused me to ignore the usual pregnancy symptoms. Even after I had discovered the secret myself I kept it from others for a long time.

The next day I did much better on the trail, even though the terrain became more difficult. I commented to Don, "Yesterday I must have been out of condition, just coming from the States." At noon we crossed the 11,400 foot pass in a downpour that did not stop, and everything was wet that night, including our sleeping bags.

The following day when we reached Wang-Be the people were bursting with excitement that we had actually come. They had a pit-cooked feast of corn and potatoes all ready to celebrate.

On our fourth day the trail led up one mountain and down the other side, then up and down again. Between Wung and Tingil we dropped two thousand feet in an hour's time. In each village the people were gathered to greet us as we passed through. "Why have you come?" they asked. They knew our plans before they asked, but they wanted to hear the answer from our own lips. "We have come to stay," I replied. With that they were satisfied and let us go on our way.

Finally we climbed over the last mountain and looked down on the Beoga airstrip. There beside it was a Damal-style house with smoke coming out of a stovepipe from our little kitchen stove. John Ellenberger greeted us very warmly, and so did the crowds of Damals. Beside the grass-thatched hut stood the pole framework and aluminum roof of a small building. Don wrapped our tent and tarps around the framework of one room to afford a little privacy for our bedroom. That was our first Beoga home.

Don and John were out first thing Saturday morning to survey the airstrip. How nice it was to have the strip in our front yard rather than having to hike an hour across the valley. Don was encouraged to find that the strip itself was almost ready for a landing, but that the holdup in a first landing was getting a fence built to keep the pigs off the strip. The Ilaga Damals, who seemed to have rubbed off some of the energy of their Dani neighbors, had helped to level the strip, but they had no wood rights to cut fence wood in the forest. The Beoga men said they would certainly build the fence sections they had contracted, but it was always "tomorrow" when they would begin. Not one foot of fence was built when we arrived.

John had laid the strip out in sections and contracted each section to a different man. Wolo took a section, and his family helped him do the work. That included Kok-Me and Delem-In, Meyong, and Novet, and all the rest of their children. A boulder protruded above the surface of their section, and that had to be chiseled away by building a fire around the rock to crack it and then digging and prying the fragments loose. To level the strip surface to an even 12 percent grade, sections of the ground had to be cut, and others were filled. When Wolo's contract was completed he received a steel ax, and all his helpers were paid shells and beads for their daily work.

Sunday was a happy day, but hardly a day of rest for us. Five hundred people gathered on the airstrip to attend church, and there was lots of singing and dancing. An epidemic of flu had struck the Beoga, and everybody wanted medicine since they had walked all the way to Milavak for church. And every last man, woman, and child, or so it seemed, wanted to see us and investigate where we were living. They came touching everything in our camp, for there was no way of securing our things, but nothing was stolen—that day or any other day.

Monday morning John Ellenberger headed up the mountain on the trail back to the Ilaga, and we were alone— that is, if you do not count the four thousand Damals living in the Beoga. A transceiver radio was to have come on the plane that took Kathy to school, but a note reached us in the forest saying the radio had not been repaired. With no communication to the outside world we rather identified with the Damals—forgotten by time and the rest of the world. But God had not forgotten the Damals, or us for that matter, and that is why we had come to the Beoga.

A man spotted Don on the airstrip and hurried over to where he was working. Realizing he had come from some distance, Don put down his tape measure, string, and carpenter's level and stood up to greet the visitor. After the formal greetings and finger snapping he said, "I've just come from Wang-Be. Now help me learn this memory verse. All I can remember is, 'The Spirit of Jesus is more powerful.'"

Don glanced at the strip where he had been surveying a section of ground for the final grading. *I'll never get this strip finished at this rate*, he thought. But he walked to the edge of the strip and squatted down, with the man following him. Breaking the verse into four short phrases, Don spoke one Damal phrase at a time, and the man repeated after him: "The Spirit who is in you/ is more powerful than the spirit/ in those who belong to the world./

From John's writings." (Scripture references did not include numbers until later, when the Indonesian counting system had been introduced.) The man continued to repeat after Don until he could say the entire verse and reference by himself. Going on his way he would teach the verse to others, line by line as he had learned it.

That sort of thing happened over and over again each day. The Beoga people demanded to be taught new truth. And so it was that two weeks after we arrived in the Beoga Don began to train the prayer leaders, who in turn taught the village people. Friday morning the prayer leaders gathered under the evergreen trees in our backyard—fifteen men who had come to learn a sermon for Sunday. Dividing them into three groups, Don taught the Bible story to one group, the application to the second, and the memory verse to the third group. After one man in each group had mastered his portion Don left them for a time to work on the strip. They continued to recite, the leader saying a sentence and the others repeating after him until everyone had learned all three sections.

The men went out by twos and threes to five church centers in the Beoga: Kelma, Milavak (right at the airstrip), Tingil, Wang-Be, and Piloma. The sermon on Sunday morning was short, only taking ten minutes, but the memory verse was taught over and over in the houses so that many were soon learning a new verse each week. From the very beginning Damal men acted as the pastors, never did the missionary, and the foundation was laid for the church of today that is self-taught, self-administered, and self-supported.

When we returned to New Guinea we were reminded that the Alliance requires all missionaries to study language—six hours a day, the book says—until they pass their two-year language exams. Although we had technically fulfilled those requirements by learning the Ekari language, Damal was now the language we had chosen for our work. John

Ellenberger, the linguist and Bible translator for the Damal tribe, had made great strides in language analysis during our furlough. Under his direction we began doing tone drills our second day back in the Ilaga, for if we were to communicate clearly in Damal we must learn the proper tone of each word, along with the sounds.

Now we were in the Beoga on our own. There was no one to guide us or check on our progress in the language. Don spent most of his daylight hours with the Damals, and for him that was language study, because always he stopped whatever he was doing if he heard a new word or phrase and nailed it down in his mind. I, like most missionaries, had no special gifts in language, and whatever I learned came through the discipline and labor of study, the hardest work of my life. I hired a lady to come and teach me, but that did not work out. She came faithfully, but she had no initiative and did not lead in a conversation.

Kok-Me stepped into my life at that point. He was one of the budding preachers who gathered each Friday to learn the Sunday sermon. He was outgoing and bubbling over with conversation—just what I needed for a language informant. For a missionary, learning the customs and culture of a people is equally as important as learning their language. Thus for language study material we went over stories of his background and family. I learned of the witch killing of his aunt and the attempts on his mother's life. I was deeply impressed with the lot in life of a Damal woman before the gospel came, and that was all such a recent page in history. Little wonder that when the women prayed they never failed to thank the Lord for their deliverance from witchcraft killings. Kok-Me continued to work with me until I passed my two-year language exam, and after that he helped me in preparing Bible lessons and other study material for the Bible school.

When Kok-Me came back to be my chief informant for the writing of this book, he returned with the same enthusiasm he had displayed almost twenty years earlier. As a language teacher he worked with me, not for what I paid him, but because he knew I must learn the language before I could teach his people. So it was with this book. At first he was reluctant to paint the full picture. He, like all the Damals, did not like to display his ugly past, but when he understood that my purpose in writing was not to ridicule their past but to contrast it with how God has changed their lives, he was eager to tell me the full story.

Can you guess what I paid Kok-Me for his help this time? It is something that he wanted very much and is quite a natural gift for a Damal. It was a pig; not a native pig, but a beautiful, pure-bred sow flown from the coast. In those sessions, as in our former ones, Kok-Me interrupted me to correct my Damal—language learning never comes to an end!

Camping among the Damals was a challenge—especially with a baby just learning to walk. Our camp kitchen had a dirt floor that was very damp, and the yard was always muddy from a combination of the daily rains and the trampling feet of the hundreds of people who came to see us. Although men had contracted to bring hand-split boards, it was weeks before they brought enough to cover the floor and walls of our ten by ten-foot bedroom. The Damals had a solution for their babies in living conditions like this—the mother or older sister carried the baby around all the time. So I hired a twelve-year-old girl to watch Lori, and much of the time she rode around on the girl's shoulders.

The ground chosen for our house site was lush, black soil. That was good for the garden that Don had planted just a week after we arrived, but weeds and brush also thrived in the warm, sunny weather. Tall grass and reeds still surrounded our campsite because all available manpower had to be concentrated on getting the strip ready for a landing. Some of the reeds were twenty-five feet high. Something else flourished there—insects by the thousands, flying and crawling all over the place. Wormlike creatures an inch or two long with dozens of legs were everywhere, and when touched they rolled up in a ball. The Damals said they were harmless, but still it was a bit disconcerting to find them in our beds. Fleas abounded, and they all seemed to prefer my blood to that of the others in the family. Ants crawled all over my dishes and pans in the kitchen even when they were perfectly clean—just checking, I suppose. Flies were thick and thicker depending on how many Damals were around at the time. The only insects we lacked were mosquitoes, and that was a special blessing because it meant there was no malaria.

Living as close to the earth as we did, our clothes really got dirty. My Damal kitchen helper took them to the cold mountain stream that ran in our front yard and scrubbed them with a bar of soap. Soon all our clothes began to turn the color of earth, no matter what color they had been originally.

The crowded quarters, the insects, and the mud really did not matter to any of us. We were in the Beoga as a family with Damals all around us who were begging to be taught the things of the Bible. Their enthusiasm more than made up for all the inconveniences.

The people had taken us in as part of their family. One way they expressed that was by bringing net bags of vegetables and always refusing any payment. If Joyce was nearby when they came, she received them and said thank-you with just the right Damal words and gestures that pleased the lady who had brought them. Joyce usually wore a string skirt over her dress and played with the Damal children. She was one of them, and yet not quite one of them. They began to tease her, and they did not stop until she became angry. Don decided to talk to the adults about that when they were all gathered after church. He explained it just as if it were a problem between family members, and the teasing stopped.

Next to our girls our most interesting possession to the Damals was our chickens. Their only domestic animal for meat was the pig. The chickens had come over the trail with us from the Ilaga, and they promptly named them "bird-pig" because they were a new meat animal. They did have a second animal in their villages—the dog. Those hungry creatures roamed everywhere, but dog meat was strictly forbidden to a Damal. On the whole they added nothing to the economy of the people. Only a few prized dogs were used to hunt *op* in the forest.

The age-old conflict between raising dogs or chickens came to a head one night when a dog got into our chicken house and killed two of our five hens. Don clobbered the dog with a rock before it could get away, but that was little consolation when we were so hungry for eggs. The next day there was a village council meeting with the decision that Don could hire a man to shoot the dogs and then give some compensation to the dog owner. Today some areas have opted to raise chickens and rabbits without dogs, and other villages have men who cannot bear to part with their dogs. I guess the chicken and the dog will not live together peacefully in the Beoga until the Millennium.

In mid February the plane flew over to see if we were ready to have the ground inspection party walk in from the Ilaga. We had to put out the *negative* signal. The surface of the strip was finished, but the fence was not complete. The Beoga strip is built in a side canyon with high mountains hemming it in on both sides and the top. That means that once the plane is on final approach, if a pig should suddenly appear on the strip the plane cannot go around for a second try. A good fence was the only answer. After the people saw that we really were in earnest and that the plane would *not* land until the fence was completed, they began to work with new enthusiasm.

Two weeks later the last vine was tied on the fence as the party arrived from the Ilaga to inspect the strip. Pilot Dave Steiger pronounced the strip hard and ready for a landing. Bright and early the next morning the Damals began to stream into Milavak to witness the first landing of the *padagalo* in the Beoga.

The Damals heard it first and sent up a shout. Then we saw it, first a tiny speck against the backdrop of the towering mountains, and then the yellow plane as it swooped down over the strip. From the plane George Boggs saw the two sheets of aluminum laid in a parallel position at the bottom of the strip and knew it was all OK for a landing. The plane flew out of sight behind the mountains and then reappeared, low and flying over the river. Turning into the side valley, he touched down to make a perfect landing. He taxied slowly up the 12 percent grade to the top and turned around. Everybody swarmed out around the plane—black and white alike. The Beoga was now open to plane service.

There have been hundreds of landings by Mission Aviation Fellowship planes in the intervening years, and each landing is charged with anticipation and excitement for all who watch. And for the passenger, the wonder of that little Cessna plane dipping down between the majestic mountains to follow the Beoga River upvalley and then to turn sharply to the left, almost before he has spotted the strip, never loses its excitement no matter how many times he has made the landing.

At first the plane brought us food supplies, a radio, household goods, furniture, and our outfit drums and crates. Next came supplies to build our house—corrugated aluminum for roofing, nails, doors, and windows along with three Ekari workmen. Two were trained in pit-sawing lumber by land, for floors and shelves, and the third man was a carpenter. He proved to be a great help to Don in building, for the bulk of the work was with crooked poles and hand-split boards that required a great deal of hand preparation.

Not many months passed before the Damals themselves were flying, too. First evangelistic teams flew to a distant point, perhaps ten days' walk away, and then they ministered along the way as they walked home. Later, families going out as national missionaries flew the first major part of their journey before they set out on foot to penetrate the rugged wilderness where no strip could be built. Today most of the pounds flown in and out of the Beoga are for the Damal people—medicine and Scripture portions; items for sale such as salt, soap, and axes; and people—to the hospital, to a church conference, to various schools, or to minister in a distant outpost. The airplane, flown by missionary pilots, has done much to spread the gospel and bring progress to the Damals.

With the airstrip open, our attention turned to the Damals, who were begging us to come and baptize them. The village of Piloma was first. Although I was midway in my pregnancy by that time, I decided to go along. We collected our camping equipment and set off on the trail. Traveling in a valley where people live is much easier than crossing a high mountain pass. If necessary, camp can be set up at any village along the way. I was familiar with the path because I hiked upriver from Piloma to Milavak on my first trek to Beoga. There was one major difference about the trail this time; there was a good bridge at Kelandi; Don made sure about that before we started out. I was not about to cross another temporary bridge! We set up camp in the early afternoon two hours short of Piloma. I was as fit for the trail as ever.

The next morning when we reached Piloma there was a crowd of excited, happy people waiting to greet us. We spent six days with them teaching the catechism, memory passages from the Bible, and lessons on the life of Christ. Don took down baptismal candidate names—108 of them— and then screened them through a group of the spiritual leaders. Those who passed were examined individually on their basic Bible knowledge and memory verses.

Our visit to Piloma had been timed to coincide with the arrival of the new witness man who had just come from the school in the Ilaga. Six men were assigned to the Beoga, one for each of the church centers. To have a man work in a specialized capacity and receive his living from the offerings of the church was an entirely new concept to the Damals. Until now every man was a farmer, and there was no specialization. But the Piloma people received their new pastor with open arms as did every other church in the Beoga.

On Sunday morning the people began streaming into the village, singing and dancing as they came, until seven hundred had gathered, a huge crowd for that sparsely populated area. The three-and-a-half-hour service began as the people marched around to lay down their offerings of sweet potatoes, cowrie shells, and beads. Until they had a pastor, there was no one to receive an offering. Everyone sat down, and the singing began. Two men with brightly painted faces stood to sing the words of the hymn, and the chant response swelled from seven hundred voices. What a beautiful part of the Damal's worship of God! Individual men had now memorized the words to the growing number of hymns. They sought out Don, John, or a Damal who knew the words, and carefully memorized them. With that learned skill they were able to take a special part of leadership in the church services.

Three men stood up from the congregation and led in prayer. The third man closed his prayer with, "Amen," and everyone responded together, "Amen." Recitation of memory verses was next, with five men each reciting a passage, phrase by phrase, and the entire group repeating after him. That was the Damal version of responsive reading of the Scripture. The witness man from the Ilaga brought the first sermon; a Beoga man, qualified as a ministering elder, the second; and Don preached the third sermon. None were long, but it had become the pattern of worship in all the churches to have two or three men speak on Sunday morning.

The form of worship sprang up quite spontaneously among the Christians. Of course there was guidance from the missionaries, but because the form was both cultural and scriptural the Damals were not so conscious of the missionary's part. The worship service was theirs, conducted by their own people.

After the service everyone went to the baptismal site. A small stream had been dammed up the day before, and the crowd sat on the sloping banks to witness the baptism of seventy-four men and women. The entire service was very quiet and reverent—a definite improvement over the first baptismal service at Kunga. Then Communion was served to those who were newly baptized and to other baptized people who were present.

Sunday afternoon we hiked fifteen hundred feet down to the Beoga River and up the other side to set up camp for the night. (In some places on earth one might say you "walked" down to the river, but not so in the Beoga. Every step you take is real work, whether up or down—it is never on the level.) The usual blisters and aching muscles of the trail were completely forgotten in the fantastic experience of witnessing changed lives and having a part in teaching these people.

26
Ever Widening Circles

When a pebble is dropped into a pool of water, the surface is broken where it falls and the ripples fan out in wider and wider circles to the edge of the pond. Even so, the Rock Christ Jesus broke the surface of timeless heathenism when Chief Den led his people in the burning of their fetishes. From that small beginning other Damals in the Ilaga followed, and then all of the Beoga turned to Christ spontaneously as soon as they heard the Bible message in their own language.

The friendly Damal tribe of 10,000 people was turning to Christ in large segments, but their aggressive Dani neighbors only watched at first. The western Dani tribe was spread out over an area one hundred miles in length, and they numbered perhaps 100,000. Four missionary societies had opened stations and begun work at a number of points, but nowhere had the Danis received the missionaries' message.

Eighteen months after Den burned his fetishes, his father-in-law, who was a Dani chief, led the first fetish burning among his people. The gospel had crossed over a bridge of kinship and business ties from Damal to Dani. The other Ilaga Danis were ready to follow. Twenty-one other groups burned their fetishes in the next year.

The Ilaga Danis were enthusiastic about what Christ had done for them and were bursting with missionary zeal. They went out witnessing not because the mission hired them, *for it did not.* Nor did the missionary organize their going. The Holy Spirit sent them. They traveled to visit their relatives or on business, but everywhere they went they communicated the excitement of their new-found faith. To the west

they walked five days to witness to the scattered Danis
living in the Dugindoga Valley. Traveling to the east they
went to the Danis of the Swart Valley, who had been their
allies in the Taganit War.

In the Swart the missionaries working with Regions
Beyond Missionary Union soon became aware of what was
happening. Although the Danis had given little heed to the
missionaries' preaching, they were now listening to the
witness of the Ilaga men. To enlarge that witness Regions
Beyond invited Gordon Larson and two of the men from the
Ilaga training school to fly to the Swart. First the Ilaga Danis
testified to the chiefs in the men's houses at night. Having
won the listening ear of the leaders, when open air meetings
were called the people gathered in large numbers. The
chiefs now felt that they were the leaders in welcoming the
new message, and they shouted to the people who gathered,
"We must all listen to the words of these men from the
Ilaga." The ice had been broken, and the RBMU missionaries were able to continue teaching through the door the
Ilaga Danis had opened. The gospel was not only a white
man's religion, it was for "real people," too.

Two Dani men who were attending the training school in
the Ilaga walked eighty miles to Pyramid in the Baliem
Valley. Their purpose in going was to retrieve some fetishes
stored there, so they could burn them. But they also sent out
word that everyone should gather and hear what they had to
say. Alliance missionary Henry Young joined the twelve
hundred Danis who gathered at the appointed village.
When the "preachers" instructed the crowd to bow their
heads and be silent for prayer, the crowd obeyed, something
that Young had never seen before. He took a tape recorder
along with him to document what the men were saying, and
well he did, for once they got started their speech was as
rapid as machine gun fire. Later, when it was transcribed,
the message was shown to be doctrinally accurate. The men
gave forth the Word in the power of the Spirit.

The prayer of an Ilaga witness man, recorded and
translated, went like this:

"Greetings, our Creator, greetings. Today we who are gathered here at Pyramid, where Tuan Young has built his house, give You our greetings. Tuan knows about You and what You have done for us. He has told these people about You, but they have not listened, and so we have come.

We are telling them carefully about Your talk. In the past we did many bad things, but today we don't do those things anymore because we have heard Your message. Since I have heard Your good talk I want to tell these people here about it. Your blood has erased our wrongdoings, our Creator. You have given Your good disposition to us. Those who do bad You will cast out. I have finished talking with You, our Creator. Amen."

As Gordon Larson watched the Dani fetish burnings in the Ilaga, taught the new converts, and baptized 500 of them during that first year, he became aware of the potential they held in leading the thousands of Danis in other valleys to Christ. In February 1960 Gordon set off on foot with a party of Christian men for the Baliem. The group traveled through all the Dani areas, preaching the message of salvation and encouraging fetish burning as the first step to be taken. The party was welcomed by missionaries from three other missionary societies as they passed through. The Danis knew nothing of separate organizations, and the missionaries also set their differences aside in giving the message they all held in common. Results were spectacular. Barriers from the Taganit War were broken down. Fetishes were burned by thousands of Danis in the Swart Valley and the Bokondini area.

At Pyramid the people had been stirred up to follow Christ by the two Ilaga men who in God's timing had arrived some weeks earlier. Realizing that the teaching of the Youngs was for the Dani too, the people had now been receiving regular instruction. For three days the Danis gathered by the thousands to listen to the preaching of Gordon and the Ilaga men. When Sunday came, nothing could stop them from burning their fetishes. In a letter to Alliance Mission Headquarters Henry Young wrote:

Sunday morning arrived, and about 11 A.M. the clans began arriving. What a sight! Groups of hundreds of people came dancing and shouting and singing, carrying taboo planks of wood, nets filled with hundreds of fetishes, and hearts full of joy and the feeling of freedom which they now possessed. As they reached the service grounds, they piled up their fetishes and then danced and sang until 2:30 P.M., when the meeting was called.

I wish you could have seen this meeting. In the center of the open space where we hold our services sat our own missionaries with one of the Ilaga Dani preachers. Around them in a vast filled-in circle sat the eager Pyramid Dani. Scattered through this vast throng stood Ilaga Dani preachers to relay the message like loud-speakers. There were somewhere between five and six thousand people seated there.

Again the people were exhorted not to burn their fetishes if they were of a divided heart. A discussion followed the sermon and some questions were answered. During the entire session the missionaries were only onlookers. Following the service there was a mighty shout, and the people divided off into their clans and began to prepare their fetishes for burning. The fetish pyre measured about two feet high by seventy feet long. When they had them all prepared, the fires were lit and soon the things that had haunted these people all their lives were going up in flames.

At this Sunday service about 50 percent of the Pyramid Dani burned their charms. On Monday another 40 percent arrived and the same procedure was carried out. A total of eight thousand people burned their fetishes in two days.

Naturally we are thrilled to witness this tremendous moving of the Spirit of God, and yet we stand in awe and are somewhat fearful at the tremendous task of teaching the people around us. Already we have organized a witness school. The Danis have chosen qualified young men whom we will teach, and they in turn will go out to teach in the villages.

Today there is a strong Christian church throughout the western Dani tribe. Forty-nine thousand of them are baptized, and an estimated fifteen thousand can read. The

Dani New Testament was scheduled to come off the presses of the Indonesian Bible Society in 1980. Those Danis have worked hand in hand with missionaries to reach thousands of other interior people in many different tribes. The waves of outreach continue to spread out farther and farther.

Once we were living in the Beoga and the Damals were learning new Bible lessons and verses each week, they could no longer contain their enthusiasm to witness. Their closest unreached neighbors were the Moni people who lived in the Dugindoga Valley to the west. Natural ties of kinship also existed, for half the people living in the top villages in the Beoga Valley were Monis, and a similar number of Damals had spilled over the mountain pass and were living in the Dugindoga.

Travelers and traders walked over the mountain, and when they returned they brought back excited reports: "Everyone is learning memory verses; all the verses from Damal are translated into Moni. On Sunday there are four points where people gather for church. The Monis want a missionary. Everybody wants to embrace the gospel."

Could this be true among the Monis? Einar Mickelson had opened a mission station at Homeyo before World War II. At various times after the war, ten other missionaries had lived and worked at Homeyo, but only a handful of Monis accepted Christ in all of those years.

Missionary conference convened at Pyramid in June 1960, and to that conference we took the glowing reports of the response taking place in the Dugindoga. The conference was of one mind that the opportunity to build the church of Christ in the Dugindoga must not be lost. Bill and Grace Cutts had just returned from furlough, planning to return to Homeyo for their third term of service, but they changed their plans when they heard the word from the Dugindoga. They were ready to pioneer again—hike over the trail, build an airstrip and a house, from the ground up—if those Monis were truly eager to accept Christ.

When pilot George Boggs landed in the Beoga he listened to our stories of opportunity among the Monis. On his flight back to Nabire he searched the Dugindoga for a possible airstrip site. The country was rugged—mountains and rivers everywhere. Then he spotted a flat area on the river bottom, the only possible site in the whole valley.

Using our transceiver radio we reported all that to our newly elected field chairman, Harold Catto. He agreed that we must act immediately. Bill Cutts had just landed at Homeyo, returning from conference, and it would take him some weeks to pack and organize things for the trek and move from Homeyo to the new mission station site at Hitadipa.

Gordon Larson volunteered to join Don to form an advance team. They would hike to Hitadipa, inspect the site from the ground, and if it was satisfactory would begin to build the strip. Bill Cutts would follow by trail when he had things organized and aluminum roofing and nails in hand to build a temporary house. Later Grace and their children would walk the three-day trail to join Bill.

The plan of action was laid out one day, and on the very next day George Boggs flew Gordon to the Beoga. It was the fourth time Don and Gordon had joined for an expedition into new country. In a few hours they had their trail gear and food supplies packed, and they set out with their carriers for the Dugindoga that afternoon. It had taken years to see the realization of their dream to open a mission station among the Damals and Danis; this new advance was launched in a matter of hours.

While in the Dugindoga Don wrote the following:

> "In my many travels . . . there have been dangers . . . there has been work and toil . . . besides all this, daily I am under the pressure of my concern for all the churches . . . Yet I run the race with joy to complete the task the Lord Jesus has given me." These words taken from the writings of Paul express some of my feelings during the past few days.
>
> Friday afternoon found Gordon and me on the trail; it was

like old times to be together and hiking in to open a new area. God gave us good weather as we traveled up beautiful mountain streams and crossed rushing rivers and high mountain passes. The two days on the trail passed rapidly, for we had such good fellowship in prayer and discussing the opportunities we would have to preach God's Word in the Dugindoga. From the reports we felt sure that at least some of the people had turned from witchcraft and magic to serve the living God.

Natives from four tribes live in the Dugindoga. Besides the Moni people and the sprinkling of Damals there is an area settled by Danis in their constant outreach to take new land, and also there is a large group of Ndugas who were driven out of the Beoga during the Taganit War.

We arrived at the first village Sunday afternoon just as the people were closing their church service. Words cannot describe the joyous, hearty welcome we received. Nearby we could see the new plot of ground they were clearing to use for worship; the present site had become too small. For five months now they had been meeting each Sunday to repeat the Bible stories and verses brought to them by travelers from the Beoga. They told us that now in eight villages people gathered regularly on Sunday. The reports had not been exaggerated!

The next day we pressed on to the village of Hitadipa and found the airstrip site to be very satisfactory. Although the trail had been hard and we were tired, the hardest strains lay ahead. From daybreak until 9:00 at night we could not get a moment of rest or quiet. My chin was sore from the Moni women chucking me under the chin—their way of expressing love because we had come.

After we purchased the ground for the strip, the people were anxious for us to give them work assignments. Also we were giving out contracts for poles and hand-split boards to be used to build the first temporary house for the Cutts. Always there were those asking us to sit down with them and help them learn a verse of scripture correctly. Once or twice a day a group gathered, and we taught them a Bible story. Often there were sick people to be prayed for or given medicine.

Yesterday and again today a number of people gathered with their charms and fetishes and burned them in a public service, declaring openly their trust in Christ. This is all the more thrilling to me, because the Monis have had a chance to hear the gospel for years but they have been the least responsive of all the tribes contacted. Now the minority groups of Danis and Damals have received the message from their Ilaga and Beoga relatives, and their Moni neighbors are joining them in burning their fetishes.

The witness of the Beoga people spread in yet another direction: to the east, to the Danis of the Sinak Valley. In 1958 Chief Kawa had walked to the Sinak just weeks after he himself had first heard. Other groups of spontaneous witnesses went there on visits in the months that followed. There was no real bond between the people of the Sinak and the Beoga except that they had both been attacked by Taganit's forces. The natural bridge of witness should have come from the Ilaga where the Danis had relatives and a common language, but that route was severed.

Early in 1958 Bill and Beverly Steiglitz arrived in the Ilaga and began studying the Dani language. A year later they hiked into the Sinak and began the cycle of pioneering another new valley. After six months of living close to the Danis—praying for them, teaching them, treating their illnesses, sharing their way of life—one village made plans to burn their fetishes. But before the scheduled event could take place a man was ambushed and killed in revenge for a death in the Taganit War, and the whole valley was thrown into the threat of war breaking out anew.

Some months later an old man invited Bill to come across the river to his home. Arriving in the village Bill found the rest of the people trying to persuade the old man to wait longer before he burned his fetishes. "I will not wait," he cried. "And I will burn them right here in public for all of you to see. I want only to follow the Jesus path."

Other individuals followed in burning their ancestral fetishes, and then village groups began to burn theirs until they were virtually gone. By the end of 1961 over a thousand people had been baptized, and a strong church began to form in the Sinak.

The island of New Guinea is divided by a high range of mountains running east to west. In Irian Jaya those splendid peaks are called the Puncak Jaya Range and boast a glacier on a mountain 16,500 feet above sea level, just four degrees south of the equator. On the north side of the range the mountains break into wave upon wave of mountains, but on the south side they plummet to the coastal plain of jungle and swamp in just twenty-five miles. Rainfall is heavy, and raging rivers rush down the rugged mountains to the sea, always carrying with them more of the precious little topsoil. It is in that rugged country south of the range, in eight mountain valleys, that half of the Damal tribe was living—in valleys that corresponded to the Ilaga and Beoga on the north side of the range. To the west five southern valleys were populated by Monis, paralleling the Monis living north of the range, and still farther west lived three valleys of Ekaris bordering their northern cousins.

The seventh Damal valley to the west is the Wa Valley, situated at 6,000 feet and directly below a glacier. Only 150 Damals lived here, isolated from their neighbors by the towering mountains on every side. Twentieth-century civilization burst in upon those Damals when a rich deposit of copper ore was discovered near the glacier, and in 1972 Freeport Indonesia built the mining town of Tembagapura in the Wa Valley.

The mountains that separate the Ilaga from the southern valley of Jila are 14,000 feet high, and the pass is 12,000 feet. But the rugged path and the bitter cold of the mountains did not deter Chief Den and the other Ilaga families from their plans to move south—away from the ever-advancing Danis. When the missionaries arrived in the Ilaga, the flow of travel was reversed for a time. Travelers came from the south to see what was happening in the Ilaga, some families moved north, and Ilaga traders traveled south, witnessing as they went.

The response of the southern Damals to the gospel was not unanimous as it had been in the Beoga, for the Roman Catholic mission was already working in the Jila Valley. Conflict of belief arose among the southern Damals. The Catholics were planning to move all the Damals from the mountains to Akimuga, a resettlement project in the tropical flatlands near the coast. That became the dividing issue. Those who wanted to become Catholics moved to Akimuga—about half of the southern Damals—and those who chose to follow the teaching of the Ilaga witness men remained in their mountain homes.

For a missionary to walk from one end of the eight southern valleys to the other end would take two weeks, and even given plenty of time the terrain is almost impassible to a Westerner. The only way the people could be reached was by Damal Christians traveling and witnessing, and yet they also needed a missionary couple to help them in their efforts.

Frank and Wilma Ross arrived in the Ilaga in 1960 and began language study. The southern Damals were thrilled that *their own* missionaries had come, and before many months had passed Frank was on the trail over the Puncak Jaya Mountains to begin construction of an airstrip. The strip site at Jila was a good one, but very difficult to build because of a huge boulder that sat right in the center of the strip. Before it was opened Frank walked back to the Ilaga to escort his wife to Jila. Wilma Ross is the only white woman who has ever hiked over the Central Range near the highest peaks. With encouragement and instruction from the Rosses the Damals continued to evangelize the southern people.

Scores of Damals from the Ilaga and Beoga can give detailed accounts of traveling to the south in an evangelistic party, experiencing hardships and dangers, hunger and sickness, miracles and fetish burnings. For the Damal every part of life was connected to the supernatural. Miracles were a natural happening to them, and indeed their way of life offered nothing scientific to aid in easing the blows of life.

In simple faith the Christians prayed to God and He answered their prayers, quite like New Testament times. Miracles also gave credibility to the true message even as they did in the book of Acts.

Of all the traveling Christians perhaps Kama-Kama was the most faithful in his witness. When Don arrived in the Ilaga, Kama-Kama was almost fifty years old, a man with social and political stature in the community although he had only one wife. When I asked him why he had not taken more wives he replied, "Many times my relatives urged me to take a second wife. They offered to help with the payments, but I just didn't want another wife with all the obligations. I think God had his hand on my life even before I heard the gospel."

It was Kama-Kama who led Don to the Beoga on the first trip after the Taganit War and gave the first clear Christian witness there. He was one of the original ten men in the Ilaga Leadership Training School. Most of Kama-Kama's clansmen lived in the Jila Valley, and it was a natural bridge for him to go to them. They repulsed him on his first visit, but on his second trip a man invited him to live in his village and he stayed there for some time.

Kama-Kama prayed for a woman who was hemorrhaging, and she was healed. The people wanted to give him a pig in payment, but he replied, "No, never! There is no price on the gospel. God healed this woman, I did not."

After the Rosses were living in Jila, Kama-Kama led an evangelistic party on a trip to the three Damal valleys to the east. Their pattern of ministry was very Damal—a message from "real" people to every man, woman, and child of the community, not to a selected group of young people or only to the men as spirit appeasement had been. When they arrived in a village the people prepared a community feast. While the food was steaming in the pits, Kama-Kama preached to them. At night the party divided up, sleeping in different men's houses, and they talked the gospel all night following the pattern of courtship sings. In several of their preaching points the people eagerly burned their fetishes.

Nigil, another one of the ten school men, traveled to the Tinga Valley in the west. He preached to the people in the afternoons and witnessed and taught in the houses at night. The Tinga people listened, but they were uncertain about which way was the *true path* to God. Nigil had been teaching them about the miracles Jesus performed on earth and also gave witness to miracles he had seen.

One day they brought to him a woman who was possessed with an evil spirit. The woman wore no skirt and babbled insanely. Some time before, she had killed her own little boy, splitting his head open with an ax and then cooking his flesh. The people said to Nigil, "Can God heal this woman? Will you pray for her?"

Nigil replied, "I do not know if God will choose to heal her or not, but I will pray for her." He talked to the woman, and she agreed to let them pray in Jesus' name. Nigil and the other men in the party joined in prayer for her. She was not healed instantaneously, but after a short time she stopped her babbling, put on a skirt, and went back to her husband as a normal woman. The Tinga people recognized that miracle came from God, and many believed because of it.

The men in Bible training in the Beoga also went out on evangelistic trips. Kok-Me headed a team of four men and one woman, the bride of one of the men in the party, to go to the Bela and Alama, the two easternmost valleys of the southern Damals. The group started out walking first to the Ilaga. They decided against taking the main trail to the south, which led into the Jila Valley. Instead they chose a more direct route to the east across a high plateau and over the Puncak Jaya Range into the Bela Valley.

Since they were all Beoga men, none of them had ever traveled on this trail before. Shortly after noon clouds descended on them right to the ground level and they were walking in a gray gloom. They could no longer see the mountains that had given them a basic sense of direction. In that high, desolate country there are no trees, only grass and

low bushes. The experienced Damal follows
former travelers where their feet have worn awa
grass or skirted a muddy bog; Kok-Me had le. ___ _uose
lessons as a boy from his father.

Late in the afternoon it began to rain, and the little group
hurried on, reassured by the knowledge that they would
soon come to the camping site for the night, build a fire to
warm their cold bodies, and cook their sweet potatoes.
Suddenly the gloom turned into darkness, and there was no
campsite, no hut or overhanging rock under which they
could build a fire. They were lost. Somewhere after the
clouds had covered them they had missed the main trail
and taken a side trail used by op hunters—a trail that led
nowhere.

The men broke some wet branches from the bushes—if
only they could get a fire started! Kok-Me took his fire-
making stick from his net bag, held the stick between his
toes on the marshy ground, and began to pull the vine, but
there was no smoke. His hands were so numb with cold that
he could hardly work the vine. He stood in a puddle of
water with rain pouring down from the sky. There was no
use to try. They were hungry, exhausted, and cold to the
point that they no longer cared whether they lived or died.

They squatted the long night in the chilling rain, and in
the morning they were still alive. Hope revived, they
retraced their steps to the main trail, and followed it up over
the Puncak Jaya Range and down into the Bela Valley.

The people received them cordially and soon fell into the
festive pattern of sharing their afternoon meal. The men and
boys gathered firewood and heated the rocks for the
cookout, singing as they worked. The women and girls
brought in nets of potatoes and greens. The men carried the
hot rocks to the women, who interlaced the vegetables and
rocks in the grass-lined pit. The final touch of covering it all
over with sod was the men's job, and then they all sat down
to listen to the sermon while the food steamed.

For several days they taught in one village before going on

to the next. Before they returned to the Beoga four villages in the Bela and three in the Alama had burned their fetishes and declared their faith in Christ.

Yet another tribe lives along the southern slopes of the Central Range. The Nduga tribe lives in ten valleys east of the Damals. They are a small tribe of nine thousand people. Most of them live in the southern valleys, but two groups live north of the range, one in Sinak, and one near Hitadipa. One wonders how they came to be so scattered in those rugged mountains and yet retain their tribal identity and language.

Kama-Kama, as no other man either black or white, had a burden to reach the southern Ndugas. His first contact with them had been on a trip to the easternmost Damals. At that point the two tribes were intermarried, and there were men who spoke both languages and could serve as interpreters. Later Kama-Kama made two trips deep into Nduga country.

The first response of the Ndugas was one of suspicion and hostility; they wanted nothing to do with Ilaga people, for Ilaga was the source of the Taganit War, a war whose settlement was not yet finalized among the Ndugas. But he went right on preaching and exhorting the people to burn their fetishes and turn to Christ.

In pregospel days Kama-Kama had not been a public speaker either as a spirit appeasement man or as a war leader, but now as a Christian God had given him the gift of an evangelist. A missionary found his sermons hard to follow because they were illustrated with native thought pictures, but the Ndugas understood and responded by burning their fetishes.

With that turning to Christ, the Alliance mission appointed Adriaan and Mijo van der Bijl to open the work among the Ndugas, with Mary Owen to reduce the language to writing and translate the Scriptures and Elfrieda Toews to serve as a nurse. An expedition was planned to escort Adriaan van der Bijl from Jila to Mapnduma, the site chosen to build an airstrip. Andy, the Ekari, went along to help build the airstrip just as he had helped in building the Jila strip. Frank Ross and Harold Catto were in the party along with Kama-Kama, who was the chief preacher, because at that point none of the missionaries were fluent in the local languages. They traveled slowly, partly because the terrain was unbelievably rough and partly because they stopped to hold baptismal services in two Damal valleys and in one Nduga valley. Those isolated Damal Christians had been taught by witness men from the Ilaga and Beoga and the Ndugas were taught by men of their tribe who had turned to Christ and been schooled at Hitadipa.

The waves of the gospel, going out from the Ilaga, had formed a complete circle. Kama-Kama was the first man to give the message in the Beoga. From the Beoga it went to Hitadipa and then jumped back to the Ndugas south of the range through men trained at Hitadipa to join with the witness that Kama-Kama had brought from the Ilaga.

Today there are perhaps 200,000 adherents to Christianity in the mountains of Irian Jaya who can trace their roots back to that first fetish burning at Kunga. (The only major church that does not include is the Ekari church, which has developed independently.) In the first five years people turned to Christ in groups; large segments of a tribe or an entire valley of people burned their fetishes as a unit. Where that happened and solid Bible teaching followed, the heathen tribal customs were replaced by Christian practices, making it much easier for a convert to stand true when he could follow Christ without breaking away from his people. In more recent years tribal Christians serving as missionaries have continued to reach out to other mountain people, widening the circle still further, and some have gone to the nomadic tribes that live in the lowlands.

From the farthest Ekari villages in the west to the Ngalum villages on the border of Papuan New Guinea there are a thousand congregations who gather each Sunday morning to worship the Lord. In God's time He has raised up a host of people to praise him in scores of languages.

27

"I Will Build My Church"

When Don and I walked into the Beoga Valley we were two people alone faced with the task of teaching the way of the Lord to 4,000 people scattered the length of a long valley. All the Beoga people had burned their fetishes in the last two years, and now they were demanding that we teach them. There was only one possible way—we must train a few who would in turn teach what they learned to all the others.

We started a Leadership Training School just five months after we arrived in the Beoga, much like the one the Ellenbergers had started in the Ilaga during our furlough. This time eighteen men and their wives, chosen from all parts of the Beoga, were the students. Many were the same men who had come each Friday to learn a Bible lesson and take it back to their villages. Now they had planted their gardens and built their houses at Milavak to attend a full-time school. For a classroom we used the newly built church. The bark roof did not keep out much rain, but it did serve as shelter from the morning sun. The Damals provided everything for the school except the teachers.

Kok-Me and Delem were students in our school. Kok-Me describes those days:

> We went to school five days a week from early morning until noon. Twice each day Damal-In taught us reading. She used a large chart and flash cards to teach us our letters and didn't like it when we said "te" for "je." It was all so foreign to us—to make papers talk—but Damal-In insisted we must keep trying. The Bible stories we learned from Damal-Neme were much easier to learn. Also he taught us a sermon to give

on Sundays and a memory verse. We memorized the verse very carefully because everyone in the Beoga was clamoring for us to teach them new verses.

On Friday noon we men all went off in pairs to preach our sermons at nine different churches. The furthest village we went to took Damal-Neme two days to walk, but we slept on the way Friday night and got there Saturday morning. When it was my turn to go there, on my return trip I slept in my father's house at Tingil on Sunday night and walked back to Milavak for school early Monday morning.

One weekend it was my turn to go to Piloma, and when I got back I found that my wife, Delem, had given birth to our first child, a girl. Delem named our baby Nimut, which means "going out," because she said I was always *going out* somewhere with the gospel and wasn't even home when the baby was born.

In September Don and I flew to Enarotali to await the birth of our fourth child, Helen Louise. School had to be closed during our absence, and the men went out in teams witnessing in other valleys. One group walked to the Sinak and another to the Damals south of the Central Range. Kok-Me joined a team that visited Moni country and then went on to the Lakes to witness to the Ekaris. Instead of walking all the way home Don arranged for a plane to fly them back to Beoga. Kok-Me's description of his first airplane flight is interesting.

I sat in the copilot's seat next to George Boggs. As we took off my breath left me. Soon we were flying over mountains— the same mountains it had taken us two weeks to hike over on our way. I saw Homeyo below us, and then we were flying over clouds. The plane began to bounce around, and I said to Boggs, "I'm afraid. Take me back to the Lakes. I'd rather walk." He just smiled and nodded his head and kept on going. I guess he didn't understand what I said. When we got to Beoga the plane circled over the strip, and I was sure we would hit a mountain. I just hid my face and vowed I'd never ride in a plane again, but I have—so many times I don't think I could count them all.

Although I was confined to the station for several months

with my family, Don continued to visit the outlying churches in the Beoga. By the end of 1960 he had baptized 1,051 people. Soon all six of the main churches were organized with qualified elders chosen from their congregations. With his elders each pastor was authorized to serve Communion to his people without the missionary's presence.

Some months later Don wrote, "Last Sunday I attended a Communion service where the pastor and elders served the emblems of the Lord's body and blood—sweet potatoes and raspberry juice—to a quiet and reverent group of 135 believers. Christ was the center of the simple service as the pastor read the Scripture from 1 Corinthians 11 in the Damal language."

Don continued in his letter, "On the way home I was walking with one of our school men when we met a man just returned from a trip to Jila. The traveler told of a nonreceptive area that was now showing an interest in the gospel. The school man commented to me as we walked on, 'Nothing used to thrill me like going on a hunt and killing a wild pig, but now my greatest joy is to hear of people turning to Christ.'"

In the fall of 1961 it was time to send out the men from our Leadership Training School for a term of practical service. Also the six men from the Ilaga who had come to serve as pastors were returning for further schooling. The elders from the churches met to assign the eighteen couples. They decided to keep only six in the Beoga even though there were sixteen regular preaching points; the other men should go as missionaries out of the valley.

First each school man stated where he would like to go. Don made a few comments, and then the elders discussed everything at length. Two of the churches stated flatly that they did not want the particular man who had asked to come to their church, and other men were nominated. They told one man he should not go to the outpost he had chosen because he spoke only Damal. Someone who also spoke

Dani should go there, for many of the people were Danis. Instead they appointed him to the largest church in the Beoga, the Wang-Be church. Kok-Me was appointed to the Ogam church. Six couples were sent to serve south of the Central Range. It was the Damals' own church, and the work was carried out under their leadership.

Witness school was dismissed for a year, Helen had passed her first birthday, Joyce had gone off to the first grade in Sentani, and we focused our attention on traveling in the Beoga. On our first trip we spent a month visiting the churches, encouraging the Christians, baptizing those who were ready, treating the sick, teaching, and preaching. We now had six men and their wives who had learned to read in our Leadership Training School, and we helped them set up schools to teach reading in each of their churches.

Four months later we were on the trail again with seventeen carriers including the two who carried Lori and Helen. Our main purpose was to work with the literacy program, spending a week in each of five centers. Our itinerary was announced well in advance, and in each place they had a twelve- by 14-foot native house built for us. That was a great improvement over living in a tent. We added a "table" built from a framework of sticks, and reeds were tied on with rattan vine to form the top.

Our second stop was Wang-Be. It rained and rained and rained, and our three-year-old Lori broke out with three-day measles, which added to the challenge of camping in a native village. However, the enthusiastic response of the Damals helped us forget the inconveniences. They were ready to do anything for us. On Sunday Don baptized 55 people, and a Communion service followed with 476 people crowded into their church building.

Weekdays I worked from breakfast to supper with the four literacy classes taught by the pastor and his wife. The students tended to memorize the primers rather than learning to read. They needed more drill with flash cards, and the pastor needed to help them break the words into syllables and sound them out rather than telling them the word. I tried to help the pastor and his wife with teaching methods, but how could I expect them to grasp all of that in less than a week, when they themselves were only barely literate?

The problem went round and round in my mind. Here we had hundreds of Christians who wanted to learn to read. Their enthusiasm knew no bounds, but there was no one to teach them. Gradually a plan began to formulate. I had found three young men at Wang-Be who had really caught onto the principle of reading. *If I could teach them myself they would be literate in a couple of weeks,* I thought. At our first church there were two young couples who were also very near to becoming independent readers. If I could gather a few gifted young people from all of the church centers, help them to become literate, and then train them in how to teach others, we would have a start toward our goal.

From Wang-Be our scheduled route led us up and over a 9,500 foot pass into Ogam. Whether I could make the trip in one day, as all the Damals did, was questionable, so we had brought our tent with us to make camp in the jungle if necessary.

Before I came to New Guinea, hiking was my favorite sport. I enjoyed nothing more than climbing a mountain in one of California's national parks. However, in my adopted land I found that superlatives abound when it comes to hiking, and they are not all on the positive side. The scenery is exquisite, but the mountains never end in going up only to come down again, and the paths are impossible!

Each path has been chosen only because it is the line of least resistance between two points, not because anyone has considered the lay of the land or cleared away any of the debris. In populated areas a trail may come into use where pigs have traveled, or the reverse may be true; pigs follow where man has walked. The path may go through, around, over, or even under the brush, logs, roots, and always through the mud that lies in the way.

Just after we broke camp we came to the Wang-Be River. The water flows over a relatively flat area at that point, and normally travelers wade across—but not that day. With all the rain the river was in flood, and not even the most daring young man was willing to wade it. Instead the carriers set about building a bridge. We had no problem crossing the bridge, but it did give us a late start.

Across the river we began to climb up toward the pass. Everywhere there was mud and jungle roots; my progress was slow. I never had been able to quite figure out how there can be so much mud in such steep country, but there it was. We reached the top just before noon and ate our lunch shivering in the cold. Don estimated that it would take me four hours to get to the base of the mountain because the trail followed a stream bed that was now in flood stage, and then it would take another two hours to go up and over a smaller mountain and into Ogam. That meant we would have to camp in the woods.

We had only gone a little way when we heard people calling to us from below. When we reached them I could not believe what I saw. There was a brand-new trail built down the side of the mountain. For three days Kok-Me and his congregation had been working in the forest. They had laid out a new path according to the contour of the mountain. A twenty-foot-wide swath was cut through the jungle. On long, steep stretches they had anchored cross poles in place to form steps down the mountain. Over the little gulleys they had built pole bridges—not the usual single-pole style that the Damals use, but four poles lashed together so that I could cross easily. That had all been done for me. I was "Queen for a Day," and I enjoyed every minute of it!

I reached the Ogam church by four o'clock that afternoon and slept in the house they had built for us instead of sleeping in the tent. On Sunday after church I stood and made a speech—something unheard of for a woman to do. I thanked them publicly for building that trail just for me.

The benefits of a good trail were now obvious to everyone.

A large crowd of people had come along with us "just for the ride," and they were as astonished as I was to find the new trail. They also saw how much easier it made traveling for them. Word spread like wildfire, and soon new trails were blossoming in all parts of the valley.

Living in a Damal village was a rewarding experience. When we were at home there was always a score of people demanding our attention "immediately if not sooner." They wanted medicine, or payment for a net of potatoes, or help in their reading primer. But in the village we were their guests. They came bringing a special gift of food or just to greet us in their affectionate way, and they were quick to grant any request we made of them.

Don had been teaching the Christians about having morning devotions; now we observed them in action. Each morning, shortly after six, the village headman gave a call, and everyone gathered in the yard. Two young men led in the singing of a hymn, and then several people prayed. Women and children had a part in prayer as well as reciting Scripture verses. One person recited a verse, phrase by phrase, and all the others repeated responsively. Someone told a short Bible story, then they were dismissed by prayer to go back to their houses for breakfast and the duties of the day.

The custom of village devotions was firmly established when the Beoga people had their first love for the Lord, and the practice continues to this day. Now they gather in the men's house around the fire rather than sitting in the cold morning air, but their faithfulness has helped them stand true to the Lord through the years even in the face of strong temptation.

In my week of teaching at Ogam I saw significant improvement in the literacy classes, but my conviction grew that we needed more and better trained teachers. I chose three young couples to attend the new school.

We left Ogam on a different trail than the one on which

we had come, so we could visit Piloma on our way home. I remembered that section of the trail very well from other trips, but I was in for another surprise. The Damals at our next stop were not to be outdone by the Ogam church. During our stay at Ogam they improved the trail so much that Lori was able to walk by herself part of the way.

Word reached us by runner from the Ilaga that the Asian flu was sweeping the interior, everyone was sick, and many were dying. That was the first world epidemic to reach the mountain tribespeople. Some were already sick in the Beoga. Before we reached home our carriers also had the flu, but we managed to complete our scheduled stops just the same.

Home had never looked as good. I longed to sit in a chair—just a straight-backed chair instead of sitting on the ground or on a carrying tin. In the evening I cut out a new dress and began sewing—an activity that helped me identify with my background. Although the girls were perfect travelers, Lori headed straight for her toys when she got home, toys she had hardly touched for months. Helen toddled around and around our living room floor; her delight was to have a smooth, flat surface on which to walk.

The Asian flu increased. Somehow it seemed to bypass the babies, but few adults escaped. The young and strong recovered with time, but many of the elderly contracted pneumonia. The stretcher was in use every day, carrying in patients to us for penicillin injections. Don spent many hours in the clinic and making house calls when the patients were too sick to walk.

Twenty died in the Beoga, and among them was Wolo. Although Kok-Me was not able to come to his father because he too was sick with the flu, he was comforted to know that the gospel had come in time and he would see his father again in heaven.

When we were at Wang-Be one man stood out above the others. That was Te-Me-Nin, an elder in the church and natural born leader. He was enrolled to enter our next Bible training school and was already a forceful preacher. On the day of the baptismal service he wore his Sunday best, which included the yellow plumes of a bird of paradise, making a very striking picture of virile manhood.

Just after we left Wang-Be, Te-Me-Nin joined an evangelistic party traveling to witness south of the Central Range. He had arrived in a valley four days from his home when the Asian flu struck. Probably weakened from crossing the high mountains near the snow peaks, he contracted pneumonia. Before Te-Me-Nin died, he said to the Beoga people with him, "Tell my wife that all is well. I'm going to God, my Father. This earth is a hard place to live, but I'm going to heaven, a truly good place." In life and in death his testimony was true.

In spite of the flu epidemic my literacy teachers' school began the week we got home. It was exciting to teach twenty young men and women, the cream of the crop from the entire valley. We met under the tall evergreen trees in our backyard. All morning I sat on the ground with them, drilling the groups of three and four.

None of the young people were fully literate when they came. When one person mastered a section I assigned him to teach someone else who was not quite as far along. The joy each experienced when all of a sudden he was reading new material all by himself was beyond description.

My next step was to show him how he could experience that joy all over again each time he taught another person to read. By teaching them, I myself got new ideas on how a Damal thinks and learns, and I incorporated those into the teaching methods I taught them. The entire six weeks was a process of "learning by doing" for all of us.

Several months later I called them all back for another session. It was beautiful to see how the local people took the students into their homes again and fed them for six weeks. Without that act of hospitality we could not have had a school. All of them had been teaching in their own villages and now they were ready for another course of teaching methods. People learned to read, and that much faster, when the teacher helped the student sound out the words rather than just reciting the written lines for him to mimic.

Three years later, in 1965, when we left for our second furlough, there were 471 men, women, and children who could read the book of Mark. John Ellenberger had translated that first portion of Scripture, another important milestone in building the church of Christ.

If you were to ask me, "What have been the hardest things in your life as a missionary?" my answer would be, "There has only been one—sending my children away to boarding school. And yet, even in that God has made the bitter sweet. The times we are together are more intensely happy than if we had never been separated."

In 1961 the Cutts family came to the Beoga to spend Christmas with us. They were still living in their little temporary house at Hitadipa, and Bill was waging a losing battle with the river as it ate away the first airstrip while he was building a new one on higher ground. They needed a break, and so did we. Christmas is an especially happy time of year because our children are home from school. Grace Cutts wrote about their visit in a letter to her mother.

> We flew to the Beoga and met the Gibbons family again. They had packed a picnic lunch, and we set off in search of a Christmas tree. Alice had prepared a cool drink, a delicious salad, Christmas cookies, and of course the picnic classic of roasted wieners. Johnny (9) took a special part in cutting the tree with the men. Before long I think he decided that it wasn't so bad after all to be the only boy among so many girls. That night we all decorated the tree, and as children always do, we decided it was the prettiest tree we had ever seen.
>
> December 22. There were five plane landings in the Beoga. Their strip is a real good one, and the planes meet here in the middle of the island between Nabire and Sentani. Gifts came in and went out; turkeys were deposited and carried every which way to missionary families; two doctors and a nurse

stopped on their way traveling through. After all the planes
had gone we decorated the house. The kids waxed Christmas
scenes on the windows. In the evening we all played games
around the tree in their lovely living room. It was so nice to
be in a real house again. The airstrip, and the sick, and the
work at Hitadipa seemed far away by this time. I enjoyed
having a baby around again. Helen (14 months) was fat and
cuddly and into everything. The older children did well
with games, but we adults didn't get on so well because of
"twin" interference. The "twins" were Amy (2½) and Lori
(3). They kept wanting to play, too. Each wore French braids
and vied for the center of attention.

December 23. Alice and I planned menus together. Kathy
(9) and Joyce (7) baked gingerbread men, and everyone
enjoyed eating them. Each evening we sang carols before
Don read from the Christmas story. The "twins" wanted to
pray every time. Joyce always impressed me when she
prayed as it was so original and uninhibited. She hasn't been
poured into the mold yet. One night she went down the list
and thanked the Lord for all the holidays in the year. It was
so cozy there as little voices thanked God—for our home and
for Christmas—and for our families.

December 24. It is the custom of the Gibbons that each day
after the tree is up more presents are put under it. The
children are allowed to sort and feel and wonder about
them. One of the cutest things I've ever seen was the way the
girls each decided which package had their dolls, and they
sat and rocked and carried them around the living room all
wrapped up. The anticipation was as wonderful as the
surprise at the final unveiling. Christmas Eve, after a buffet
supper around the tree, everyone opened presents. Gifts
were stacked high when we began, and after they were all
opened each child had just what he or she wanted.

December 25. Christmas Day while the children played
with their things, Alice and I worked on dinner. We had
turkey, shipped frozen all the way from the States, with
dressing, mashed potatoes and gravy, cranberry sauce,
candied sweet potatoes, green beans, cauliflower, Waldorf
salad a la Beoga, and ice cream sundaes. Everything was
super. Our whole week in the Beoga couldn't have been

better. Being together as families is what really made it special.

During the last few months of 1962 the accepted students for our new Bible school were back at the mission station digging gardens, building fences, and repairing their grass-thatched huts. All of the twenty-eight men who came from both the Beoga and Ilaga had passed an examination demonstrating that they could read the gospel of Mark independently, and many of their wives were also literate. A new school building was erected just across the airstrip from our house. It boasted an aluminum roof and desks enough to seat all the men. Since the women and their babies were inseparable, their classes were held separately from the men's.

School opened on the first of January. Gradually we built up to a five-hour school day. I was teaching Old Testament stories. It was a red-letter day when they learned a new story from the duplicated notes I had given them instead of hearing it given orally. They were also learning to print. That led to the day when I gave them their first test—just a true or false quiz, but gradually the difficulty of the tests increased.

Formerly all the teaching from the New Testament had been from the gospels and the book of Acts, but now Don branched out into teaching 1 Corinthians and doctrine of the Bible. Another semester he taught 1 and 2 Timothy, making a rough translation of the books to serve as text for the course. Reading an abstract text, digesting the teachings, and then putting them into one's own words is a great achievement for adult men who had spent all their youth in primitive superstitions.

Still later we taught arithmetic, Indonesian language, and writing instead of printing. Arithmetic has always been the most difficult subject of all because the Damals had no background in the concept of numbers. In fact, all the secular subjects were on a much lower level than their Bible subjects. God the Holy Spirit enlightened their minds in a special way to the truths of His Word.

Years went by and the first Bible school class completed two years of study followed by two years of practical ministry and two final years of study to graduate. A new class entered when the first group was sent out, and the training has continued until four classes of graduates have gone out to all parts of the Damal tribe to pastor churches.

We were always on the lookout for qualified Damals whom we could train as teachers in the school. Gradually three men and one woman began to teach. At first we guided them in daily classes, and then they took over more and more subjects until the turnover was complete in 1977 when Daniel Alom became the principal of the Bible school.

Singing has always been an integral part of the life of the Damals, and from the very beginning it played an important role in building their faith. The Damal chant form was an excellent medium for teaching new biblical truths as well as expressing praise to the Lord. John Ellenberger, with the help of Christians, wrote the first substantial block of hymns. But soon the Damals, inspired from learning new truth, were composing songs themselves. Before we had any readers, the words had to be memorized and passed on just like Scripture verses. As people learned to read, one of the first things they wanted was a printed hymnal. At their request I collected the hymns, wrote them down, and mimeographed them in a book containing fifty-two songs.

Words of an Easter hymn, "As Jesus Arose We Too Shall Rise," go like this:

Because Jesus rose from the dead let us praise Him
They crucified Him on the cross
When He died they buried Him
But it was impossible for death to hold Him captive
God untied the vines of death that bound Him
When He arose from death the earth shook
An angel came and rolled the stone away
Jesus the Savior arose. Hallelujah.

As Jesus arose we too shall rise
We shall leave this body that is subject to decay
We shall receive an eternal body
As Jesus arose we too shall rise. Hallelujah.

One of the classes in the Bible school was a singing class.
The men not only sang hymns, but they also brought new
songs, that they had written, to class, and we worked on
them together.

During a break from school one of the students went to
the lowland people to the north. (Those people had had no
contact with mountain tribes before the gospel came, and
they truly represented a mission field to the Damals. They
were cannibals and wore nothing—not even the traditional
gourd and grass skirt worn by the highland people.) Here is
a "Missionary Song" written by that school man. (The
"grain field" and "bread" of the Bible are both pictured by
the sweet potato for the Damal.)

Come, Holy Spirit, and fill us with Your power
Come, Oh Counselor, and give us help
Send us forth with the message of Jesus' resurrection
That we Damals may tell the message boldly
Send us to people who have not tasted the sweet potato
of life.
Many sweet potatoes are mature and ready to be
harvested
Come, my comrades, let us dig the potato harvest
When the last sweet potato has been dug
We will enter the beautiful gate with joy and singing
Come, Holy Spirit, and fill us with your power.

The number of songs the men produced grew rapidly, and
they wanted a new hymnal. That time we had it printed.
Our present song book contains 123 hymns, and it has
become the most popular Damal book sold.

As more and more people learned to read, they also
learned to write. Here was another new world of communication open to them. Much of that writing, or I should say
printing, was self-taught. But it was surprising how well

they learned to print by practicing on scraps of paper. Their spelling was creative, but with a bit of imagination usually the recipient figured out the message.

Don received more letters than anyone else. Often the writer was outside the door waiting to discuss the matter more fully, but a letter quickly caught Don's attention, and the writer was also using his newfound skill. One interesting use of writing found by several young men was to send a letter proposing marriage to the girls of their choice—an interesting adaptation of the bitter leaf tucked in a piece of pork that Kok-Me had used.

We stayed on in the Beoga for five and a half years, and during that time Lori grew from a year-old baby to a little girl ready to enter first grade. One evening shortly before our furlough she prayed this prayer, "Dear Lord, help the people here to be strong so they will go to the woods and kill birds there but not kill birds in the trees in our backyard. And bless the birds because they sing for us."

Lori was caught between two cultures. She saw the point of view of her Damal age-mates and their need to eat birds or rats or any bit of meat. If our cat killed a rat and the people stole it from her, Lori's response was not, "The poor rat got killed," or, "The poor cat was robbed," but rather it was, "Good, that means hungry people got something to eat."

At the same time Lori was also an American girl, so she appreciated the many birds that sang from the tall evergreens in our backyard. We declared those trees to be a bird sanctuary and did not allow the people to shoot birds there. Thus Lori not only asked God to lead her friends to other birds, but also to bless the birds for the joy they brought to us. So goes life when a little girl is caught between two cultures.

Damal church leaders from every part of the tribe gathered in the Ilaga for their first meeting. Thirty-one official delegates attended, representing twenty-nine church and seventeen unorganized groups. They came from all three districts, and some from the Jila district had walked ten days to get there. Such a gathering was unheard-of by the Danis and Damals of the Ilaga, for they had never before seen a group gather from such distances, and everyone arrived on the appointed day.

The meetings did not follow parliamentary procedure, but nevertheless all was done in order. Damals do not actually vote. They discuss a matter until conflicting opinions are no longer voiced and only one idea remains. A constitution was drawn up which included a good doctrinal statement and a description of the operation of the churches on the local and district levels.

The Damal church is self-propagating—spontaneously they go every direction, witnessing. It is self-supporting—all of their churches and schools were built from their own resources. The church is self-governing—the Damals are an independent people, quite desirous and capable of carrying out their own affairs. But more than that, the Damal church is meeting its own needs within the framework of how Damals have expressed themselves for centuries. The gospel is not a foreigner's religion—it belongs to them!

28
The Damals Today

What of the Damal church today? Was their decision to follow Christ real? The answer to that question is a resounding yes! At the same time the Damal church is not perfect—quite like Christian churches anywhere in the world. In these more than twenty years a new generation has grown up in a changing world. The young are following in the faith of their elders for the most part, but the path becomes increasingly difficult with foreign pressures and the allurement of materialism.

I could write of their temptations and stumblings, but I will not. I neither deny their existence nor try to hide them; but as Paul did, we missionaries preach and teach against sin to those involved, but always encourage them to new growth in Christ.

The past is irrevocably linked to the future. Even during the months I have been writing this book the Damals living south of the Central Range, and to a lesser degree those living in the Ilaga, have gone through a deep valley of rebellion stemming first from their old beliefs in *hai*. "If only the key could be found," they reasoned, "we would unlock the door to material wealth, and paradise would be on earth." Other problems also stemming from the old Damal culture continue to surface from time to time: taking a second wife, divorce after a trial marriage, and war indemnity payments.

Freeport Indonesia is now mining copper from the mountain west of the glacier in the Puncak Jaya Range. That is traditional Damal territory, and the company built a town in the Wa Valley just below the mine. All the material goods, the wonders, and the vices of a modern city can be seen by any Damal who travels to Tembagapura. No man can turn back the hands of time as the Damals merge with the modern world. Yet we missionaries face the task of cushioning the shock caused by a "stone age" people coming face-to-face with the twentieth century. Through changing times our approach has been the same, and it still works—teach the Word of God first.

After the early years when so many learned to read out of sheer determination, the number passing the literacy test slackened off. I wrote new phonic primers, organized the program, and turned it all over to the Damals to carry out, but only a handful were learning to read. They wanted our personal involvement with them, not just our direction. When we said, "You all get busy and learn," no one did anything, but when we said, "Learning to read God's Word is an exciting thing for Christian young people. Come on, we'll work with you. Let's plan to have a Literacy Festival two years from now, and we'll give out prizes to the churches with the most new literates," then things began to happen.

If you were to visit us in the Beoga you would see our reading program in action. Every Tuesday our backyard is crowded with people who have walked up to two days to get here. They have come to be tested on their progress in learning to read. I sit on the ground with them, testing them one by one. Most of the students pass the test, and I send each to Don to exchange his book for the next one in the series. A few cannot read the material independently, and I spend some time with them analyzing their problem and showing them what to study.

The goal in all of this is to become an independent reader in Damal. When the four primers are mastered, the student can read. Then he goes through four readers to improve his speed.

It is a happy day when I give a student his final test. He receives a "reader's card" entitling him to purchase, at a token fee, the various books of the New Testament that have been translated by John Ellenberger. Don records the student's name, village, and the name of the teacher who taught him to read. Then he rings a bell and announces to the crowd, "Rejoice with us! We have a new literate from Tingil. His mother taught him to read. All of you keep working, and soon we'll ring the bell for you, too."

Once the program got underway, valleywide enthusiasm mounted. The Piloma people did not want to make a poor showing when they learned that the Jugu people had more new literates than any other village. Even people who spoke Damal as a second language, or not at all, joined in and as a result the Beoga people were so involved in competition that they did not join neighboring valleys when fighting broke out there.

One thirty-year-old Dani man had been studying for some time. He was a man of prime warrior age, who always dressed in colorful native attire. Every month or two he walked four hours from his village to be tested. Sometimes I had to tell him, "You're making progress, but you haven't mastered that primer yet. Go home and study some more." Finally the day came when he passed his final exam, and with real pride of accomplishment received the gospel of Mark. At the same time his relatives in the Ilaga were engaged in a war. Instead of joining them as might be expected, he resisted the temptation and continued on, putting God first in his life.

In the last three years 550 have passed the reading test, and most of those are "second generation" Christians in their teens and twenties. The grand total in the Beoga is 1,400, which means that almost one out of every two Damals over ten years of age is literate. Being able to read opens the door to so many new possibilities in life. For children attending the government elementary schools, learning to read in the Indonesian language becomes much easier. Other schools are open to young people who want to study the Bible, learn Indonesian, or become medical workers; and learning to write follows easily after a person has learned to read.

However, the primary purpose in all of that is to read the Bible, each person for himself. Damals are quite like the rest of us in that they fail to read it even when they are literate. To encourage them we mimeograph a calendar and include a Bible reading schedule on the back. The Damals are still very much a people of group action, and everyone likes to be doing the same thing as his neighbor. Once a month the pastor reads off the list of literates in his church, and the people answer if they have been reading their Bibles. Peer pressure helps many get started. Scripture sales are booming, and books have to be reprinted to keep up with the demand. Although the Damals do not have enough money to actually pay for the cost of their books, they do pay a portion, which makes them value their Bibles more highly.

Sunday school is the most exciting church growth tool we have today—not Sunday school for a few little children, with lessons translated from quarterlies written for Americans, but a four-year Bible study course of dated lessons, covering the life of Christ, the book of Acts, and Old Testament stories, for every person in the village.

Five years ago I was teaching a course on teaching methods to a Bible school class of men. I assigned each of them to go out and teach a Sunday school class using the methods of teaching we had been studying. None of them fulfilled the assignment, so I began to visit different churches to see what was happening during the Sunday school hour. I found that a man told a Bible story selected at random to a group scattered in the village yard. Most of the children present were too far away to even hear the words being spoken. The Damals needed help, that was certain!

I began writing Sunday school lessons for the Bible school men and required them to fan out into nearby churches and teach classes of eight to ten students. At first the village people did not want to leave their old routine. "This is how we've always done it," they said. But gradually with lots of enthusiastic promotion on our part, the new program began to catch on. I continued to duplicate lessons and included all the men and women in the Bible school as teachers in the pilot program. When one method did not seem to work, I dropped it and tried another.

Our Sunday school lessons now have a four-part format: the story, application, memory verse, and review questions. The teacher first tells the Bible story in his own words and then relates it to two or three applications pertinent to today's living such as marriage, witnessing, a proper attitude toward the government, or trusting God in all circumstances. Next comes the dozen or so questions written out in the teacher's manual designed to help the students repeat the story and application.

The memory verse is the most important part of the lesson. It expresses the theme and application of the lesson in no more than five easily memorized phrases, and the Beoga people are really memorizing Scripture verses again, as they did before they learned to read. To encourage memorization and retention of God's Word we offered a small certificate to each person who could recite fifteen or more of the twenty-six memory verses used in a six-month period. The response was overwhelming. The first time, around 850 earned a certificate, and six months later the number went up to 1,050.

After the Sunday school lessons caught on in the Beoga, the Damals of the Ilaga and the southern Damals living in the Jila and Tembagapura areas also wanted to be in on the program. The terrain south of the Puncak Jaya Range is simply too rugged to permit missionaries to travel to the villages, but the pastors come in for Sunday school seminars. We reviewed methods of presenting the lesson and encouraged the pastors to gather all their teachers on Monday and Tuesday mornings to study the lesson together. They took back enough copies of the Sunday school manual to give a copy to every literate teacher. We now mimeograph 950 books every six months for the Damal tribe, and they are always gone right after the starting date of the lesson book.

Classes are small, which means that every student gets involved in answering the questions and reciting the Bible verse. Sunday morning in the larger churches there are twenty-five to thirty classes, all scattered around the churchyard enjoying the morning sunshine. Women teach children and women's classes, and that has opened a new and very fulfilling ministry to the tribal women.

Any Christian who can read is welcome to teach, and the teachers range from teenage boys to gray-haired grandmothers. Desiring to become a Sunday school teacher has motivated some to learn to read.

The Ilaga Danis once again watched their Damal neighbors. This time it was the Sunday school lessons that they wanted in their own language. Betty Wilson took over the production of the Dani books. She trained a Dani pastor, who also spoke Damal, to translate the lessons. At first Betty mimeographed the books, but more and more Dani areas wanted the material, not only those served by the Alliance but those related to other missionary societies. Recently 1,400 copies of the Dani manual were printed. The Ilaga Danis, true to their style of doing everything with more enthusiasm than their neighbors, are also using the Sunday school stories and questions in daily village devotions.

One Sunday after the sermon in the Milavak church, a visiting Ilaga pastor stood and said, "I want to tell you of how the Lord protected me as I was walking from the Ilaga. The landslide that I had to cross near Wung was active, and I was afraid when I crossed it, but the Lord was with me and I crossed safely." He paused a moment and then went on. "There is something else that I am thankful for, and that is the Sunday school lessons. For some time now we have not had a missionary to teach us in the Ilaga, but now we have printed Bible lessons. Many of the people are faithfully studying these lessons. I want to thank Damal-In for writing them for us." Those words meant much to me, for words of appreciation come less frequently today than they did in the beginning.

One Christian lady in the Ilaga was faithfully teaching her Sunday school class, although her husband was not following the Lord. He made arrangements to marry their daughter to a man who already had a wife. As a result of her Sunday school studies, the mother and daughter firmly resisted the marriage, and in time the father gave up.

Now the daughter has been given in marriage to a fine young man. Applications in the lessons encourage women to stand up for their convictions in a marriage arrangement even if the men of the family are thinking only of their own interests and the bride price. Systematic teaching of God's Word is bearing fruit.

Anticipation increased as the days for the Literacy Festival drew near. The church leaders announced baptismal services for the week before the festival. They selected four points in the' valley: Milavak, Piloma, Wang-Be, and Ogam, as centers for baptisms. We knew of all the plans, but Don had no part in examining the candidates or baptizing them. Ordained Damal pastors took the complete leadership. Three hundred sixty-six Damals followed their Lord in baptism. Most of them were young people and children, but there were adults in the group, too. Kelma had eleven adults baptized—men and women who had bypassed that decision all these years.

The big day came for the Literacy Festival. People began gathering by the hundreds on the airstrip. They were all dressed in their best—whether it was western dress or tribal finery. The young people painted their faces with red and black greasepaint, and colorful feather plumes adorned the heads of a few.

While people from nearby waited for more distant church groups to arrive, they chanted and marched up and down the strip. Each group carried a banner with its church name, and the number of new literates they had gained during the contest.

Every few minutes a lookout peered down on the airstrip

from the mountaintop upvalley. They were waiting for the group to gather from downvalley. Finally the dramatic moment arrived. People began to pour in waves over the mountains on both sides of the airstrip like warriors running to battle. They entered the airstrip running and yelling in rhythm. Every little distance a group would stop to circle-dance.

Finally they sat down on the strip by churches, with their banners waving over them. Hundreds of visitors from other valleys and tribes lined the sides of the strip. Some of them had walked five days to attend the celebration.

For judging, the churches were divided into three classes according to their size. We gave out prizes to churches with the most new literates. In all, 270 had learned to read in twenty-one months. The first and second-place churches in each class chose a prize; either a volleyball, a sheet of aluminum for church roofing, or salt. We pinned a red flag on the six church banners in the first division. Then all the new literates gathered and danced in a circle, shouting in rhythm as they danced.

The next prizes were for churches with the most individuals following the Bible-reading schedule. Blue flags were given out in that category, and everyone following the reading program from the whole valley circle-danced.

Awards for Scripture memorization came next. Yellow flags appeared on the church banners to indicate the winners. What a sight to see over a thousand people circle-dance!

The fourth group of awards were given to the churches with the most Sunday school teachers. Green flags were given out, and all the Sunday school teachers danced together.

The crowd broke up at midday to prepare for the feast the next day. Groups of young men and boys ran down the airstrip bringing firewood and rocks for the cooking pits. Men carried in their squealing pigs while women went off to the gardens to gather greens and sweet potatoes.

One select group of men went downvalley to butcher a bull. Tasting beef for the first time was the specialty of that feast. Four years earlier a community cattle project was begun with two heifers and a bull calf. The herd had grown to nine head. Just at dusk the men came back singing and carrying the hunks of the seven-hundred-pound bull. Nothing was left behind, from the horns to the tail!

At dawn the men began to butcher the pigs they had brought from all parts of the valley. That was the biggest pig feast ever in the Beoga; they slaughtered 268 pigs. The Lord's blessing was evident when the pigs were butchered because only one had pork tapeworm—an infestation making the meat unfit to eat. (In some areas in Irian Jaya up to 20 percent of the pigs are infested.)

The rack of firewood to heat the rocks for cooking stretched four hundred feet down one side of the airstrip. On the other side of the strip, pits were dug and lined with banana leaves. By noon all the meat, greens, and potatoes were steaming in the pits.

While the food cooked the people gathered in the middle of the strip for a service. Don spoke to them, reviewing how the Word of God was growing in their hearts. Then he recounted the ways the Lord was blessing them as they sought to put the Lord first in their lives.

God has given good health in a time when neighboring valleys have been stricken with epidemics.

The pork tapeworm, which brings to humans a disease that can be fatal, has almost disappeared from the Beoga. (That came about after pointed teaching on hygiene and sanitation, and the entire valley joining in cooperation.)

Gardens are flourishing as are the pigs, chickens, and cattle.

The pastor who closed in prayer expressed the praise in the hearts of all the people. "Heavenly Father, You have caused the gospel to grow large in all of our hearts. This celebration is the most important time in our spiritual lives since we burned our fetishes. To You, oh God, be all the glory!"

The food was ready, and the four thousand people sat down by church groups at the bottom of the airstrip. (I realized in a very vivid way that when Jesus fed the four thousand that was a lot of people!) Teams of a dozen men ran with the food, serving first the greens and later the meat. Everyone received a portion—even visitors who had had no part in providing the food.

About two o'clock there was rain on the mountains, and it looked as though it would move down to the airstrip, but the rain never came. For three days we did not have a drop of rain—most unusual for the Beoga. That was an obvious benediction from God's hand on our praise festival.

The strip was the *only* place a crowd that size could gather. The dirt field took a terrific beating with eight thousand feet walking, running, and dancing on it for two days. Had it rained, the planes could not have landed the next day.

The day after the feast the twin engine turbojet Nomad made two landings, taking thirteen passengers each time, and Cessnas took four more loads. Graduates of the Bible school and their families were flown out to minister in distant areas. Airplanes serving their own people made an outstanding ending for the Damals to a celebration of rejoicing and praise to God.

A worried couple hurried down the trail from Kelma. The husband walked in front and his wife followed, bent down with the weight of her baby, which she carried in her net bag. As they passed through the village of Jugu a man called to them, "Where are you going?"

"Our baby is very sick," came the response, "and we are going to the clinic at Milavak."

"Wait! I will pray for your baby." The Jugu man, a church elder, prayed in Jesus' name that God would heal this child, and the couple continued on their way.

Obed, a Damal medical worker, took the baby's temperature and listened to the chest sounds with his stethoscope.

"It is very hard for your baby to breathe," he said. "His chest is all filled up with fluid. Why didn't you come sooner?"

The mother began to explain, but Obed broke in. "Never mind about that now. I am going to give him penicillin shots, and you must not return home until he is completely well."

In the Beoga today there are four clinics, each manned by a medical worker who took training under a missionary nurse. Naturally the scope of their training is limited to treatment of the most common diseases, but through their work many hundreds of lives have been saved. When a case is beyond their training they bring the patient to Don, and he calls Dr. Bromley, our mission doctor, on the radio. Often she is able to diagnose and prescribe treatment over the radio, but sometimes she says the patient should be flown to a hospital.

Whooping cough broke out among tribal people to the east of Beoga recently. Thirteen years ago an epidemic swept through the interior, and hundreds of babies and children died. This time, before the whooping cough spread, we began an innoculation campaign in the Beoga, just as many others did across the island. Vaccine was purchased and flown in to us. Two medical workers walked to all the villages in the valley, giving injections to every baby and small child. Six weeks later they made the rounds again. As a result of our campaign and many others like it, whooping cough never got to the Beoga; it simply disappeared from the interior.

When we walked into the Beoga there were scores of women with huge goiters hanging from their necks, and most of the other women had small goiters inside their throats. All of them lacked iodine in their diet. But more pitiful than women with goiters were the cretinous children that those women bore, children with serious mental and motor control handicaps. There is no medical help for those retarded children.

Iodine is lacking in the soil of the Beoga, so the vegetables grown here were also lacking in that mineral. There are no other natural sources such as fish or salt containing iodine. In the early years we gave out iodine tablets once a month to all women of child-bearing age. That was not a complete success, but it certainly helped. Then medical science came up with an injection of iodine suspended in an oil base. It releases the iodine slowly in the body to supply a woman's needs for three years from one injection. After a campaign covering all the women there were no more cretinous children born, and only a few very old women show any signs of a goiter.

As the Damals advanced in education and contact with the rest of the world, their longing increased for money to purchase things they cannot produce—clothing and axes, kettles and soap, books, and aluminum for church roofs. A few of them are employed at Tembagapura, but most of the jobs require a technically skilled person, which eliminates hiring the Damals. In 1979, Freeport initiated a weekly helicopter flight to Beoga to buy vegetables. That has given the people a cash income, not a handout, and a sense of sharing from the benefits of the mine. Beside vegetables, the Damals have been marketing baskets and artifacts. Weaving rattan baskets is a newly learned art, but one that is closely related to weaving a war-vest.

Don is never without a project or two designed to help raise the Damals' standard of living. The greatest lack in their diet is protein. Through the years he has introduced various kinds of beans and peanuts as well as promoting a variety of sweet potato that is as high in protein. He brought in chickens and rabbits, goats and cattle, distributing them on a plan whereby part of the offspring is returned to the project to be given to others.

Don's current project is distributing rabbits to men who build pens, according to his design, that will keep the dogs out. The rabbit lives on sweet potatoes and greens and is a nice size to provide meat for a family.

But no other animal thrives as well or is as highly valued in Damal society as the pig. Don's project of flying in pure-bred stock to upgrade the local pigs seems to be working better than anything else he has tried.

In December 1978 the Ilaga Damals, with the help of their Dani neighbors, hosted a national church conference at Kunga. Invitations were sent out well in advance to eight districts of the KINGMI Church of Irian Jaya.* Two hundred thirty-two churches from Mapnduma, Sinak, Beoga, Hitadipa, Homeyo, Tembagapura, Jila, and Ilaga were each invited to send two official delegates besides their District Superintendants and other officers. Everyone else was welcome to come along, but only the official delegates were allowed to vote and be served the main meal each day.

On the opening day the valley sponsored a mo feast for everyone, and there must have been eight thousand people gathered in the abandoned gardens set aside for the feast. There was not enough mo to serve them all, but that did not dampen their spirit of rejoicing. To the tribal people nothing could be more graphic than to see that mass of people, for all who gathered had come to express their support of the church of Jesus Christ.

The Kunga people built an addition to their church, doubling its seating capacity, and put up extra dormitory-style houses. All morning the kitchen crew labored over its cooking. Rice was boiled in a huge pot, emptied into a drum, and the process was repeated until they had cooked enough. Cabbage and greens were steamed and then seasoned with red peppers, peanuts, and fried pork. At noon the government guests were seated at tables while the 525 official delegates sat in rows in the churchyard.

* KINGMI is the title the Indonesians use for their national church organization. Each letter represents an Indonesian word from the title "Gospel Tabernacle Christian Church of Indonesia." It is the Indonesian equivalent of the Christian and Missionary Alliance.

Everyone was served a heaping plate of food in a surprisingly short time.

Morning and evening the delegates attended church services, and during other hours they listened to reports and testimonies and carried on lively discussions during their business meetings. Everything had to be translated into four languages. The delegates were seated according to tribe, and translators spoke simultaneously to each group. The final evening thirty men, graduates of five different Bible schools, were ordained to the ministry.

For us as Damal missionaries the highlight of the week was the Sunday service held for all the Damals before the conference officially convened. Leaders and pastors from all four of the Damal districts had come from near and far. Chief Den and the others who led in the Kunga fetish burning were there, and Sam had flown from Wamena. Kama-Kama, Tita, Kok-Me, Nigil, Jak-Niti, and scores of others whom we had trained in the Bible school and knew and loved as Christian brothers were all there.

Those men and women represented seventy-five Damal churches scattered all around the Puncak Jaya mountains. They are now brothers and sisters in Christ; love has replaced killing and war; God's purity now reigns instead of adultery and fornication. Freedom to serve a merciful God has replaced the fear and bondage of spirit appeasement. And the women have been released from the lifelong threat of being killed as witches. A positive faith in a living God had set the Damals free.

At the close of church we shared the sweet potato and raspberry juice of the Communion service together. My mind flashed back twenty years to the first Communion service I partook with some of those same men and women right here at Kunga. For all that God had done in those years I could only praise Him.

Epilogue

The Damal story is still going on, and it will continue until time becomes eternity. In writing this book I have relived the events of the past twenty-five years, and I am filled with awe and wonder that I should witness and even have a part in this fantastic adventure for God—one that is unique in this changing world; one that is more exciting than going to the moon, and more worthwhile.

People sometimes ask me, "How can you live all alone in the Beoga? Don't you get very lonely?" First, I know the Lord has called me here to serve Him, and there is always much to be done, from teaching the women how to sew and make dresses for themselves to writing and producing Sunday school lessons. I am not by nature a person who could ever be separated from my children and send them away to school, but God has given grace for each day, and more than that He has given extra good things in the lives of our girls.

Each of our five girls loves the Lord with all of her heart. The four older girls are back in the States now. Each has reflected on her life as a missionary kid—that life of sharing the world of the Damal children during preschool days and then going off to boarding school for eight months every year, from the first grade through high school graduation. The four have written to us expressing their love and appreciation for the opportunity to grow up on the mission field.

The Lord has paid back to us a hundredfold for any seeming sacrifice we have made in following His call to the foreign field. One of those blessings has come in the form of our fifth daughter, Darlene Alice. Darlene is now an eleven-year-old who adds a lot of joy to our lives with her love for people, her delight in playing the piano, her pastime of writing stories reflecting her life as an MK, and her excitement in discovering something new in God's creation.

Don is still the man who always has time for every individual and his needs. More often than not the Damal's topic of conversation is pigs or money, or a plane flight rather than "spiritual" things, but Don always has time to talk—just because he loves people and enjoys talking to them. After he has made their friendship, they listen and respond to him as he teaches and counsels from the Word of God. Don originally envisioned the Damals as blocks of people, a valley or a whole tribe, but he has won them as individuals, one by one.

Recently I had the privilege of flying by helicopter to Duma, a valley south of the Puncak Jaya Range, that is the home of three hundred Moni people. The flight was arranged for Don to check out the airstrip that the people had been building for two years. I could hardly believe my eyes when we arrived at Duma. There it was—a twelve hundred-foot airstrip engineered with an even 8 percent grade. From the center crown there was a 4 percent side slope to prevent erosion caused by the frequent rains. It was hard and ready for a landing.

Don had surveyed the strip using a carpenter's level, a tape measure, and a ball of string; and the people had built it using digging sticks, their bare hands to move the dirt, and a couple of sledge hammers to break up boulders. Now the strip would make it possible for national missionaries to fly in and out as well as take Monis to Bible school and bring a medical worker to this isolated area.

For ten years Don has been making trips into the three Moni valleys south of the Range—valleys that were bypassed in earlier years. When he first walked through the area looking for a village that would receive two Damal missionary families, not one area would have them. Every six months or so Don hiked over the Central Range making further contacts. In time Damal missionaries moved in; six churches were established with converts being baptized, people learning to read, and young people walking over the range to attend school. Now they have their own airstrip.

When someone asks Don, "How much longer will you continue working here in Irian Jaya? Have you worked yourself out of a job?" his reply is, "As long as the Lord keeps the door open I'll continue working until I retire. True, most of the things I did for the Damals in the early days, they are now doing for themselves, but they still need an older brother in the Lord to give spiritual directive, innovative ideas, and materials to reach the current generation for Christ. And there are other projects like reaching the southern Monis and building an airstrip, which still require a missionary's help."

On a recent visit to the Ilaga I went looking for Den—to take his picture. I found him planting mo in his garden some distance from Kunga. His steps are slower than they used to be, and one of his sons has taken his place as village chief, but that is to be expected since Den was born in about 1900. As we were walking back to Kunga together he surprised me by carrying a fifty-pound piece of firewood balanced on his shoulder. "If the gospel had not come to the Ilaga," Den said, "I wouldn't be living today. I'm getting old now, and one of these days I'll be going to heaven."

Kama-Kama moved to the Beoga a year ago to be near his son during his final illness. He lived in constant pain the last six months of his life, even though he took medication to help correct his problem. When I asked him to give me the details of various preaching trips he had made, his face would light up and his pain was forgotten. Serving the Lord was always most important in his life.

Kama-Kama's son, Timotius, serves as a Bible translator. Timotius learned to read and write as a young boy sitting beside his father in school. Kama-Kama never learned to read, but Timotius got a head start at a time when there were no schools for children. He went on to gain an excellent command of the Indonesian language and graduated from an Indonesian language Bible school. Today he is translating selected portions of the Old Testament from Indonesian into Damal. Don helped check the book of Genesis, and it is now at the printers. Other books will wait for publication until John Ellenberger returns from furlough and can double-check the translation.

Chief Kawa is a very active man at sixty-five, and all five of his wives are still living. He never misses a district meeting when the chiefs are invited to join the pastors, and he stands firm in serving the Lord. Recently he escorted a fourteen-year-old daughter the long day's walk from Piloma to Milavak so I could test her on her progress in learning to read. Kawa had no living children when we first came; now he has a large family, and he gives the Lord all the credit.

One of the men whose arrows helped to kill Imi and her mother was Yaiya Markus, (John Mark), now an ordained pastor. He told me the story with reluctance and shame, admitting that the only crime of those two women was to mourn the death of their loved ones. Yet he has the assurance that that sin of the past has been forgiven by God through the death of Jesus Christ.

Today Yaiya Markus is the assistant district superintendent for the Beoga Valley. Had the gospel not come when it did he would have become a chief with several wives, and would have followed the traditions of his fathers in spirit appeasement. Now he is using those same leadership qualities to direct others into the true path of following Christ. When a problem from the old culture arises in lives today, he is right there counseling and presenting the Bible way to resolve the situation. He knows where he has come from and where he is going.

"Will you ever turn back from following the Lord?" I asked Kok-Me one day.

"No, I never will," he said, "and most of the Damals will not turn back either."

Kok-Me is not a model Christian, and he is quite subject to the usual human weaknesses. Like his father, he has a roving spirit. He is not content to stay at home and pastor the small church where he is assigned. Sometimes he mixes business and traveling for the joy of it coupled with witnessing for Christ.

Kok-Me had just finished relating the gory details of a battle in the Taganit War. He turned to me and said, "What about all those who died without hearing the gospel? Are they in hell? What about my ancestors who died before you came with the gospel message?"

I nodded and said, "That's a hard question to answer." *And, I thought, people ask this same question in the States, but they are only asking a theological question that does not pertain to them directly. Anyone there who has a true desire to hear the Bible message of salvation can find it.* But I was sitting in my living room talking to a man who was asking a question that was very personal to him. His uncle, whom he knew and loved, had died in the battle we had just been talking about, and he had never heard God's Word.

Another question I had heard before from Damals, though not verbalized that day was, "Why didn't your fathers come to my people with the good news?" Why didn't they? "And why don't more of your brothers and sisters come today?" What could I say?

I could not pass over Kok-Me's question without discussing it, but I felt it was too much for me to try and answer by myself, so I asked Don to join us.

First Don asked Kok-Me what he believed was the answer to his question. He replied, "Since Jesus preached to the people who died before the Flood, wouldn't He give some way of salvation for my ancestors?" We looked up the passage he was referring to and found it in 1 Peter 3:19-20, reading it in the Damal translation. "In his spiritual existence Christ went and preached to the imprisoned spirits. These were the spirits of those who had not obeyed God when he waited patiently during the days that Noah was building his boat."

That is an interesting conclusion, I thought. When Kok-Me had studied in Bible school I taught 1 and 2 Peter verse by verse. I remembered that we had not spent much time on those verses, because even with the help of commentaries I could not give any explanation of that difficult passage. That was Kok-Me's own original thinking.

As our discussion continued I came up with the principle that a person who knows the teaching of the Bible and does not act on it will be punished severely in the judgment, and the person who has little light will be judged accordingly. Don found the reference on this one: Luke 12:47-48. "This certainly applies to the Damals who never heard," I said.

"God has revealed specifically to us how He will punish those who reject the gospel," said Don. "Mark sixteen, verse sixteen, is one of the many passages stating this truth. 'He who believes and is baptized will be saved; but he who does not believe will be condemned.' But there is no verse that deals specifically with the question of those who died without hearing. This is one of the things that God has not revealed to us." Don took his English Bible and gave a free translation of Deuteronomy 29:29, "'There are some things that the Lord our God has kept secret, but he has revealed his law, and we and our descendants are to obey it forever.'" Don added, "Some things are not made known to us, but we *are* to follow the teachings written in His Word.

"Many times in Scripture we are told to go and preach the gospel to all people. There are some who follow their own reasoning at this point and say there might be less punishment for those who do not hear than for those who hear and reject. Therefore we should leave the heathen as they are. That is simply an excuse to disobey Christ's clear command to preach the good news around the world."

Kok-Me accepted what had been said and then nodded. "Now I want to say something," he began. "We Damals had nothing before you came with God's message from the Bible." His voice rose with emotion as he continued. "We thank God that He sent Gordon Larson and John Ellenberger and you, Damal-Neme, to bring us the words of Jesus. *Hai,* the hope of eternal life, has come to us through Jesus Christ.

"The coming of the gospel has stopped our wars. Women are no longer killed as witches. Before the gospel came many babies born here were handicapped and dumb. The sores from yaws covered so many people that travelers from the Ilaga used to sit on their own rain mats lest they be contaminated with this diease. People were always hungry, and our pigs didn't prosper. Spirit appeasement filled every part of our lives, but still it didn't help us. The younger generation doesn't even know what it was like in the Beoga before the gospel came, but my generation does. This was the only way of life my ancestors knew.

"Now you have come with the gospel, and we want to thank the Christians in America who sent you to us. Damal-Neme and Damal-In, when you grow old and leave us, we want new missionaries to take your place. We will give these new missionaries the same symbolic names we have given you. We will love them as we have loved you, and they will continue to teach us and lead us on God's trail."